Policy Consultancy in Comparative Perspective

T0381651

Many Western countries have seen an increase in the volume and importance of external consultants in the public policy process. This book is the first to investigate this phenomenon in a comparative and interdisciplinary way. The analysis shows who these consultants are, and how widely and for what reasons they are used in Britain, the United States, Canada, Australia, the Netherlands and Sweden. In doing so, the book addresses the positive and negative implications of high levels of external policy consultancy, including its implications for the nature of the state (transforming into a contractor state?) and for democratically legitimized and accountable decision-making (transforming into consultocracy?) It provides valuable new insights for students and practitioners in the fields of public administration, public policy, public management, political science and human resource management.

CASPAR VAN DEN BERG is Professor of Governance at the University of Groningen. His work has appeared in journals including *Governance*, *Public Administration* and *JPART*. He received the prestigious Van Poelje Prize for best dissertation in the administrative and policy sciences in the Netherlands and Flanders. He was a visiting fellow at Princeton University (2013–2014). He received a prominent four-year Veni scholarship from the Dutch Science Organization (2015).

MICHAEL HOWLETT is Burnaby Mountain Professor and Canada Research Chair in the Department of Political Science at Simon Fraser University, Canada. He specializes in public policy studies, with an emphasis on natural resource and environmental policy-making. He is currently editor of *Policy Sciences, Policy Design and Practice, Journal of Comparative Policy Analysis, Policy & Society* and the *Annual Review of Policy Design*.

ANDREA MIGONE is Director of Research and Outreach at the Institute of Public Administration of Canada. He specializes in public policy and public administration. His academic career includes work on decision-making, globalization, innovation policy, procurement and governance. He was a post-doctoral research fellow at Simon Fraser University.

MICHAEL HOWARD is a Conjoint Lecturer at the University of Newcastle, Australia. His career has spanned teaching and research in public policy in both academic and advocacy settings, along with policy development and service delivery within innovative government programmes. His publications have centred on historical aspects of policy-making and contemporary commercialization trends in the public sector, with a focus on consultants.

FRIDA PEMER is Assistant Professor at the Stockholm School of Economics. Her research centres on how organizations use professional services, and on digitalization in professional service firms. She has published her work in highly ranked journals such as *JPART*, *Governance*, *Human Relations*, *Industrial Marketing Management* and *Journal of Business Research*.

HELEN M. GUNTER is Professor of Education Policy at the University of Manchester. She is a Fellow of the UK Academy of Social Sciences, and recipient of the BELMAS Distinguished Service Award 2016. She published *Consultants and Consultancy: The Case of Education* (2017; co-authored with Colin Mills) and her most recent book is *The Politics of Public Education* (2018).

Cambridge Studies in Comparative Public Policy

The **Cambridge Studies in Comparative Public Policy** series was established to promote and disseminate comparative research in public policy. The objective of the series is to advance the understanding of public policies through the publication of the results of comparative research into the nature, dynamics and contexts of major policy challenges and responses to them. Works in the series will draw critical insights that enhance policy learning and are generalizable beyond specific policy contexts, sectors and time periods. Such works will also compare the development and application of public policy theory across institutional and cultural settings and examine how policy ideas, institutions and practices shape policies and their outcomes. Manuscripts comparing public policies in two or more cases as well as theoretically informed critical case studies which test more general theories are encouraged. Studies comparing policy development over time are also welcomed.

General Editors M. Ramesh, *National University of Singapore*; Xun Wu, Hong Kong *University of Science and Technology;* Michael Howlett, *Simon Fraser University, British Columbia and National University of Singapore*

Policy Consultancy in Comparative Perspective

Patterns, Nuances and Implications of the Contractor State

CASPAR VAN DEN BERG
University of Groningen

MICHAEL HOWLETT
Simon Fraser University

ANDREA MIGONE
Institute of Public Administration of Canada

MICHAEL HOWARD
University of Newcastle, Australia

FRIDA PEMER
Stockholm School of Economics

HELEN M. GUNTER
University of Manchester

CAMBRIDGE
UNIVERSITY PRESS

Shaftesbury Road, Cambridge CB2 8EA, United Kingdom

One Liberty Plaza, 20th Floor, New York, NY 10006, USA

477 Williamstown Road, Port Melbourne, VIC 3207, Australia

314–321, 3rd Floor, Plot 3, Splendor Forum, Jasola District Centre, New Delhi – 110025, India

103 Penang Road, #05–06/07, Visioncrest Commercial, Singapore 238467

Cambridge University Press is part of Cambridge University Press & Assessment, a department of the University of Cambridge.

We share the University's mission to contribute to society through the pursuit of education, learning and research at the highest international levels of excellence.

www.cambridge.org
Information on this title: www.cambridge.org/9781009376242

DOI: 10.1017/9781108634724

First published 2020
First paperback edition 2023

A catalogue record for this publication is available from the British Library

ISBN   978-1-108-49667-4   Hardback
ISBN   978-1-009-37624-2   Paperback

Cambridge University Press & Assessment has no responsibility for the persistence or accuracy of URLs for external or third-party internet websites referred to in this publication and does not guarantee that any content on such websites is, or will remain, accurate or appropriate.

Contents

Figures

Tables

Author Biographies

Caspar van den Berg is Professor of Governance, and Director of the Graduate School Campus Fryslân at the University of Groningen, the Netherlands. He holds a PhD from Leiden University, on the impact of European integration on the national civil service systems of the Netherlands, Britain and France, which was awarded the Van Poelje Prize for best dissertation in the administrative and policy sciences in the Netherlands and Flanders. He was previously a visiting fellow at Princeton University (2013–2014). His work has appeared in journals, including *Governance*, *Public Administration* and the *Journal of Public Administration Research and Theory*.

Michael Howlett is Burnaby Mountain Professor and Canada Research Chair (Tier 1) in the Department of Political Science at Simon Fraser University. He specializes in public policy analysis, political economy, and resource and environmental policy. His latest books are *Designing Public Policies* (2019), *The Policy Design Primer* (2019), *Collaboration and Public Service Delivery* (2019), *Making Policies Work* (2019), the *Routledge Handbook of Policy Design* (2019) and *Policy Styles and Policy Making* (2019).

Helen M. Gunter is Professor of Educational Policy at The Manchester Institute of Education, University of Manchester. She is a Fellow of the Academy of Social Sciences, and recipient of the BELMAS Distinguished Service Award 2016. Her work focuses on the politics of education policy and knowledge production in the field of school leadership. Her most recent books are: *An Intellectual History of School Leadership Practice and Research* (2016), *Consultants and Consultancy: The Case of Education* (co-authored with Colin Mills; 2017) and *The Politics of Public Education* (2018).

Michael Howard is a Conjoint Lecturer in the School of Humanities and Social Sciences at the University of Newcastle (UoN) in Australia, having been a continuing lecturer at UoN in social and public policy from 2000 to 2018. His research publications have centred on commercialization trends in the public sector, with a focus on the use of consultants, together with historical aspects of policy-making in Australia. At UoN his teaching has spanned courses in Politics and Policy, Social Science and Human Services. Prior to 2000 he held lecturing and research positions at the University of Sydney and the University of New South Wales, together with positions in policy development and programme delivery in community welfare and health in the NSW Public Service.

Andrea Migone has taught at Simon Fraser University and York University; he is currently Director of Research and Outreach at the Institute of Public Administration of Canada (IPAC). His research and publications focus on the intersection of public policy and public administration as a space where design and implementation come together. He is interested in a variety of subfields, including policy advisory systems, procurement, innovation, public sector leadership and governance.

Frida Pemer is Assistant Professor at the Department of Management and Organization at the Stockholm School of Economics. She holds a PhD in Organization Theory from the Stockholm School of Economics, and has been awarded the Wallander grant for best dissertation in business administration. Her research centres on how public and private organizations use professional services, and on digitalization in professional service firms. She has been a visiting researcher at the University of Oxford, and has published her work in highly ranked journals, including *Journal of Public Administration Research and Theory, Human Relations, Industrial Marketing Management, Journal of Business Research* and *Journal of Supply Chain Management.*

Acknowledgements

This work is part of the research programme *Patterns of Politicization*, which is financed by The Netherlands Organisation for Scientific Research (NWO) (project number 451-14-009), and of the *Consultancy and Knowledge Production in Education* project, which is funded by the British Academy (project number SG121698).

Abbreviations

4Cs	Consultants, Consulting, Consultation, Consultancy
ABN	Australian Business Number
ABS	Australian Bureau of Statistics
ALP	Australian Labor Party
ANZSCC	Australian and New Zealand Standard Commodity Classification
APS	Australian Public Service
APSC	Australian Public Service Commission
ASIC	Australian Standard Industrial Classification
ASIC	Australian Securities and Investment Commission
ATO	Australian Taxation Office
BIS	Department for Business, Innovation and Skills
CATS	Consultants and Temporary Staff
CCS	Crown Commercial Service
COFOG	Classification of the Functions of Government
DAS	Department of Administrative Services
DCSH	Department of Community Services and Health
DEET	Department of Employment, Education and Training
DEFRA	Department for Environment, Food and Rural Affairs
DFAT	Department of Foreign Affairs and Trade
DfEE	Department for Education and Employment
DFES	Department for Education and Skills
DG	Director General
DITAC	Department of Industry, Commerce and Technology
DMO	Defence Materiel Organisation
DND	Department of National Defence
DoD	Department of Defence
DoF	Department of Finance
DoFA	Department of Finance and Public Administration
DPS	Defence Procurement Strategy
DSS	Department of Social Security
DUO	Dutch Executive Agency for Educational Affairs

DWP	Department for Work and Pensions
EIPP	Evidence-Informed Policy and Practice
EU	European Union
EY	Ernst & Young
FCO	Foreign and Commonwealth Office
FMV	Swedish Defence Material Administration
GaPS	Gazette Publishing System
GDP	Gross Domestic Product
GSIN	Goods and Services Identification Number
GST	Goods and Services Tax
HMRC	Her Majesty's Revenue and Customs
ICT	Information and Communication Technology
JBR	Annual Management Report of Dutch Central Ministries
JCPAA	Joint Committee on Public Accounts and Audit
MAF	Management Accountability Framework
MinBZK	Dutch Ministry of Home Affairs
MinFin	Dutch Ministry of Finance
MoD	Ministry of Defence
NAO	National Audit Office
NHS	National Health Service
NPM	New Public Management
OECD	Organisation for Economic Cooperation and Development
P&S codes	Product and Service Codes
PPA	Public Procurement Act
PPPs	Public–Private Partnerships
PwC	PricewaterhouseCoopers
PWGSC	Public Works and Government Services Canada
R&D	Research and Development
SCP	Dutch Social and Cultural Planning Office
SEK	Swedish Krona
SOU	The Government's Official Investigations
SSCFPA	Senate Standing Committee on Finance and Public Administration
TEP	Temporary External Staff
TINA	There Is No Alternative
TSBPS	Task and Solutions Based Professional Services
UNSPSC	United Nations Standard Products and Services Code

1 | *Policy Consultancy in Comparative Perspective*

1.1 Introduction: Between Consultocracy and the Contracting State

While the role of consultants in the policy process has long been a concern for scholars of public administration, public management and political science, empirical studies of policy-related consulting are scarce, with little quantitative data. The country-level case studies in this book shed light for the first time on a number of important but as yet under-researched questions. The first is the actual extent of the use of government consulting in a number of countries, and what have been cross-time developments: to what extent has the use of consultants grown over time, and what are the (political, fiscal-economic, society, policy-related) factors that explain greater or lesser growth in a particular country or sector? The second is the question of what role(s) consultants play in the public sector and how large is the share of these consultants in policy work (policy analysis, policy advice, implementation and evaluation). A third is how large is the portion of consultancy work that is management consultancy, or other types of consulting, such as ICT-architects, legal advisers and accountants? The fourth is how much of consultants' work is concerned with substantive policy advice, and how much is procedurally oriented, i.e. organizing policy support, collecting input from external stakeholders, communicating the policy, etc.?

The core arguments of the book are: 1) policy consultancy has been a problematic blind spot for scholars, politicians and other commentators who are concerned with the substantive and procedural quality of the policies that shape our societies; 2) policy consultancy is a far more important and sizeable component of the work that happens within government than the literature currently acknowledges; 3) the use of policy consultants is unevenly distributed across types of policy

1

organizations and policy sectors; 4) the use and role of policy consultancy needs to be understood in terms of the political-administrative culture and structures of a given national polity.

The chapters in this book examine governmental use of consultancy services from a comparative perspective. They aim to bring more conceptual and empirical clarity to the type and extent of policy consultancy, the role and impact of consultants on public policy, and the similarities and particularities in the use of policy consulting in and across various countries and political-administrative systems including the UK, the USA, Australia, the Netherlands, Canada and Sweden. Thus, comparatively, the book will provide insights into the importance, role and implications of policy consultancy in

(a) Westminster-style systems (UK, Canada and Australia);
(b) a traditionally contracting-oriented system (USA);
(c) Weberian, consensus-driven systems (the Netherlands and Sweden).

This selection of cases gives a firm spread across Western developed nations with a good variety of characteristics in their political-administrative and policy advisory systems that are likely to have an impact on the use and implications of policy consultancy. Therefore, each chapter gives ample attention to country-specific mechanisms and dynamics. In the concluding chapter, the authors reflect on the comparative findings and contribute to theory development relevant to the aforementioned academic fields.

Conceptually and theoretically, the book addresses the current debates in a number of relevant academic disciplines:

– public administration (the relationships between consultants and the standing administrative apparatus),
– public management (particularly public personnel management),
– policy sciences (how do policies come about and on what substantive and political input are they based?),
– political science (what political factors explain the increase in policy consultancy, and what are the implications of increasing policy consultancy for political accountability and government legitimacy?).

In order to understand and explain policy consultancy, we draw on theories and literature from a number of disciplines. First, the rising use of policy consultancy may in part be explained by mechanisms central to the study of *public administration.* Weber's (1968) and Merton's

(1949) work on bureaucratization suggests policy consultants would in part be a remedy for the excesses of bureaucracy (rigid, inward looking, over-protected, minions), although in another sense consultants are even more prone to lapse into the pitfalls of bureaucracy (defending their own interests rather than those of the organization, let alone the public cause). In addition, public administration highlights the political-administrative considerations that help explain the rise of policy consultancy, such as civil service politicization, a lack of trust between political leadership and the standing administrative apparatus (Suleiman 2003), and the perceived benefits of appointing outsiders to give legitimacy to a specific policy programme (Peters and Pierre 2004, Aucoin 2012).

Second, from a *public management* angle, policy consultancy can be understood as the manifestation of an alternative public sector human resource management (HRM) system that of classical government. That is, one more closely inspired by the business-like and short-term results orientation of New Public Management (Hood and Peters 2004; Pollitt and Bouckaert 2011), addressing the fiscal pressures on governments when policy consultancy is a welcome answer to shrinking standing policy capacity.

Literature from the *policy sciences* would suggest that policy consultancy is a part of the administrators' toolkit for taming wicked problems, and sudden and urgent policy challenges (Head 2008; Ferlie et al. 2011). Temporary added expertise and capacity may help to forge windows of opportunity to promote otherwise unrealistic policy solutions (Kingdon 1993; Howlett 1998).

Lastly, *political science* informs us of political considerations that may explain the rise of policy consultancy, including an issue's political salience, the political symbolism of hiring external experts and considerations of timing regarding the electoral cycle (Hood 2013). In addition, comparative political science helps us to understand cross-national variation regarding policy consultancy: i.e. differences in the degree of reliance on consultant: their specific roles: and how they are perceived by politicians, administrators and the public at large. Here we expect to find a marked difference between those countries that have a strong tradition of contracting (USA) (Howlett et al. 2016), a Westminster-style system strongly impacted by New Public Management (UK, Canada and Australia) (Halligan 2003) and Weberian, consensus-driven systems with an open policy-making system in the *neo-corporatist* tradition (Lijphart 1999; van den Berg 2011, 2017).

Setting out to address the above questions leads us to a number of more reflective and theoretical questions. In general terms, this study examines the consulting phenomenon as falling between the popular notion of 'consultocracy' and that of the 'contracting state'. Arguably, the former is the notion of the implicit or explicit rule of an ever-increasing legion of consultants who have replaced many traditional administrative and civil service positions on a more or less full-time and permanent basis, thereby usurping their decision-making power and ability to influence governments, without the traditional means of accountability of civil servants to elected representatives (Davies 2001; Freeman 2000). Meanwhile, the latter is a more dispassionate critique of the results and impact of various forms of contracting, such as private–public partnerships (PPPs) and the different forms of contracting various types of goods and service delivery and internal government processes to private sector firms (Vincent-Jones 2000, 2006).

This perspective informs each chapter's evaluation of a series of subordinate questions about to what extent the use of consultants and the size of the standing civil service apparatus are related (Saint-Martin 1998a, 1998b, 2005, 2013) and whether consultants replace permanent public servants when bureaucracies shrink (waterbed effect), or if they are hired in policy areas in which political priorities shift in much the same way as the standing apparatus grows in those areas (proportional add-on). The chapters investigate phenomena such as how many temporary external practitioners are consultants and how many work on policy issues. They use various data sources (such as budgetary) to assess the length of contracts and the range of suppliers of various kinds of services. They also – for the first time – attempt to assess the price of consultancy in financial terms (compared to permanent hires), the extent to which the use of consultants erodes departments' and agencies' control over their policy agenda, and the costs involved in the erosion of in-house knowledge, continuity and institutional memory.

1.2 Policy Consultants and Policy Advisory Systems

It is very useful to examine professional policy work as existing within larger *policy advisory systems* which transcend the boundaries of internal government expertise and knowledge transmission (Nicholson 1997). Recent studies from New Zealand, Israel, Canada and Australia argue that government decision-makers sit at the centre of a complex web of policy advisers (Dobuzinskis, Howlett and Laycock 2007; Maley 2000; Peled 2002; Eichbaum and Shaw 2007), which includes 'traditional' political and policy advisers in government, non-governmental actors in NGOs, think tanks and other similar organizations, as well as less formal or professional forms of advice obtained from colleagues, friends and relatives, and members of the public and political parties, among others.

At their most basic, we can think of policy advice systems as part of the knowledge utilization system of government, itself a kind of marketplace for policy ideas and information, comprising three separate components: a supply of policy advice, its demand on the part of decision-makers and a set of brokers whose role it is to match supply and demand in any given conjuncture (Lindquist 1998). We can see these systems as arrayed into three general 'sets' of analytical activities and participants linked to the positions actors hold in the 'market' for policy advice.

The first set of actors is composed of 'proximate decision-makers' acting as consumers of policy analysis and advice: actors with actual authority to make policy decisions, including cabinets and executives as well as legislatures, and senior administrators and officials delegated decision-making powers by those other bodies. The second set are those 'knowledge producers' located in academia, statistical agencies and research institutes who provide the basic scientific, economic and social scientific data upon which analyses are often based and decisions made. The third set comprises 'knowledge brokers' serving as intermediaries between the knowledge generators and the proximate decision-makers, repackaging data and information into usable forms. These include, among others, permanent specialized governmental research staff, their temporary equivalents in commissions and task forces, and a large group of non-governmental specialists associated with think tanks and interest groups. Although often seen as 'knowledge suppliers', policy consultants almost by definition exist in the brokerage sub-system, which is where most professional policy analysts can be found (Verschuere 2009; Abelson 2002; Dluhy 1981).

This model suggests that different types of 'policy advice systems' exist depending on the nature of the knowledge supply and demand, and that what consultants do in brokering information, how they do it, and with what effect, is largely dependent on the type of advisory system present in a specific government or area of interest. This helps to explain why we find different policy analysis styles in different policy fields (Mayer, Bots and van Daalen 2004; Lindquist and Howlett 2004), since these can be linked to cultural *doxa* and practices of political actors and knowledge suppliers conditioning how policy advice is generated and deployed (Peled 2002; Howlett and Lindquist 2004; Bevir and Rhodes 2001; Bevir, Rhodes and Weller 2003; Aberbach and Rockman 1989; Bennett and McPhail 1992; Gunter 2012).

Some of this variation in advisory systems is temporal in nature, and is due to the fact that the introduction of elements of formal or professional policy analysis into the brokerage function has a different history in each jurisdiction (Prince 1983, 1979, 2007). Given its reliance on existing institutional arrangements for political decision-making, however, an advisory system's exact configuration can be expected to vary not only temporally, but also spatially, by jurisdiction, especially by nation-state and, somewhat less so, by policy issue or sector. That is, personal and professional components of the policy advice supply system, along with their internal and external sourcing, can be expected to combine in different ratios, in different policy-making situations (Prince 1983; Wollman 1989; Hawke 1983; Rochet 2004). Understanding these variations is critical in understanding the role consultants play in the policy advisory, and policy-making, processes.

Generally, however, four distinct 'communities' of policy advisers can be identified within the policy advice system depending on their location inside or outside of government, and by how closely they operate to decision-makers: core actors, public sector insiders, private sector insiders and outsiders (see Table 1.1).

The actual jobs and duties performed by each set of policy advisers in either type of organization must be empirically determined in each instance. Understanding how the four communities do or do not relate to and reinforce each other is a critical, and very much understudied, determinant of the system's overall capacity and effectiveness. Important aspects of the functioning of policy advice systems include factors such as whether or not, or what type of, 'boundary-spanning' links exist between governmental and non-governmental organizations (Weible 2008). Additionally, attention is given to whether or not employees have opportunities to strengthen their skills and expertise (O'Connor, Roos and Vickers-Willis 2007), or to outsource policy research to personnel in private or semi-public organizations and consultancies.

Table 1.1 *The four communities of policy advisers*

	Proximate Actors	Peripheral Actors
Public / Governmental Sector	Core Actors: • *Central Agencies* • *Executive Staff* • *Professional Governmental Policy Analysts*	Public Sector Insiders: • *Commissions, Committees* • *Task Forces* • *Research Councils/ Scientists*
Non-Governmental Sector	Private Sector Insiders: • *Consultants* • *Political Party Staff* • *Pollsters*	Outsiders: • *Public Interest Groups* • *Business Associations* • *Trade Unions* • *Academics* • *Think Tanks* • *Media*

Consultants form one of these types of actors to whom policy research can be outsourced. They are non-civil servants brought into governments on a more or less temporary basis to augment existing internal expertise and personnel, including that related to public policy-making. Generally, consultants can play a highly significant role as 'privileged outsiders' similar to that of political party staff or pollsters with special access to key insiders, thereby linking the external and internal parts of the advisory system (Clark 1995; Druckman 2000). Like the other members of this quadrant, this makes them potentially highly influential in policy debates and outcomes. Unlike the other two, they have been studied little.

The scale of the use of consultants is a key issue, and the use of a threefold typology, distinguishing small-, medium- and large-scale use of policy consultants, is helpful in understanding the variation in the use of policy consultants (see Table 1.2).

Understanding the nature of this 'external' source of policy analysis, its various types and their influence, and its effectiveness in different analytical contexts involves discerning how a policy advisory system is structured and operated in the specific sector of policy activity under

Table 1.2 *Three types of consultancy*

	Type I Consultancy	Type II Consultancy	Type III Consultancy
Level of policy or structural disruption	Small	Moderate	Large
# of consultants involved	Small	Moderate	Large
Description	Small-scale, one-off, time-limited consultancy, not intended to be ongoing / repeated	Instrumental or process consultancy work changing rules / norms / legislation, etc.	Major consultancy exercise of massive scale, which changes the landscape / culture / political-administrative dynamics
Aim (example)	Advising on a particular issue; fixing a specific problem	Legislative change or changing a policy setting in regard to a constituency	Paradigm changes from old-style regulation to self-regulation

examination and how professional policy work is conducted within this system. The role that analysts and advisers existing *outside* of government play in policy-making has been less studied and is little understood, although the common wisdom concerning consultants is that for-hire consultants play a significant role in policy-making, arguably one that has increased significantly in recent decades (Dent 2002; Guttman and Willner 1976; Kipping and Engwall 2003; Martin 1998; Wagner and Wollman 1986). European studies, for example, have noted their explosive, though unevenly distributed, growth in use across countries and policy sectors (FEACO 2002). A 2007 UK government survey estimated their cost at approximately £5 billion in 2005–2006 (House of Commons 2007: 1), representing a 30 per cent increase in this estimate over the three-year period 2003–2006. Similar figures have been reported in New Zealand and Australia (see State Services Commission 1999; ANAO 2001). However, information on budgets and contracts is generally scarce, and more research studies are required to situate policy workers more firmly within the context of alternate sources of policy advice to governments (Adams 2004; Gunter and Mills 2017).

1.3 Policy Consultants, Consultocracy and the Contracting State

Due to a variety of issues around decision-making secrecy and lack of transparency in the interactions of external advice-givers, little is known regarding non-governmental policy advice in most countries (Hird 2005), except for the general weakness of actors such as think tanks and research institutes in most jurisdictions (Smith 1977; Stone and Denham 2004; McGann and Johnson 2005; Abelson 2007; Stritch 2007; Cross 2007; Murray 2007). Page's (2010) study of regulatory policy-making identified four types of expertise relevant in government: (1) scientific expertise; (2) policy expertise; (3) process expertise; and (4) instrument expertise. In earlier work, Page and Jenkins (2005) stressed how internal government experts are usually process experts, and more recent work confirmed a distinct lack of scientific, policy and instrument expertise among bureaucrats, opening the door, again, for external experts to exercise influence in these areas (Page 2010). However, due to a lack of data (and often, until recently, privacy and other laws around contracts), even less is known about the growing legion of consultants who work for governments in the 'invisible public service' (Speers 2007; Boston 1994). Much more research into these areas has been needed, and is provided in this book.

While the exact dimension of the policy consulting phenomenon is unclear, the *use* of external policy consultants in government has been an increasingly important focus of concern among governments in the USA, the UK, Canada and Australia, among others (ANAO 2001; House of Commons Committee of Public Accounts 2010; Bakvis 1997; MacDonald 2011; Project on Government Oversight 2011). Some (e.g. Saint Martin 2005) have written about the 'new cult of the management consultant' in government and have described consultants and 'intellectual mercenaries' as 'hired guns' that 'politicians can use to bypass reluctant civil servants', while others, such as Hood and Jackson (1991), have coined the term 'consultocracy' to underline the growing influence of consultants on the public management process. Another point of focus emerged with more fine-grained analyses of spending patterns related to the difficulties governments encountered in assessing precisely how the money has been spent (Macdonald 2011), and in creating structures capable of monitoring this activity (House of Commons Committee of Public Accounts 2010).

Some of this concern arose over the costs incurred by governments (Craig and Brooks 2006) as an offshoot of 'the contracting state', while others have suggested that the rise of the *consultocracy* has led to a diminishment of democratic practices and public direction of policy and administrative development (Saint-Martin 2004, 2005). Some accounts include policy consulting in a more general shift in overall state–societal relations – away from the 'positive' or 'regulatory' state (Majone 1997) and towards the 'service', 'franchise' or 'competition' state (Butcher et al. 2009; Perl and White 2002; Radcliffe 2010; Bilodeau, Laurin and Vining 2007). This approach centres on the idea that the contemporary 'service state' is based on many more external–internal links in the provisions of services – where contracting is often the norm – than the pre–WWII 'autarkic state', which relied on 'in-house provision of all kinds of services' aiming to deliver 'consistency, reliability and standardization' in service provision (Butcher et al. 2010:22). This old system has been replaced, they argue, by the contemporary service state: 'a hybrid mixture of part public part private activities, delivery chains that do not remain in neat boxes or organizational settings, loose combination of actors and providers who are each necessary to see something delivered' (Butcher et al. 2010: 31). Here, the state is the chief contractor, and the extension of contracts to policy and administrative matters should be neither surprising nor unexpected including that for-hire consultants play a role in policy-making, arguably an increasingly significant one (Dent 2002; Guttman and Willner 1976; Kipping and Engwall 2003; Martin 1998; Wagner and Wollman 1986).

Others see the use of consultants in policy-making as less significant, linked to the normal development of policy advisory systems in modern government as business groups and others require specialized expertise in their efforts to lobby governments, and government agencies in turn require similar expertise in order to deal with businesses, NGOs and other active participants in policy-making processes as interest intermediation grows increasingly professionalized and institutionalized (Halligan 1995; Lahusen 2002: 697). Czarniawska and Mazza (2003), for example, suggest that consultants are likely to play a limited mandate role, arguing that they are too poorly organized to exercise any kind of permanent policy influence, and therefore rely strongly on a variety of appropriate political and institutional characteristics to exercise influence.

This view is supported by van Houten and Goldman's (1981) and Saint-Martin's (1998a, 1998b) findings for Canada and provides the main working hypotheses proposed herein. That is, regarding professional governmental policy analysts in the internal policy advice supply network, we know that their activities are very closely tied to available resources in terms of personnel and funding, the demand they face from clients and managers for high-quality results, and the availability of high-quality data and information on future trends (Howlett 2009a; Riddell 2007). Non-governmental analysts are likely to share these same resource constraints and thus not to automatically influence government deliberations. Consultants' influence on policy-making is therefore likely to vary by issue and circumstance, and the sources and direction of these variations are important information for both policy theorists and practitioners interested in understanding the role of the 'hidden' or 'invisible public service' (Speers 2007).

1.4 Methodological and Data Limitations in Researching Policy Consultants

As this discussion suggests, policy scholars have a range of evidence and positions about the role of consultants in the policy process. Their views vary from estimations of their 'strong' influence on policy-makers to suggestions that this influence is at best diffuse and weak (Bloomfield and Best 1992). Both policy and management consultants are seen as either independent 'agents of change' (Lapsley and Oldfield 2001; Tisdall 1982) or as weak, 'liminal' subjects, dependent for any potential influence on allowances made for this by their employers (Czarniawska and Mazza 2003; Garsten 1999; Bloomfield and Danieli 1995).

Such dichotomous views should be easily resolvable through empirical analyses (Clark and Fincham 2002). These not only should more accurately assess the quantitative questions, such as how many consultants there are and if these numbers have grown over time, but would also carefully examine the qualitative questions around the nature of their influence on governments, from the provision of direct advice to the more indirect creation of specific kinds of knowledge and its mobilization/utilization in policy deliberations (van Helden et al. 2010; Weiss 1977 and 1986). However, both empirical and conceptual understandings of the origins and significance of the development of policy consultancy are mixed.

As Speers (2007) noted in her study of Canada's 'invisible private service', for the past several decades management consultants have been involved in every stage of the policy process. But despite this prominence, because of difficulties in generating empirical data on the subject few studies assess this question in purely policy terms (for notable exceptions, see Saint-Martin 1998a, 1998b, 2004, 2005, 2006). Rather, most draw upon studies of management consultants in government, or more generally, in making such assessments. Several significant methodological and data problems stand in the way of clarifying this debate, which the authors of this volume have sought to overcome.

First, concerns about the use of consultants in government are not recent, as numerous publications on the subject from the 1970s attest (Wilding 1976; Meredith and Martin 1970; Rosenblum and McGillis 1979; Guttman and Willner 1976; Kline and Buntz 1979). However, more recently concerns emerged not just about the size and number of consultancies, but about their apparent growth as a percentage of both government employees and expenditures (Speers 2007), and concomitantly about their increased influence and impact on the content and directions of government decision-making (Saint-Martin 1998; Speers 2007).

Second, as noted, generally the quality of existing data is poor (Howard 1996; Perl and White 2002; Lahusen 2002), as it is highly inconsistent and relatively rare while generally stressing the growth of the expenditure involved (FEACO 2002; House of Commons Committee on Public Accounts 2007; State Services Commission 1999; ANAO 2001). This problem affects the question of accountability and efficiency: that is, whether contracts are competitively priced (MacDonald 2011). At times, governments are hard pressed to assess these situations. The UK House of Commons Committee of Public Accounts (2010: 5) argued that it was '[not]'convinced by the Cabinet Office's argument that it is impossible to measure whether government's use of consultants represents value for money'.

Third, it must be possible to separate out 'policy consulting' from categories such as engineering or technical services consulting, as well as from 'management consulting' – the category often used to capture policy consulting in official government reports and documents (Saint-Martin 2006; Jarrett 1998). However, many 'consulting' activities are difficult to distinguish from those related to more general government goods (and especially services) 'contracting' (Davies 2001, 2008; Vincent-Jones 2006). Moreover, it is also often difficult in official statistics to distinguish 'consultants' from 'temporary and part-time workers' (MacDonald 2011; Project on Government Oversight 2011). These important distinctions, which are often glossed over in the limited literature on policy consultants and consultants in government, lead to over-estimation of the number of consultants when counting them together with 'contractors' and especially 'part-time' employees, which include large numbers of temporary office workers (MacDonald 2011; McKeown and Lindorff 2011). Policy consultants' numbers are also over-estimated when using the numbers of management consultants, which include figures for IT consultants and others not ranked separately in many government databases (Perl and White 2002; MacDonald 2011). In Canada, for example, the new Proactive Disclosure project (which publicizes federal contracts with a value of more than $CDN10,000) provides information for the departments and agencies of the federal public administration. However, only a very small percentage of these include a more detailed breakdown of the services provided that would allow researchers to assess whether the contracts have a policy dimension at all.

Fourth, while there may be concerns with the growth of policy consultancy in terms of the impact on public service unionization, professional standards and accountability for funds, it is difficult to determine the extent of *policy* influence from such numbers of consultants. Even when policy consultants are properly identified – a far from simple task – the question of their influence over policy processes and outcomes remains unclear. Some studies have stressed the role played by a few large companies in monopolizing the consultancy market and suggested the record of these firms in providing good advice is shaky at best (O'Shea and Madigan 1998). On the other hand, others have noted the large numbers of smaller firms involved in the industry and the often very weak position they find themselves in when advising large clients such as government departments (Sturdy 1997). Similarly, while some studies focus on the reputational aura that some consultants can muster given their status as experts and professionals (Evetts 2003a, 2003b; Kipping and Engwall 2003), others note the disregard in which their credentials are held by many employers (Czarniawska and Mazza 2003; Bezes 2011; Brint 1990).

1.5 What This Book Contributes to the Study of Policy Consulting and Chapter Outlines

This book gives centre stage to the study of the 'invisible public service' consisting of externally hired consultants. First, we develop and consistently apply a definition of policy consultancy that isolates the policy roles consultants fulfil from other categories of consulting. Based on solid empirical data from each of the six countries, we then assess the growth in numbers and expenditures of policy consulting per country and, wherever possible, per policy sector. We then explain the role policy consultants perform in the marketplace for policies, ideas and information. We aim to shed more theoretical light on the questions of under what circumstances core actors will be more likely to rely on policy consultants than on other advice-givers within the policy advisory system, and under what circumstances these policy consultants are more or less likely to influence or shape the content of policies. What evidence can be found for assertions that consultants are hired because the standing bureaucracy lacks scientific, policy and instrumental expertise? In doing so, we address what evidence can be found for assertions that core actors use consultants to bypass reluctant civil servants, and to what extent contracting has become the norm in the business of government. While addressing these questions, we are keenly sensitive to variations in our dependent variables (use of consultants and influence of consultants) across time, political-administrative systems and policy sectors. We thereby lift the topic of policy consultancy to a higher scholarly level and contribute significantly to theory-formation on the important, context-dependent role of policy consultants within the policy advisory system.

This introductory chapter has set out the motive for the book and has mapped the theoretical terrain of what is to come. It has set out the conceptual and analytical framework of the country studies, firmly embedding the phenomenon of policy consultancy into the topical debates in public administration, public management, policy sciences and political science. It has described the variation in different countries' overall political-administrative systems and, related to it, their policy advisory systems, the role(s) played by consultants within them, and the definitions and demarcations of the range of consultants to be examined in the study.

Each country-level chapter examines what the general tasks and activities of policy consultants are in a country-specific case. Categories of activities are identified according to two logics: first, related to the various stages of the policy cycle (analysis and preparation through to evaluation); and second, to professional disciplines and fields of activity (substantive/technical, legal, ICT, communications). Each case study examines in detail where consultants are employed within governments. However, the book will focus on the central government level, which is typically the only level for which any reliable data exists. Within that, there are variations by country across both policy sectors and types of organizations (core departments, executive agencies at arm's length and regulatory agencies). Some sectors and organization types make more use of consultants than others, and the patterns within and across jurisdictions will be displayed and explained.

Each chapter also addresses the reasons why consultants are employed. The literature cites various motives for hiring consultants, such as to legitimize a course of action an agency wishes to make, to help develop ideas of how to proceed, to clean up a scandal, to review agencies or programmes, to provide external feedback on government performances, or to create room to manoeuvre for politicians and others. Over time, these reasons for ongoing reliance may change. Independent variables that could explain variations include the nature of the political-administrative system, the degree of market-orientation of the state, the country's fiscal and economic situation at a given point in time, and the degree to which the incumbent government has set goals for major policy or system overhaul. The individual chapters examine how these variables play out, or not, in specific jurisdictions.

Chapter 2 examines the United Kingdom, where there is increased concern in critical policy studies about the use of consultancy services at central government level, through to the governments of the four nations (i.e. England, Northern Ireland, Scotland and Wales), local government and public service delivery. Such concerns are focused on the replacement of publicly appointed and accountable experts, through to profit making strategies at a time of austerity and the promotion of privatization. Empirical studies tend to focus on broad critical reviews of the entry, role and impact of consultants, or provide in-depth case studies of companies or policy changes. This chapter describes and explains the complexity of the emerging consultancy industry and how the government engages with it. It reports on a review of what research is saying about consultants and consultancy in UK government systems at the UK level, with a view to providing a new assessment of trends and impacts. The analysis shows the increase in consultancy within and for central government, with an emphasis on revealing the diversity in size and role of those who offer services and are contracted by government.

Chapter 3 examines the case of the United States. The USA forms the largest and most archetypal case of government contracting. Nonetheless, it has received little detailed empirical treatment, despite a plethora of anecdotal and popular accounts claiming to have documented a pattern of exponential growth in the size and impact of policy-related government contracting. This chapter reports on the distribution of the American federal government's contracting of policy services in the context of several initiatives on the part of the Obama administration, which provided for the first time reasonably accurate data related to questions about the size, trends and other aspects of US federal government policy consulting. The analysis shows that concerns about sizeable increases in consulting activity possibly undermining many 'core services of government' raised in earlier government and popular reports are not without merit, however, with significant variations across agencies in terms of the extent to which this has occurred. This uneven pattern of policy contracting is analysed and explained.

Chapter 4 examines Australia. The focus of the chapter is an analysis of the summary details of consultancies and contracts over the past three decades, as these were listed in mandatory official reporting systems of the national government. It contrasts a consistent and strong long-term growth in total spending on consultancies and contracts with stagnation in the level of in-house staffing and related running costs. It examines the 'take-off' years of the late 1980s and early 1990s and argues that a significant proportion of consultancies directly addressed 'programme content', as distinct from administrative arrangements or corporate services. It also establishes a much larger level of spending on policy-relevant contracts in the decade from 1997 and a further doubling-to-trebling of this spending in the decade from 2007. The chapter also analyses the distribution of this consultancy and contract spending on the supply side. Both for the 'take-off' years (late 1980s and early 1990s) and the period 1997–2017, it finds a polarized distribution: a corporate end where a very small proportion of suppliers get much of the spending, and with a huge array of sundry operators undertaking very small amounts of work. It argues that the long-term market share of successful contractors puts them in a position to influence many aspects of programme development. The chapter also examines the demand side of the consultancy and contracting relationship. It finds that the Department of Defence is a standout spender throughout the period, especially during 1997–2007, and that departments tend to fall into three bands of absolute spending both in the earlier and later parts of the period. At the same time, it also establishes that the overall pattern of growth in spending is replicated right across Commonwealth departments, both in the earlier and later decades. The chapter ends with some discussion of the implications of these patterns for the notions of 'consultocracy' and the 'contractor state'.

Chapter 5 examines the case of the Netherlands. In line with its consensus-driven and neo-corporatist political-administrative tradition, the policy advisory system in the Netherlands has been characterized by a great openness to external sources of advice, including policy consultancy. The country's government has often been described as the world's second largest per capita consumer of public sector consultancy, after the USA. Two main factors account for the increase in the use of policy consultants since the early 1980s. First is the relative decrease in the standing of institutionalized advisory councils and boards, a gap that has in part been filled by policy consultants from a number of large international, as well as Dutch, independent consultancy firms. Second, New Public Management-style reforms and subsequent rounds of government austerity since the 1980s have resulted in a decrease in the volume of internal policy advisers within departments and agencies. Here too, consultants have in part compensated for the loss of internal policy advisory capacity. The Dutch case therefore points to externalization and politicization of the policy-making process, both of which have worked to increase the demand for policy consultancy. From a political point of view, hiring consultants has been a preferred route to increasing policy competence in the Netherlands since: (a) at the top level of the organization, external consultants can be handpicked and better politically controlled than permanent civil servants; (b) external consultants provide a greater external legitimacy to a given policy than does the permanent civil service alone; and (c) the costs of external consultants are accounted for within the budget of material costs rather than under personnel costs, which makes it easier to conceal the real expenditure on human resources. While consultants fulfil roles in each phase of the policy cycle, the process- and management-oriented tasks are most prominent. Sectoral differences are significant, whereby in certain sectors seasonal peaks in implementation are absorbed by means of consultants and in other sectors technical policy innovations are designed by consultants. The analysis is based on time series of government data, secondary Dutch literature and research reports, and primary survey data among top civil servants and policy consultants themselves. The analysis gives rise to important normative questions related to the real cost of policy consultancy, the damage consultancy may do to internal expertise and continuity, and the identification and regime loyalty temporary staff has towards the government as a whole.

Chapter 6 discusses the Canadian case. Analysis of the use of policy and management consulting in the Canadian federal government based on the new Proactive Disclosure data reveals a picture of a highly skewed process in which several departments dominate the demand for consulting services, and the significance of large and repeat contracts. It suggests a pattern of long-term ongoing interactions between suppliers and purchasers of these services – one which reinforces in this area of government activity the same pattern of the 'permanence of temporary services' found in earlier aggregate studies of government contracting and temporary help. This pattern of expenditures is consistent with the idea put forward by Speers (2007) and Saint-Martin (2006) that consultants comprise a hidden or 'invisible civil service'. In other words, despite their legal status being temporary and ad hoc in nature, they have a more or less permanent and fixed character, which largely escapes traditional reporting and accountability measures, operating without even the limited transparency provisions that allow some insights into the world of the visible public service and its impact on public policy-making.

Finally, Chapter 7 addresses Sweden, a country long characterized by its large public sector and welfare system. However, following the rise of NPM, activities formerly performed by public sector organizations have become increasingly privatized. As a consequence, the responsibility for services such as pensions, health care and schools has partially been transferred from the state to private organizations and individual citizens. As part of this development, government agencies' use of policy and management consultancy services has increased. The consultants have been recurrently described in academic literature and Swedish media as carriers of NPM ideals, and as playing a central role in the privatization efforts in the public sector. That said, detailed information about the use of consultancy services in the Swedish public sector has been lacking. Building on longitudinal quantitative data on government agencies' spending on consultancy services and interviews with policy-makers, this chapter provides a rich illustration of how the use of consultancy services has developed over time and has been distributed over different government agencies. The chapter ends with an analysis and discussion of the identified patterns.

The final chapter summarizes the findings of, and draws comparative conclusions from, the preceding chapters. It highlights the main conceptual and theoretical contributions our work aims to make to the related academic fields more broadly. This is where patterns across similar political-administrative systems will come to the fore, and other, previously unexpected patterns revealed in the book's examination are set out and discussed.

2 | Consultancy in the UK Government: Modernizing Privatism

2.1 Introduction

Demands made by the UK government for external policy support are big business, where the highest spend on consultants has been calculated at £2 billion in 2003–2004 (NAO 2006), and currently major consultancy firms are active in bidding for six months of Brexit work with a price tag of £1.5 million (Martin 2017). At the same time, the focus has been on review and retrenchment, with a fall in spending to £1.8b in 2005–2006 (NAO 2006), whereby 'the government is determined to make every taxpayer penny count' and the 'Cabinet Office is working to help departments reduce reliance on everything from expensive consultants to print cartridges' (Gov.uk 2015). Thus, it seems there is recognition of a contribution to public policy that is beyond 'in-house' capacity: 'when used correctly and in the appropriate circumstances … [they] … can provide great benefit to clients – achieving things that clients do not have the capacity or capability to do themselves' (NAO 2006: 4). At the same time, there are concerns about a failure to deploy and manage efficiently and effectively: 'When used incorrectly, consultants can drain budgets very quickly, with little or no productive results' (NAO 2006: 4). While this matter of utility and value for money has been a major feature of official scrutiny (NAO 2006; 2010), research and investigative journalism have sought to raise questions regarding modes of entry about and impact on democracy (Hood and Jackson 1991; Craig with Brooks 2016; Saint-Martin 2000). Consultants can be benign 'change agents' (Lapsley et al. 2013) as well as 'intellectual mercenaries' (Leys 1999) who are characterized as 'demons' who trade in 'sharp practices' (Lapsley et al. 2013: 118).

This chapter focuses on the Whitehall UK government to examine the modernization of *privatism*. Privatism refers to 'club government' (elite generalist civil servants) in relation to practitioners (such as teachers, lawyers and medical professionals), whose respective roles within public policy have been fractured and modernized through the entry of a range of 'external experts' as illuminated in Chapter 1 (Green 2015; Moran 2003). Experts include political advisers and think tanks, as well as 'Tsars' with specialized knowledge deemed able to make a difference to the economy, health or welfare; for instance, the work of Mary Portas and the rejuvenation of the high street, or Emma Harris (A4e) and getting people back to work. Additionally, experts are also individual consultants, teams and global firms, such as PricewaterhouseCoopers and McKinsey & Company.

What is modern about modernization through the work of external experts is the normality and vitality of change, driven by attitudes, languages and strategies that are focused not only on restructuring and reculturing public services, but also on the policy processes, institutions and advice networks that frame and deliver such services. Consequently, knowledge production for and within modernized and modernizing public policy is about 'relevance', 'utility' and 'dynamism' – in regard to both the realities of 'know-how' and the symbolism of those who are recognized as being 'in the know' in ways that are considered modern (Radaelli 1995). The state is therefore rendered knowledgeable through how knowers, knowledge claims, knowledge sites and knowledgeabilities are identified and procured, and how privatism is reworked from the 'club' to the 'contract'. In this modification of privatism, networking may have shifted to the transparency of the remit and delivery, but the deal-making and operation of private interests remains. Integral to the contract is the financialization of knowledge production, whereby what is deemed to be of value, or worth knowing and using, is that which can be commodified and sold. Hence, the packaging, transfer and implementation of a product with the legitimacy of having worked in corporate organizations becomes fundamental.

While a range of knowledge actors have been brought into Whitehall to both frame and deliver modernization, this chapter focuses specifically on the '4Cs': 1) *consultants* – contracted to give policy advice and deliver policy outcomes; 2) *consulting* – the practices that respond to and direct client demands; 3) *consultation* – the interplay of consultants and clients through consulting; 4) *consultancy* – what is to be done, who by, when, with what impact, and at what price (Gunter and Mills 2017). What is interesting about the 4Cs is how particular people, practices and programmes can be considered to have challenged and replaced civil servants and public professionals as 'experts'. Moreover, of interest is how this is being questioned and debated, not least how 'it is not self-evident that corporate management consultants or party political "fixers" are necessarily better placed to give advice on how to reshape ministries and major public services than civil and public services themselves' (Pollitt and Bouckaert 2011: 66). Hence the 4Cs are not settled and remain controversial in regard to their cost, role, contribution, and, in particular, the impact on democracy.

This chapter offers an analysis that begins with the examination of the contextual shifts in knowledge production in Whitehall and the location of the 4Cs within the design and enactment of public policy through the knowledgeable state. The chapter will then examine in detail the specific role of consultants as knowledge actors, before charting their particular role in knowledge processes, particularly how they carry, embed and normalize privatization through data, ideas and argumentation.

2.2 Modernizing Knowledge Production in UK Public Policy

The research reported here locates UK government public policy processes within a variant of the contractor state as outlined in Chapter 1, and follows Pearton (1982) to adopt the concept of the *knowledgeable state*, regarding how and why government takes up a particular position within knowledge production. Contracting as a formal and relational process begins on the basis of the state. First, as 'overall policy-maker' through outlining and leading on purposes by 'defining the ends'. Second, as provider through the provision of services and accreditation of a workforce (e.g. engineers, doctors and teachers) that translate 'ends into specific demands'. Third, 'as the national revenue-raiser' because in the final instance, public investment 'finances the whole process' (Pearton 1982: 254). Consequently, the people, institutions and processes of the state are knowledgeable, demand knowledge, and seek out ways of knowing and relationships with knowers, through contractually identifying, commissioning and deploying goods and services.

The dimensions of the knowledgeable state are:

Knowers: Those within government as elected politicians or as appointed officials, who present knowledge (in the form of an election manifesto or a

CV) and have 'know-how'. They seek to know better and/or differently through contractual exchange relationships with those in civil society who have experiential, theoretical and empirical evidence, with various stand-points, ideologies and positions.

Knowledge sites: Knowers as knowledge actors locate in a range of places and spaces regarding policy-making. These can be formal public institutions, such as 10 Downing Street and the Cabinet Office; various Whitehall departments, as well as the wider system(s) of government (such as Parliament, devolved governments in Scotland, Northern Ireland and Wales); or socio-political arenas (meetings, teams, social events) that are constituted for a particular purpose. Networks that reach externally into companies, universities, think tanks, lobby groups and supra-national organizations (e.g. World Bank, OECD) and govern-ments (e.g. the EU) can relocate the site of knowledge production in regard to public policy, and hence regulation is through contracts (and confidentiality agreements).

Knowledge claims: Knowledge actors in a range of sites seek to gen-erate and access knowledge in the form of ideas, evidence and arguments in order to develop, support and confirm an intervention in civil society and/or a reform of a public service. Claims are about framing a case (sometimes with normative statements about the world, linked to ideo-logical standpoints) and using data (statistics, case narratives) that are convincing and robust.

Knowledgeabilities: The veracity and viability of knowers, with claims developed and used in particular sites, is through both demonstrating that they know and can be trusted, and through recognition and acclaim for that knowing. Such knowledgeability is located in language and skills, but also in embodied deportment, accent and status. For example, a minister has the legitimacy of the election mandate and can exhibit this at the despatch box in the House of Commons or on a TV programme. Such a communication strategy is about making policy legible, where the prime focus is on declara-tions about the challenges to be faced and the simplification of the solutions articulated (Scott 1998).

Successive UK governments have sought to modernize the knowledge-able state by presenting modernizing reform strategies (e.g. Tony Blair in 1999 and David Cameron in 2011). *Modernization* is a multi-faceted word that encapsulates notions of transformation, progress and innova-tion, based on a break with the past, as well as asking questions such as: *what is holding Britain back?* Addressing such matters tends to focus on structures, systems and the people who inhabit them, with claims about red tape, in addition to elite interests seeking to maintain a hold on power. Hence, claims for the modern are packed and unpacked as a means of ensuring that Whitehall departments and co-ordinating processes at 10 Downing Street and the Cabinet Office not only enact manifesto commitments as an election mandate for government, but also have the right people, doing the right things, in order to deliver the necessary changes. The BBC comedy programme *Yes Minister* (1980–1984) characterized the problems of the modernizing reforms of Whitehall and the civil service. The show depicts fictional character Jim Hacker as the Secretary of State for Administrative Affairs; Hacker is manipulated and under the control of Sir Humphrey Appleby, the permanent secretary. The idea of the 'mandarin' culture of a ruling class of hierarchical and procedural generalist civil servants was made visible through this realistic fiction, and it spoke to governments on both the left and the right who were concerned not only about policy failure, but also about the workings of 'club government'. Furthermore, the programme sparked interest in how the civil service set out to thwart reforms in order to maintain their own purposes and practices as a privatized 'state within a state' (Kellner and Crowther-Hunt 1980).

The 'Sir Humphrey Appleby-ization' of Whitehall has been a strong feature of reform initiatives from the 1960s onwards, where modernization has variously featured reviews and changes to structures and systems, the composition of the civil service and relationships with external experts (see Hood 1990). For Prime Minister Harold Wilson (1964–1970 and 1974–1976), the modernization imperative of the 1960s was about realizing the post-colonial identity of the UK and meeting the demands of scientific progress. This is encapsulated in the Fulton Report (1968), regarding the need for policy planning driven by outside experts and talented civil servants as the antidote to an essentially Victorian–Oxbridge, elitist and generalist administration. Edward Heath (1970–1974) put emphasis on outside experts through the creation of the Central Policy Review Staff (a think tank) designed to provide the prime minister with knowledge separate from the operation of the Whitehall machine. Margaret Thatcher (1979–1990) recognized the potential of civil service advice and processes to obstruct conviction politics, and integral to her strategy was to challenge an overloaded government through sell-offs and outsourcing of public services and assets, but also to bring in people with private sector financial management cultures and methods to shake up Whitehall. Sir Derek Rayner (chairman of Marks & Spencer) headed up the Efficiency Unit

(1979–1983), where 'Rayners Raiders' set out to make visible changes that saved public money through planned and forensic scrutiny (Haddon 2012). Restructuring following the Ibbs Report (Efficiency Unit 1988) enabled the changes to go deeper through focusing on the skills of the Whitehall core, and the relocation of activity and civil servants to arms-length agencies, such as in the HM Stationery Office and Meteorological Office (Panchamia and Thomas 2014). More recently, this emphasis on investment delivery and outcomes during the Blair and Brown governments (1997–2010) has accentuated not only performance skills and cultures, but also how the standards of public services matter more than structures (Barber 2007). However, the Conservative–Liberal Democrat coalition (2010–2015) and the subsequent Conservative governments (2015–present) have set out to disinvest through austerity and intensified privatization. Echoing Thatcherism, David Cameron (2011) argued: 'There are things government does today that it will stop doing'. In other words, while delivery matters, the idea of universal services through public provision (rather than through the private or voluntary sectors) is being questioned, sold and outsourced.

This brief overview has identified some major trends in the modernization of the knowledgeable state:

Knowers: The prime knowers remain elected politicians who are directly accountable to the public through elections, but there has been increased recognition of the importance of particular types of 'expert'. Successive governments have set out to reform and replace 'neutral' but 'private' expertise, as typified by 'Sir Humphrey Appleby', where new forms of 'private' (from the corporate world or the City) individuals, networks and companies currently dominate. Following Jessop (2002), it seems that the 'Schumpeterian Competition State' is shifting, challenging and overtaking the 'Keynesian National Welfare State', whereby the latter is attacked and rolled back, and the former is enabled and developed through the focus on economic growth and capital accumulation. Consequently, knowers are outsiders to the Whitehall 'village', and it is only by being outside that experts know how to compete to generate competition. Thus, by entering Whitehall they can 'institutionalize' and legitimize the modern (Pollitt and Bouckaert 2011). Importantly, such outsiders have brought a dynamic change imperative, where the focus is on restructuring – or what Pollitt (2007) has identified as endemic 're-disorganisation'.

Knowledge sites: The prime sites for public policy-making in the form of public institutions remain, but there have been three main trends. First, the shift from the provision of services through public institutions (hospitals, schools, transport, etc.) to the commissioning of those services at 'arms-length' through 'trusts' (e.g. Multi-Academy Trusts in education), as well as the practice of outsourcing through procurement contracts, where public institutions have taken on slimmed-down, management (Clarke and Newman 2007) and regulatory roles (Moran 2003). Second, the intensified shift to outsourcing based on the contractual purchasing of goods and services. Flynn and Asquer (2017) identify this as the challenges and differences from buying a nuclear submarine to school stationery. Competition is involved in regard to the operation of provider–purchaser arrangements. Third, the shift away from government to forms of networked governance, where the combined effect of sourcing external 'competition knowers' and the restructuring of the state to authorize and deliver competition has impacted on what Bevir and Rhodes (2003: 6) identify as 'the hollow state and the differentiated polity'. The removal of decision-making from political representatives in public institutions to agencies 'at one remove' (Burnham 2001: 128), or outsourced to contracted providers, are forms of depoliticization. These processes reach all the way down to the individual and the family, who now have to choose and pay for supply–demand services (such as health, education, pensions and elderly care), which were previously provided by the state.

Knowledge claims: The prime claims regarding public policy remain located in the conviction ideologies of political parties in the adversarial Westminster system, but where the focus has shifted from political debate to performance delivery. Importantly, the trend features two related processes: New Public Management (NPM), and Evidence-Informed Policy and Practice (EIPP). NPM is based on explicit standards (benchmarks) combined with audits and evaluations, where there is a shift from the normality of management to new forms of power relationships (Hood 1991). Technical accountability for the delivery of an outcome is related to claims regarding 'what works'; thus, the operational practices on enacting public policy require robust and defendable evidence underpinning what has been done and what will be done. The *reculturing* of public service means that 'there is no alternative' (TINA) to what Rose (1991) identifies as 'governing by numbers', whereby NPM operates on the basis of performance measurement and EIPP supplies ideas, strategies and data to make the case for improving the numbers (see Gunter et al. 2016). Whitehall contract suppliers can operate within and contribute to the development of this knowledge regime, as well as 'nudge' and be 'nudged' in order to realize policy goals (Thaler and Sunstein 2008). Calls have been made for unmodern knowledge producers in higher education to cooperate (see DfEE 2000), or face being labelled as 'enemies' of progress (Hyman 2005).

Knowledgeabilities: The prime knowledgeabilities in public policy remain located in historical traditions with regard to the demonstration and communication of political party values and visions, but with a shift to modern branding that puts making a pitch for funding and process delivery above contested debate. This means risk management is a key consideration regarding investment (of money, reputation, career, etc.), and if a policy does not achieve the required outcomes, the focus is on avoiding or relocating blame (see Hood et al. 2004). Importantly, while digitalization and social media give more direct access to public servants and services, with the opportunity for more choice in relation to individual needs, the concerns over security mean that direct access is controlled through procedural checks (see Hood and Margetts 2007). Within this context, Whitehall knowledgeability is related to corporatized problem management as technical identification and solution implementation, where security of data and personal standing is about handling the media with regards to questions about numbers. However, integral to risk within public policy is recognition of a swing away from the dependent citizen to the aspirational consumer that relocates responsibility away from the taxpayer and towards the insured and active 'self' (Peters 2016). Self-reliance is challenging party identification towards individualized calculations of 'what's in it for me?' or 'who does what for me?' For, the unmotivated and dependent citizen, the safety net is provided by charities, the voluntary sector and philanthropy.

Movements within the knowledgeable state illuminate the importance of the contract as a formal agreement to deliver services in ways that are timed and funded, with outcomes evaluated. This enables ministers to have the right type of numbers in order to demonstrate performance at the ballot or despatch box, and the numbers in turn are produced by Whitehall through the focus on targets, benchmarking, scorecards and outcome measurement data. Contracts can be renewed or terminated as a means of securing efficient and effective government. Forms of contractualism are developing where practices that are not governed by contracts are actually thought about, organized and enabled through a contract ethos. This challenges the binaries and segregations of insiders and outsiders (as noted in Chapter 1) and suggests the pervasive adoption of consultancy dispositions by those who are not contracted consultants. As Yeatman (1997) argues, what is developing is a form of 'contractual personhood', where particular types of knowers – in accepted sites with approved claims and forms of communication – are enabled to have an impactful voice with authority and legitimacy.

Integral to this redesign in power relationships is the financialization of knowledge production: what you know and how you know is now primarily about whether such knowing is worth knowing. Such calculations of 'value' are based on price and cost (resources such as time, money and reputation) in relation to the functionality of what works by the prescription of outcomes, and how exchanges impact on dispositions about what can be said and done, and what can be claimed. Financialization of knowledge means that what is known and can be known is commodified into a product that is designed, produced, retailed and purchased on the basis of functional fit. Therefore, the consumption of knowledge meets and shapes the ideas, assumptions and predilections of the 'consumer', where designing knowledge for sale requires manufacturing and 'value-facturing' for a market. Moreover, other forms of knowledge production that cannot be commodified are excluded and potentially denounced (see Ward 2012).

The growth and orientation of the 4Cs needs to be understood within this context, whereby firms and individuals have positioned themselves to take advantage of – and to participate within – modernizing privatism in public policy knowledge production. For example, PA Consulting (2017) makes the following declaration:

Our mission is to transform and improve public services. We work with the full spectrum of government and the public sector, from central departments through to universities and local service providers. We can help you create or remodel services, making the most of the latest technology, getting value for money and making life easier for the people who use them. Here's what we can do:

- Understand and interpret what people need from your services.
- Build and prove cases and sourcing strategies for the changes and investments you want to make.
- Redesign organizations to make them more effective and more agile.
- Deliver major change: from implementing new IT to developing the workforce and embedding complex culture change.
- Improve budgeting and sourcing processes and outcomes.
- Help you exploit the opportunities and deal with the risks involved with digital technology, including delivering innovative and award-winning services.

Indeed, the Management Consultancies Association (MCA 2016) responded to the NAO (2016) report on consultancy and public policy by stating:

The NAO report highlights that management consultancies bring much needed skills and expertise to the public sector. The UK's world-class consulting industry's partnership with central government is helping deliver policy promises and transform and improve public services. Our evidence is that this vital collaboration increasingly delivers value for money for the taxpayer. Typically, consulting projects across all sectors deliver benefits worth around £6 for every £1 spent. But we can make this good news still better. The consulting industry is pressing government to accelerate the use of more innovative ways of working and to focus clearly on achieving the best outcomes for taxpayers. Partnerships between management consultancies and government are improving the management of long-term health conditions, delivering reductions in crime and greater public safety, introducing new digital services, and helping to make government itself more efficient and effective. We increasingly expect public services to be easily accessible, particularly as digital technology opens up opportunities to deliver them in new ways and short-circuit expensive processes. That's why over a third of the consulting services provided to central government involve designing and delivering digital services and technology innovation.

These examples of the individual firm and the network that represents firms illustrates the private role of the 4Cs in modernized public policy-making. The framing of the contribution through the use of the label 'management' suggests urgent and relevant technical know-how that is not, as Chapter 1 outlines, the key focus of this book. However, it is important to note how such claims are located in wider policy processes that are contributed to and enabled through what might be called 'management'.

Knowers: The 4Cs are presented as the prime knowers – they can construct and deliver contractual competitiveness, and so retail expertise in ways that enable the right type of difference to be made to public services. Their responsiveness (through billability and espoused flexibility) means that they are motivated, fleet-of-foot and experienced in corporate processes. Their 'can do' and 'know how' dispositions can replace the privileged 'Sir Humphrey's' (and other publicly trained, accredited and appointed professionals) that have dominated Whitehall and public services, and thus 'get things done' in ways that 'make a real difference'.

Knowledge sites: The 4Cs can enter public institutions and relocate decision-making to more productive arenas in ways that render political debate inefficient and obsolete, and that introduce templated procedural checklists and delivery schedules. Consultants as teams, or as part of teams or advisers to teams, mean that they and/or civil servants can get on with the job without interference, allowing consumers to access the services they need according to their priorities and resources.

Knowledge claims: The 4Cs have tried and tested organizational and people-control processes (e.g. Business Process Re-engineering, or 360-degree performance review) that can be brought in to reform the government machine (including local services), or can be bespoke and bought in for special reforms. The latter have in place data production that will monitor and measure impact and change, in order to guarantee numbers that demonstrate what is working and why, as well as why not, with clear chains of accountability and responsibility.

Knowledgeabilities: The 4Cs have ways of thinking, talking, being and doing that enable convincing and robust approaches to the change imperative and where the consumer–citizen can access services and insure the self, and others can be supported (or not) through gifting.

Attention is now paid to mapping the role and impact of the 4Cs as knowledge actors within UK government public policy.

2.3 Consultants as Knowledge Actors

Public policy in the UK government is the remit of politically neutral, publicly appointed and remunerated civil service, where there are two main trends. The first trend shows reduction in size: in September 2016 there were 384,950 (full-time equivalent) civil servants in post, and it is reported that this is down 18.5 per cent since 2010, the smallest since World War II (Whitehall Monitor 2017a). The second trend aims to improve capability and flexibility through intensified challenges to the generalist culture and practice of the civil service, based on the argument from the 1960s that more specialists should be brought in in order to advise and support programmatic changes in public services. The contracting of the 4Cs is integral to both the slimming down and the cultural change in the civil service, where a range of 4C companies are actively involved.

Table 2.1 shows the top ten consultancy providers.

By 2016, the NAO outlined that the largest suppliers include the Big Four: Deloitte, PricewaterhouseCoopers, Ernst & Young and KPMG (Consultancy.uk 2016), as well as PA Consulting Services Ltd and

Table 2.1 *Government's use of consultants*

Supplier	Spend 2005 (£ million)
IBM	275
LogiaCMG	175
Accenture	130
PA Consulting	102
Capgemini	85
Matt MacDonald	77
PwC	65
Atos	59
KPMG	57
Deloitte	50

Source: From NAO (2006): 7.

McKinsey & Company (NAO 2016: 15). Furthermore, there is a complexity of individuals and their companies (including sole traders and universities) involved in contracted supply of services (see Gunter and Mills 2017).

Reviews of the use of consultants in UK public policy-making have identified three reasons for their normalized and vital contributions:

1. People – access to specialist skills;
2. Process – knowledge on how to approach a task;
3. Perspective – an independent view; new innovative thinking. (NAO 2010: 10)

It is argued that projects are highly complex and of such a scale that in-house staffing cannot deliver, and to 'employ' this range of staff as a salaried workforce is seen as an inefficient use of public funds. Furthermore, this type of 'external' expert can bring objectivity and be responsive to intense demands on government, where their roles may vary from policy advice and the drafting of legislation through to a temporary appointment to a project team, or the management of outsourced services. *Consultants and Temporary Staff* (known as CATS or C&TS)[1] are defined as follows:

[1] Also styled as Consultancy and Contingent Labour CCL – House of Commons, 2014: 14.

Consultancy: 'The provision to management of objective advice relating to strategy, structure, management or operations of an organisation, in pursuit of its purposes and objectives. Such advice is provided outside the 'business-as-usual' environment when in-house skills are not available and will be time-limited. Consultancy may include the identification of options with recommendations, or assistance with (but not the delivery of) the implementation of solutions.'

Temporary staff or contingent labour: 'The provision of workers to cover business-as-usual or service delivery activities within an organisation.' This includes:

- Temporary workers – administrative and clerical staff employed casually or through an agency;
- Interim managers – normally middle-to-senior grade staff; and
- Specialist contractors – usually middle-to-senior grades providing expertise not available in-house. (NAO 2016: 14)

Nevertheless, parliamentary scrutiny reports show variations in spending on consultancy. At the turn of the century the focus was on cost, with a reduction from £1.8 billion in 2005–2006 to £1 billion in 2009–2010 (House of Commons Committee of Public Accounts 2007: 3). While the plan was to reduce spending on CATS, the NAO (2010) review shows increases in spending by Education, Communities and Local Government, DEFRA, FCO and Transport. Meanwhile, there were reductions by DWP, BIS, Heath, Culture, Defence, HMRC, Cabinet Office, Justice and International Development (2010: 14). Indeed, the most recent review demonstrates the rise in spending overall:

Since 2009–10, the government has used spending controls to reduce its use of consultants and temporary staff, and by 2014–15 spending had fallen by £1.5 billion. However, spending has increased by between £400 million and £600 million since 2011–12, suggesting that this was more of a short-term reduction than a sustainable strategy. (NAO 2016: 4)

Thus, the use of CATS remains a major public cost:

The main 17 government departments and their agencies paid permanent staff salaries totalling £17 billion in 2014–2015. Departments also spent between £1.0 billion and £1.3 billion on consultants and temporary staff, who are paid as independent suppliers rather than as employees. They can fulfil anything from highly specialist roles through to providing cover during peaks in demand for less skill work, and the approach to managing these resources needs to be tailored accordingly. Both consultants and temporary staff are sometimes used to fill gaps in the skills of the civil service. (House of Commons Committee of Public Accounts 2016: 4)

Spending does vary between departments, where in 2009–2010 the top five spenders were health (£108m), transport (£96m), education (£74m), the Home Office (£73m) and defence (£71m) (NAO 2010: 12). More nuanced recent analysis considers such spending variations in relation to the costs of permanent staff:

On average, departments and their arm's-length bodies spent 6 per cent to 8 per cent of their permanent staff salary-related costs on C&TS but this varies widely between departments and individual bodies. Two of the largest employers, HM Revenue & Customs and the Department for Work & Pensions, spend only the equivalent of 1 per cent to 2 per cent of their permanent staff costs on C&TS. In contrast, some smaller departments can be proportionately high users of C&TS: HM Treasury and the Cabinet Office spend 17 per cent and 35 per cent respectively of their permanent staff costs on C&TS. The Cabinet Office is a particularly large user of temporary staff (representing 24 per cent of its permanent staff costs) as it has a strategy of recruiting private sector expertise for fixed terms, for example, for the Government Digital Service, Major Projects Authority and Crown Commercial Service. (NAO 2016: 17)

This close attention to detail has raised questions about the contracting process, where in 2006 the National Audit Office was concerned about differences between departments regarding tenders, and the range of ways in which consultants were contracted and paid (NAO 2006). In 2014, the Crown Commercial Service (CCS) was created, and this brought together the 'delivery of policy, managed services and advice' in order to introduce coherence across Whitehall:

Sharing services and expertise will enable us to provide a high quality, flexible and resilient service for departments and customers across the wider public sector. Most importantly, it underpins our commitment to ensuring maximum value is extracted from every commercial relationship. (House of Commons 2014: 7)

Reporting shows savings; in particular, ' we have operated the central government consultancy and contingent labour, spend controls and saved £1.55 billion in 2013/14 compared to the 2009/10 baseline' (House of Commons 2014: 8).

While the case for the 4Cs is clearly made, the emphasis has been on value for money, where there is a need to consider the work that is undertaken and its impact. We now turn towards this matter.

2.4 Consultancy as Knowledge Processes

UK public policy-making has various demands regarding knowledge production, and – importantly – this means that trusted policy actors as knowers can be accessed and relied upon to undertake important activities. The NAO (2016) review is summarized in Table 2.2, where the most common types of consultancy spend procured through CCS agreements are *Multi-Specialism* and *Finance*:

What this means in reality can be explained by two case studies of the 4Cs in action – one at the level of the department, and one at the level of the project – as shown in Cases 1 and 2.

Case 1: Ministry of Defence (MoD), (House of Commons Hansard 2013)

The total spend on consultants by the MoD between 2007 and 2012 is presented in Table 2.3, showing a fall of 84 per cent.

The contracts awarded between May 2010 and November 2012 are listed in Table 2.4, providing an overview of the range of projects and suppliers with the contract value. The largest contract is for £12 million

Table 2.2 *Types of consultancy spend by departments, 2014*

Type of Consultancy Spend	Percentage (%)
Multi-specialism	49
Finance	17
Audit	10
Change management	8
Strategy	8
Human resources	6
ICT	2
Procurement	0

Source: Based on NAO 2016: 20.

Table 2.3 *Total MoD expenditure on consultancy*

	£ million
2007–2008	120
2008–2009	106
2009–2010	79
2010–2011	26
2011–2012	19

Source: House of Commons Hansard (2013). Contains
Parliamentary information licensed under the Open Parliament
Licence v3.0.

and the smallest for £638. Notably, the information shows that the Big
4 consultancies (Deloitte, PwC, E&Y and KMPG) have just under £31
million – or an 86 per cent share – of the contracts.

Case 2: *Improvements to London rail transport (House of Commons Hansard 2012a)*

Below there are two examples of transport projects:

First, the *Thameslink Rolling Stock Project* managed by the Department for
Transport, with the aim to have longer and more frequent trains in order 'to
provide additional capacity and remove passenger bottlenecks on the
London commuter network' (Gov.uk 2011). Table 2.5 provides a list of the
companies involved.

The second transport project example is the Thameslink Programme,
which focused on improving the railway lines, stations, rolling
stock and general integration of travel (Thameslink Programme
2017). Table 2.6 shows the companies involved.

Importantly, while PwC of the Big 4 is represented, there are a wider
range of consultancy firms outside of the top global players.

Examples from parliamentary scrutiny along with primary research
demonstrate the global status from big management companies
through to specialist companies (e.g. transport), and the importance
of the individual consultant who has moved from having done the job
within Whitehall (or agencies/services) and is now working in the
consulting context (e.g. Leys 1999). In addition, it seems that large
global companies have a brand and are required to speak to a template,

Table 2.4 MoD consultancy contracts awarded since May 2010

Start Date	Consultancy Name	Description of Requirement	Contract Value (£)
1 May 2010	Harness IT Consulting	Enterprise Resource Planning (ERP) Project – Implementation and Development – Project Team Costs	200,907
20 May 2010	Criterion	Leadership Forum design	16,800
21 May 2010	Cap Gemini plc	Barcoding Project – Transition and Project Management Consultancy	43,236
21 May 2010	Cap Gemini plc	Barcoding Project – Third-party services and software	41,150
21 May 2010	Pinsent Mason	Legal services for Project Delphi	60,000
27 May 2010	KPMG	Operational Efficiency Programme/Asset Management Review	101,592
7 June 2010	Criterion	Amendments to questionnaire	18,500
7 June 2010	Criterion	Update the Managing Performance V3 course	5,600
29 June 2010	Dr Mukulika Banerjee	Provision of subject matter expert advice to the Chief of the Defence Staff Strategic Advisory Forum	2,000
12 July 2010	Libra Advisory Group	External Assistance (EA) for Afghan Counter Insurgency Centre	18,250
23 July 2010	Criterion	Creation of Abstract Reasoning Test	17,000
1 August 2010	Cap Gemini plc	ERP Project – Implementation and Development – Technical Services	15,000
1 August 2010	Worldwide Technology UK Ltd	ERP Project – Implementation and Development – Project Team Costs – Cutover Management	148,779
1 August 2010	Ipsos Mori	Fleet Auxiliary Flotilla Survey	17,990

Date	Company	Description	Amount
10 August 2010	Inventures	EA on Defence Training Rationalisation Fall Back Plan	15,000
10 August 2010	Concerto Consulting Ltd	EA on Defence Training Rationalisation Fall Back Plan	11,000
16 August 2010	Pinsent Mason	Career Levelling – Legally Privileged	1,675
16 August 2010	Zenst	Provide coaching to support nominated senior managers	999
24 August 2010	QinetiQ	Support to Develop IA Training Courses	17,663
8 September 2010	Criterion	One Day Consultant design	2,800
27 September 2010	KPMG	Cost Assurance and Analysis Development Programme	12,000,000
5 October 2010	SCS Ltd	Field Army Stock Efficiency	31,500
6 October 2010	InterCultures Ltd	The provision of cultural advice and guidance to Commander Task Force Helmand and his staff covering political, economic, social and development environments, as well as civil-military issues	49,770
11 October 2010	CPCR	To tweak and update current Line Managers course	3,220
12 October 2010	Atkins Ltd	EA for Defence Acquisition Reform Programme (DARP) Partnering for skills Project Management Scoping Study	218,144
20 October 2010	TMP	Review of AIB	25,450
31 October 2010	Cranfield University	NATO Capability Culture Scoping Study	49,000
1 November 2010	Deloitte	External Assistance to the Re-Negotiation Process	120,000
5 November 2010	SCS Ltd	SO2 mission specific training resource management	100,000
23 November 2010	C. O. I	BFBS Media Broadcast Tech Support	40,000
20 December 2010	CPCR	Development of a one-day Bringing the Business Plan to Life event	1,610

Table 2.4 (*cont.*)

Start Date	Consultancy Name	Description of Requirement	Contract Value (£)
7 January 2011	Quatrosystem Ltd	Carry out a soft issues assessment of the six bidders competing for new ISP contracts	103,177
10 January 2011	KPMG	EA for Puma Mk2 Simulator and Synthetic Training Upgrade	64,578
14 January 2011	Transcend	To undertake work for the new operating model for DIO	48,500
4 February 2011	Criterion	Design of first Learning Community session	2,800
4 February 2011	Criterion	Design of one day event for Line Managers of Technical Consultants	7,000
15 February 2011	Criterion	Graduate Development line manager training design	1,400
16 February 2011	Mayo Learning	Training design	3,500
28 February 2011	In Partnership	Coaching and Organisation change projects	4,344
2 March 2011	Catalyze Ltd	Request for Technical Support to Assist in Down Selection of Site Options	15,000
10 March 2011	Bray Leino	Graduate Development Programme – Team build design	638
15 March 2011	Criterion	Design of a two-day training event for technical consultants	9,000
15 March 2011	Criterion	Research and development of simulation	9,000
21 March 2011	Freight Transport Association	External Support for Driver Certificate of Professional Competences	7,051
25 March 2011	KPMG	Admiralty Holdings Limited strategic review	110,762

Date	Company	Description	Amount
1 April 2011	Deloitte	External Assistance for Defence Infrastructure Transformation Programme	441,000
19 April 2011	In Partnership	Coaching and Organisation change projects	12,150
20 April 2011	Criterion	Additional development costs for the extension of the Building Technical Consulting Excellence event	4,200
29 April 2011	Serco Ltd	Continued Provision of Technical Support to Defence Crisis Management Centre	177,760
9 May 2011	Deloitte	Assist in the design and delivery of Defence Infrastructure Organisation (DIO) Transformation Programme	5,000,000
26 July 2011	Ernst & Young	Future Defence Storage and Distribution Project (FDSDP) EA Support	222,000
14 November 2011	QiResults	Provision of a Phase 2 Efficiency in Support Leader to Support the Materiel Strategy – Business Case/Investment Appraisal	72,000
29 November 2011	Deloitte MCS Ltd	Sale of Marsh wood	99,900
29 November 2011	Ernst & Young	EA for the Commercial Development of RAF Northolt	94,000
1 January 2012	Pricewaterhouse Coopers	SDSR Renegotiation of PFI Projects	169,465
4 January 2012	Deloitte MCS Ltd	EA to the Army 2020 study	106,000
16 January 2012	Ernst & Young	External Assistance Support to The FDSDP Tender Exercise	470,000
17 February 2012	Deloitte LLP	The provision of a Benchmarking exercise for the Royal Fleet Auxiliary against the Royal Navy and commercial operators	850,000
1 April 2012	Ernst and Young	Analysis of the capabilities required to deliver future Fleet management services within Defence Support Group (DSG)	39,000

Table 2.4 (*cont.*)

Start Date	Consultancy Name	Description of Requirement	Contract Value (£)
12 June 2012	Detica Ltd	Delivery of Cross Government ICT Strategy Outputs	149,430
13 June 2012	Deloitte LLP	The provision of consultancy support services to deliver improved leadership behaviours	1,529,912
1 July 2012	Prof. J. F. Alder	Provision of specialist support and advice on chemical and explosives activities	5,000
6 July 2012	Catalyze Ltd	External Assistance to the Change Programme Team at RAF Lyneham	10,000
9 July 2012	Deloitte MCS Ltd	EA to support Army 2020 Study	70,000
13 July 2012	LEK	Business Strategy Partner for Materiel Strategy	1,950,625
18 July 2012	Change Partners	Provision of services to support Corporate Intervention 2	20,000
31 July 2012	Atos Ltd	External Assistance for Logistic Commodities Category Management Assessment	16,500
10 August 2012	Maxxim Consulting LLP	Corporate Strategy Review and Development	51,325
14 August 2012	Deloitte MCS Ltd	Consultancy for the provision of technical advice and support to progress management and liabilities and rationalization in the warship build sector	599,836
10 October 2012	Bell Pottinger Public Affairs Ltd	The provision of consultancy support services to the MoD DIO transformation Project to support the Change Leadership and Communication requirements of the transformation programme	995,000

Date	Firm	Description	Amount
10 October 2012	PwC	The provision of consultancy support services to the MoD DIO transformation Project to support the Portfolio Integration and Management requirements of the transformation programme	942,560
10 October 2012	Deloitte	The provision of consultancy support services to the MoD DIO transformation Project to support the Enhanced Operating Model and Technology Solution Implementation requirements of the transformation programme and the Strategic Business Partner Procurement	5,922,928
15 October 2012	Deloitte	The provision of consultancy support services to the MoD DIO transformation Project to support the Footprint Strategy of the transformation programme	253,341
18 October 2012	Deloitte	EA for the Defence Fire and Rescue Project	426,474
19 November 2012	KPMG	The provision of consultancy support services to the MoD Material Strategy Project to support the construction of business cases, investment appraisals and benefits realizations for the transformation programme	1,145,250
			35,627,041

Source: House of Commons Hansard (2013). Contains Parliamentary information licensed under the Open Parliament Licence v3.0.

Table 2.5 *Thameslink rolling stock project*

	Costs Incurred to May 2010 (£ million)	Cost Incurred June 2010 to September 2011 (£ million)	October 2011 to March 2012 Forecast
Arup	4.0	1.7	0.5
Freshfields	6.6	1.9	1.3
PwC	2.5	0.9	0.6
Interfleet	1.5	0.1	0
Booz	0.5	0.3	0.1
Total	15.1	4.9	2.5

Source: House of Commons Hansard (2012a). Contains Parliamentary information licensed under the Open Parliament Licence v3.0.

Table 2.6 *The Thameslink Programme*

	Costs Incurred to May 2010 (£ million)	Cost Incurred June 2010 to September 2011 (£ million)	October 2011 to March 2012 Forecast
Atkins	0.5	0.1	0.1
EC Harris	0.2	0.1	0.25
SDG	0	0.1	0.03
Nichols	1.4	0.3	0.04
Bovis Lend Lease Consulting	0.7	0.4	0.09
Eversheds	0.07	0.01	0
Willis	0.036	0.004	0.01
Total	2.906	1.014	0.52

Source: House of Commons Hansard (2012a). Contains Parliamentary information licensed under the Open Parliament Licence v3.0.

or a particular way of doing things, or what Rasiel and Friga (2002) call 'The McKinsey Mind'. By way of contrast, those who operate as sole traders may well have been civil servants or professionals and now operate externally, but are regarded as 'more down to earth, they do not come with all the lines like "we aim to bring about positive change", they just do what they have to do and get on with it, without the need to be constantly justifying and pushing themselves' (Lapsley and Oldfield 2001: 541). However, whether a global or local product is on offer, and whether there are contingent and varied exchange relationships (Fincham 1999), the key to what the 4Cs are about is problems, problems, problems. The 'what works' and 'we make a difference' approaches from the private sector may not always be appropriate for public services, but in order to keep costs down the superiority of modernizing privatism continues.

Problems are concerned with the identification of a puzzle or obstacle that needs to be identified, understood, confronted and then fixed. The 4Cs are actively involved in:

Problem scoping: How a problem might be recognized (or not), where consultants are active in identifying a situation as a problem that can and should be solved.

Problem framing: How a problem might be understood, where consultants are active in characterizing and naming a problem using particular spaces, time and processes. For instance: 'the same idea, or rather what is perceived as the same or similar idea, may come back to the same place several times'. (Czarniawska and Mazza 2013: 124)

Problem solving: How a problem may be sorted through a particular strategy where consultants are active in moving decisions into and out of arenas, and using particular beliefs, strategy packages and delivery enactment schedules.

Problem re-solving: How a problem may be beyond 'solving' and so is part of an ongoing strategy where consultants are active in re-entering a situation and providing serial strategizing and product options.

How this operates around particular policies is evident in primary research, particularly regarding the impact of the 4Cs in the privatization of public assets:

Education: A range of research continues to examine the place and contribution of the 4Cs in the privatization of school provision by the UK government in England (Gunter 2017; Gunter et al. 2015; Gunter and Mills 2016, 2017).[2] Notably, this includes the role of international companies such as McKinsey and Company (Coffield 2012), in addition to individuals such as Ruth Miskin and literacy (Clark 2014, 2017) in winning contracts, influencing what can be imagined and levered in changes to the classroom and

---

[2] N.B.: Education policy for England is the responsibility of the UK government.

professional practices shaping reform agendas. The restructuring of school provision has generated between 70 and 90 different types of schools in England (Courtney 2015), with the 4Cs actively involved in advising government as well as schools on conversion, set up and sponsorship (see Ball 2011 on the role of KPMG and academies). In particular, professionalism has been re-agented as transformational leadership, where the 4Cs have not only framed the purpose of running a school as a business, but how through entrepreneurship national standards can be reached (or exceeded) with school expansion or failure (Gunter 2012; also see Coopers and Lybrand 1988; DfES/PwC 2007; Forde et al. 2000). Importantly, analysis is showing how the 4Cs are active in excluding research evidence and working with Whitehall to ignore or discredit alternative ways in which public services education might be imagined and enabled (Gunter 2018).

Health: O'Mahoney and Sturdy (2016) report on the role of McKinsey and Company in the privatization and deregulation of the NHS, citing various relevant aspects. First, challenges to the underlying purposes of universal and free cover based on need. Second, support for the creation of an internal market with completion and choice. Third, active involvement in the production of policy documents and legislation. Fourth, the movement of senior staff into and out of government and McKinsey (see Leys 1999), and with 'free' advisory staff and secondments into public administration. Fifth, networking, facilitating meetings and provision of advice to NHS Trusts, alongside the funding of dinners, flights and entertainment for senior NHS personnel (see Rose 2012). Notably, McKinsey is able to mobilize different types of power through resources, meaning-making and process design, not least their role 'in reproducing the ideologies and structures of capitalism such as neo-liberalism' (O'Mahoney and Sturdy 2016:261), where ideas travel, are diffused and impact in ways that require forensic mapping to identify and conceptualize. Most recently, Kirby (2017) reports on how £17.6 million has been spent on consultants (including KPMG, McKinsey and PwC) to plan cuts to NHS services.

Medway Ports: Arnold and Cooper chart a management and employee buy-out of 10,000 shares at £1 each, based on the advice of Price Waterhouse, followed by redundancies and the sell-back of shares valued by KPMG at £2.50. The Medway Ports were then resold at £37.50 per share to the Mersey Dock and Harbour Board. This case illuminates a wider trend in the promotion of 'popular capitalism', where the authors draw on Ernst & Young's (1994) claim of building a 'constituency for privatisation' (1999: 16). The attractive but unprotected and unstable offer of share ownership is based on 'The employment of private sector accounting firms and investment bankers as advisors', where pricing is used as 'the material basis of economic enticements offered to potential opponents of privatisation in the electorate and workplace' (1999: 140).

Prisons: Mennicken argues that the privatization of prisons is linked to ideas from outside of the service, where consultants were one of a number of organizations that identified and articulated opportunities for investment. Therefore, 'these firms pushed for policies seeking to establish prisons as separate economic units, governed by the market, economic calculation and objectives of profit making' (2013: 209). Consultants have been actively involved in evidence collection about and for the privatization of prisons, and the research shows how, from the 1980s onwards, consultants have been involved in getting ready for such a change through the transformation of 'prisons into managerial, performance-oriented entities' (2013: 221).

Railways: Jupe and Funnell show how consultants presented themselves as neutral experts and gave advice to UK ministers as 'key purification devices' (2015: 82). Neo-liberal ideas dominated where people who might oppose were excluded and critiques were discounted, networks in support of privatization were built with consultants and the 'revolving door' brought senior consultants into formal posts through secondments. Any problems were characterized as implementation failures rather than design flaws, and conflicts of interest were elided: 'Consultants were given crucial influence on policy-making by the initial tender documents whose visible agenda explicitly required consultants to report on how, rather than whether, British Rail should be privatised' (2015: 82).

These cases illuminate the impact of the 4Cs on knowing about and for competition, where the sites of activity were relocated and claims that were used to promote privatization through the use of ideas, data and language. Indeed, the Efficiency Unit (1994) reported on this modernizing privatism by identifying the particular role of consultants in promoting commercial practices, and 'in particular they have made a significant contribution to the achievement of several important government objectives – notably privatisation' (1994: 3).

The cases also show how the financialization of knowledge production by and for the 4Cs is about segmenting, packaging and mediating a situation in ways that allow it to be costed, priced and followed by value-for-money calculations regarding change imperatives, outcomes and impacts. The dominant technology that lends itself to financialization is that of *the problem*, and this enables espoused neutrality combined with the urgency of radical transformation to be promoted and bought into. Common patterns are evident in the cases with regard to how the 4Cs operate in securing privatization:

Problem scoping: The problem is identified as the workforce (teachers, engineers and doctors) who have a stake in retaining their control of public funding, where their pay and credentials are not subject to real-world performance.

Problem framing: Such a problem is caused by a lack of competition regarding the supply of service and the failure to incentivize demand from the public as customers and as shareholders.

Problem solving: Such a problem can be solved by introducing internal and external markets for the service, as well as by removing professional codes and trade unions that protect inefficiencies and prevent capable people without professional training and accreditation from entering the workforce.

Problem re-solving: Solutions may be resisted by professional groups and unmotivated members of the public, where implementation failure may need new reform strategies that can be addressed by 'new' packages of support.

Importantly, the 4Cs are positioned in such a way as to be able to control entry to and embeddedness within government, where the use of confidentiality agreements means that a consultancy team negotiates a contract in ways that 'effectively exclude ... the rest of government and the parliament from the negotiation of the sale price' (Beveridge 2012: 64). In this sense, the 4Cs are not only about supplying a service, they are also about bringing ways of thinking and practices from the commercial sector into government as normalized activities. Consultants are enabled to bring in expertise such as ICT or engineering, but their work demonstrates the interplay between technical savviness in the operation of accounting and advisory processes, and the complexities of day-to-day engagement. Consultants therefore operate as 'cultural intermediaries' (Moor 2008: 408), and, as such, 'consultants are cultural performers, cultural artists, whose product should not be judged in terms of its supposed practical ends' (Stirrat 2000: 43). Consultants connect, speak, influence and shape-shift in order to fit and rework a situation, standing both within and outside, creating words, strategies and outcomes through the use of symbols – key people, situations and successful outcomes – as a means of creating effectiveness (Negus 2002). The purposes of contractual exchange relationships are not just about agreeing the terms and conditions, but also about how beliefs, values and priorities are changed, particularly to knowledgeabilities and ways of thinking about – and being in – the organizational world.[3] Consultants become embedded through the social, trusting ties of friendship and intimacy – or secrecy – as a form of 'marriage' (Kitay and Wright 2004: 12).

2.5 Debating the Knowledgeable State

There is evidence of the positive contributions to public policy by the 4Cs, where, for example, 'the Ministry of Defence is saving on its procurement having used consultants to help implement a new approach and develop internal procurement capabilities' (NAO 2006: 5). However, there are characterizations of the 4Cs as a 'colonising force' (Lapsley et al. 2013: 119) that is 'plundering' public resources (Craig with Brooks 2006) and that is so entrenched that democracy is being damaged (Saint-Martin 2000).

Importantly, select committees can undertake scrutiny (e.g. Parliament 2000), where the reports from select committees (House of Commons Committee of Public Accounts 2007, 2010, 2013, 2016; House of Commons Public Administration Selection Committee 2011, 2013; House of Commons Health Committee 2009) and the National Audit Office (2001, 2006, 2010, 2016) have enabled assessments of how recommendations have been responded to over time. However, parliamentary scrutiny can be reactive through how parliamentarians read something in the press and provide anecdotes that lead to questions with formal answers and limited debates (e.g. House of Lords Hansard 2012; House of Commons Hansard 2012b).

Investigative journalism has produced a range of accounts (see Cohen 2006; Toynbee 2011): for instance, where a former consultant teamed up with a journalist (see Craig and Brooks 2006) to forensically outline the predatory nature of the 4Cs and the folly of the government. Primary research located in the social sciences has used a range of independently funded data (documents, interviews and observations) to put such accounts into a historical context, and has analysed the contribution the 4Cs are making to policy and the impact on the government system. Major studies by Bakvis (1997) and Saint-Martin

---

[3] As well as in relation to career opportunities in the outside world, as civil servants do cross over.

(1998a, 1998b, 2000) have charted and analysed role and impact across government; these studies have never been equalled in the scope of the data and level of analysis that brought together the major insights into what was unfolding at the turn of the century.

Mapping, analysing and the formation of judgements by parliamentarians, officials, journalists and researchers are beginning to provide contextual evidence and argumentation regarding the current situation. It is not possible to be definitive about the 'who', 'what', 'how' and 'why' as the evidence is time-bound and incomplete and the situation is subject to flux, not least in terms of how the 'policy' contribution cannot necessarily be distinguished and separated from 'management', as outlined in Chapter 1. However, it is possible to use the focus on the knowledgeable state and the 4Cs to examine the trends and the debates that are taking place:

Knowers: It remains the case that the primary knowers in public policy are elected politicians, who demand and invite into Whitehall a range of external expertise (Saint-Martin 2000). More than twenty years ago, Bakvis (1997) identified the range of knowledge actors involved in public policy, and while consultants are a significant part of this community they are not the only external experts who are brought in to proactively impact policy-making. Since then, important mapping work has been undertaken by Ball and Junemann (2012) regarding education, wherein they lay out the interconnections and modes of contact between a range of people and organizations on knowledge flows and exchanges, in the shaping of education policy and practice. What is emerging is a knowledge complexity where the separation out of the 4Cs may be vital for parliamentary and journalistic scrutiny with regard to project evaluation, as well as researching and conceptualizing experts and public policy. Thus, there is a need to locate the 4Cs alongside and in relation to knowledge actors in other employment contexts.

Knowledge sites: It remains the case that the prime sites for public policy-making are public institutions, where research is identifying trends away from accountability processes and towards depoliticized delivery through agencies and templates. Important analysis has identified the growth of what Hood and Jackson (1991) characterized as 'consultocracy', regarding the 4Cs as indicators of a 'new class' who bring in managerialist ideas for the reform of the civil service, and privatization strategies for public services (Saint-Martin 2000, 2001). This has been influential in political studies as it has enabled the relationship between contracting and contractualism, in addition to the conduct of government to be examined – and particularly for the health of democracy to be assessed. What is emerging is a clear view that the 4Cs are important, but that there is something more dynamic than an 'ocracy' where the 4Cs take part in, but have not taken over, government (Saint-Martin 2000). This is related to a number of insights, where the argument is made that the 4Cs are 'more a lubricant in public sector reform than the policy reform machine itself' (Hodge and Bowman 2006: 114). Therefore, consultants make government work more like a corporation than actually infiltrate and turn government into a corporation. Furthermore, the specific 'lubrication' contribution of the 4Cs as knowers is recognized through research outside of the UK (see Beveridge 2012), where the notion of arena-shifting has put the focus on the 4Cs as a 'business deal'. In other words, solutions are retailed and – importantly – the control of negotiations can happen in 'places' and 'spaces' that may not be institutional, and that are removed from public scrutiny. The transnational nature of knowledge production means that the 4Cs not only travel to UK policy-making, but also that arena-shifting may well be off-shore regarding globalized consultancy companies, as well as networked with supra-national organizations (e.g. World Bank) or governments (e.g. the EU) (Souto-Otero 2015; Stone 2008).

Knowledge claims: It remains the case that the prime claims regarding public policy are located in ideologies and the party system. What is under-researched is the coincidence with the impact of neo-liberalism and neo-conservativism on party political agendas in relation to the 4Cs. In other words, the drive to introduce and evidence what works has cut across the political divide, where the role of numbers in NPM and EIPP has been a feature of successive governments.[4] In this sense, the 4Cs are part of, have created and have been enabled through other knowledge actors in public policy (political parties/advisers, think tanks, professors and research centres). These actors have worked on and demonstrated shared dispositions in what a knowledge claim is, and how knowledge flows around networks regarding how claims can be framed and articulated in a range of ways and places. While NPM and EIPP are ageing, are seen as problematic and, at times, are more rhetorical than real (see Gunter et al. 2016), there does remain active investment in numbers that are about costs, accounting, ideas and answerability, along with outcomes and accountability.

Knowledgeabilities: It remains the case that, while modernization has shifted much in identities, culture and practices within Whitehall, the traditions within which this happens have remained resilient (see Barber 2007). What Livingstone (2007) identifies as 'spaces of speech' are important, whereas particular venues (office, café, corridor, meeting room and online)

---

[4] For example, the symbolic and resource investment in leaders and leadership in public services; see Gunter (2012).

impact on what is and is not speakable. Consequently, the processes of *depoliticization* and arena-shifting, which the 4Cs have been implicated in creating and using to great effect, has impacted the type of spaces where decision-making is located, and hence how bodies, speech and language are integrated into claims. In particular, risk management is a key feature, where the commercial risk of the 4Cs in public spaces (based on democratic consent and transparent accountability) has impacted on claims, not least whether they are veiled by confidentiality agreements. What is emerging is a form of trust that is located in 'responsibilization' or how everyone (not only consultants) is expected to take on responsibilities that previously the state acted as provider and guarantor for (Shamir 2008). The drafting, negotiating and signing of a contract means that the individual provider or consumer is powerful through their individuality. Thus, consent is based on being responsible for payment, delivery and accepting evidence by numbers. The 4Cs are directly involved in constructing this form of contracting, where the risk is in not accepting responsibility for the risk, whether as a private citizen or in public office.

In conclusion, it seems that the 4Cs are major providers of costly services as a means of modernizing knowledge production for public policy. In the concerns over the club elite conservation of 'Sir Humphrey Appleby', the approach was to challenge, cut and replace a civil servant with a functional 'independent contractor' who can enable change by 'introducing superior management skills at the same time as they challenge orthodoxy' (McLarty and Robinson 1998: 256). However, the concerns are that while spending on the 4Cs is discretionary, the civil service itself 'was like an addict hooked on consultancy' (Shah 2016). Therefore, costs soared despite civil service numbers declining (Flynn and Asquer 2017). Evidence demonstrates that their problem-solving expertise may actually be a problem in itself, with concerns over conflicts of interest and the promotion of fads at the expense of professional expertise (Paton 1999), as well as how reforms may not be in the public interest (Leys 1999). Concerns over value for money regarding control and deployment of the 4Cs continue to be raised (House of Commons Public Administration Select Committee 2011), alongside wider concerns about democratic accountability (Saint-Martin 2000). Three trends stand out. First, concerns about the role of the government as client and contractor, or how those in government are active participants in the construction of the 4Cs. Second, how inefficiencies and a failure to evaluate the contribution by the 4Cs may be generated by political turf-wars between departments in Whitehall (e.g. Brexit; see Whitehall Monitor 2017b). Third, how central to the management processes underpinning public policy are arguments for the active use, capacity building and development of in-house civil servants (NAO 2006) who have learned the ways of the 4Cs.

The debates have come full circle: the privatism of club government has been challenged by the modernizing privatism of the 4Cs, and the experiences of the cost, impact and outcomes of this is to give more attention to in-house staff as internal consultants. Perhaps this is the biggest impact of the 4Cs on public policy-making as a form of modernizing privatism: that even when they are not there or have been replaced by other knowledge actors, they continue to shape the purposes and practices of those who are employed as public servants.

3 | *Policy Consulting in the USA: Significant but in Decline?*

3.1 Introduction: Policy Consulting in the Public Sector as a Problematic Phenomenon

As the Introduction to this book has argued, governmental use of consultancy services has long been a concern for scholars of public administration, management and political science (Howlett and Migone 2013a, 2013b; Kipping and Engwall 2003; Graeme and Bowman 2006; Guttman and Willner 1976; Rosenblum and McGillis 1979).

Although the impact of policy consulting is generally expected to be fairly broad, most of these studies have focused on a narrow set of questions related to the effect of contracting out on levels of public service employment and budgets (Dilulio 2016; Guttman and Willner 1976; GAO 2011) rather than on policy outcomes. Much existing research has focused either on placing this expansion in a historical perspective (McKenna 1995, 1996, 2006), or assessing its underlying causes and consequences (David 2012; Berit and Kieser 2002; McGann 2007).

A number of recent studies, however, have begun to look at other questions, such as the increasing use of consultants for work related to policy analysis, advice, implementation and evaluation – activities thought to be the core work of policy workers in government (Saint-Martin 2001, 2005, 2012).

The existing small literature on the subject acknowledges the simultaneous growth of the policy consulting industry, and the growing share of the public sector as a client of this industry (Pattenaude 1979; Hodge and Bowman 2006; Gross and Poor 2008). Empirical studies are scarce, however, with little analysis of quantitative data. To date, these studies have also only examined the situation with respect to the activities of

Thanks go to Caroline Brouillette, Jack Coleman and Roman Skorzus for invaluable data collection and analysis for this chapter.

consultants in a relatively small number of countries, including New Zealand (Boston 1996), Australia (Howard 2006), Canada (Howlett and Migone 2013a) and the UK (National Audit Office 2016). Moreover, many existing statistics are often idiosyncratic and do not allow for comparison between departments or countries, or for an assessment of trends. Few studies outside of Saint-Martin's thesis of policy consultancy's contribution to neo-liberalism and preferences for market-based policy alternatives (Saint-Martin 2012) draw any conclusions as to policy impact and effects.

Somewhat surprisingly, the largest and most archetypal case of government contracting, the United States, has received very little detailed treatment, despite a plethora of anecdotal and popular accounts claiming to have documented a pattern of exponential growth in the size and impact of policy-related government contracting (Gutman and Willner 1976; Pattenaude 1979; Rosenblum and McGillis 1979; Hodge and Bowman 2006; Saint-Martin 2007; McKenna 2006; Gross and Poor 2008; David 2012).

Some of the reasons for this gap between popular and scholarly treatments of the subject have to do with the difficulties associated with gathering detailed information on contracts and consultants' activities (Howard 2006; Howlett and Migone 2013a, 2013b). These data difficulties are serious and range from no reporting of contracts in some jurisdictions, high dollar figure cut-offs for reporting in many and time lags in others. Additionally, there are serious variations in reporting across departments and governments, variations in such practices across time, secrecy provisions regarding contracts, and general inability to identify contractors from publicly available contract information. Furthermore, there are difficulties in separating out policy-related versus administrative or management consulting activities and contracts, among others (British Columbia Office of the Auditor General 2001). While many of the problems listed above persist in the US case, and continue to make it difficult to track changes in consulting practices, recent reform efforts make it possible to sketch out a general view of the pattern in US government consulting over the past decade and promise increasingly accurate accounting and greater detail in the future.

This chapter reports on these challenges in the context of the distribution of the American federal government's contracting of policy services and discusses how, thanks to several initiatives on the part of the Obama administration only partially rolled back by the Trump government, many such issues can now be overcome, or partially overcome, to provide reasonably accurate data related to questions about the size, trends and other aspects of US federal government consulting.

3.2 The US Situation in Comparative Perspective

The UK National Audit Office defines consultancy as 'The provision to management of objective advice relating to strategy, structure, management or operations of an organization, in pursuit of its purposes and objectives. Such advice is provided outside the "business-as-usual" environment when in-house skills are not available and will be time-limited' (National Audit Office 2016).

This definition emphasizes the management nature of much consulting. Much 'privatization' activity in the 1960s, '70s and '80s – in many jurisdictions – extended well beyond the sale of public enterprises to the creation of contracts and other kinds of arrangements, to deliver services from human resources management to auditing and other functions (Doern 1994; McIntosh 1997; Ford and Zussman 1997).

Traditional practice in most governments, including that of the USA, was to have in-house service provision in the public policy realm. Policy analysis and other kinds of policy development activities, such as the preparation of briefs and background papers, policy statements and the like, remained largely an internal function until recently.

Under the influence of various reform movements since the 1960s, however, this has now given way in many areas to the 'service state', where the state acts as a contractor for the external service delivery of services previously delivered internally (Butcher, Freyers and Wanna 2009).

In the past two decades, the use of consultants for these kinds of activities has grown in many countries, including contracting out data collection and analysis, polling and the provision of other kinds of background information by a plethora of consultants, including academics, think tanks and private firms, both large and small (Saint-Martin 2006, 2007; Boston 1994).

Policy-makers and academics in many countries, including the USA, have expressed increasing unease about this outsourcing of policy-related services and its implications, for four main reasons

(Saint-Martin 2007; Howlett and Migone 2013a). First, public spending is ballooning while government employment remains stable (Dilulio 2016), for which reason control over costs in all areas of contracting is a source of discussion. This includes assessments of the effectiveness of outsourcing services to consultants. Second, the phenomenon could provoke an erosion of departments' and agencies' control over their policy agendas (Howlett and Migone 2013b). Third, this may undermine their operational capacity (Saint-Martin 2007) in the event of an emergency or crisis, where they may find themselves without adequate in-house personnel or data to deal with an issue. Fourth, such activity may involve a loss of control over data collection and access to private purveyors (Smith and Desouza 2015).

Pemer, Börjeson and Werr (2014) sum up existing arguments for and against managers' use of policy consultants under two main rubrics. The first, a 'rational' or transaction-cost paradigm, sees the decision to contract services as the result of a weighing the pros and cons of external provision against the costs of internal resources required to perform the same job. This view largely ignores long-term issues such as privacy and capacity losses. A second, more critical paradigm, on the other hand, is concerned with these issues and also emphasizes changes in decision-making processes which can result from such contracting: for instance, managers attempting to avoid blame and enhance perceptions of certainty by employing external consultants to support their ideas, or decision-makers inheriting any biases which consultants may have through blind consumption of their reports and data, however collected and written.

Both perspectives require empirical analysis in specific jurisdictions, as does the evaluation of the answers to the issues raised. Some answers are emerging in some of the countries cited above. First, external policy consulting may not be growing as fast as is often alleged (Howlett and Migone 2013). Second, on the demand side, a small number of agencies might generate the majority of contracts while others generate relatively few (Howard 1996a). Third, on the supply side, the field is divided between a few large companies which dominate large contracts in a quasi-oligopolistic fashion in particular fields and with specific departments, and a large number of small contractors who perform bespoke services. And fourth, many policy-related contracts are linked to focus groups, polling and other kinds of consultative activities rather than directly affecting the generation of internal reports and briefs

(Howlett and Migone 2013a, 2013b). However, most of these studies are of countries with Westminster-style systems, which traditionally have been slow to engage in contracting processes and which face accountability and other challenges in doing so (Knill 1999).

Studies of other systems, such as the USA and other US-inspired republican systems and countries, which have been much more prone to contract activity throughout their history, may reveal a different pattern. The United States is the archetypal model of such a state (Spoehr 1999). Historical accounts position management consulting as an American-based industry kick-started through contracts issued during World War II, and subsequently exported to Europe. Hodge and Bowman (2006), for example, named the US penchant for contracting out as having resulted in the creation of *consultocracy*, where the business of reforming government in the 1980s and 1990s was driven by the US Big Four accounting firms: Deloitte, Ernst & Young, KPMG and PricewaterhouseCoopers – a phenomenon also detailed in Saint-Martin (2006). McKenna (2010) also noted how military efforts triggered alliances between professionals and the administrative state, which were institutionalized in the post-war era. With pressure to decrease the government's size and scope in the post-war era, the Truman-era Hoover Commission was created in 1947. This Commission attempted 'to solve the organizational dilemma by doing just what corporate executives would have done – hiring management consulting firms to restructure the Executive Branch' (McKenna 2006: 878). Subsequent high-profile assignments, such as the reorganization of the Post Office, the task force on federal personnel management and McKinsey & Co.'s involvement in the space race, created a contractor state not only in goods procurement for the military and other entities, but also in services.

More recently, Saint-Martin (2012) reported that the available evidence seems to indicate that consultants in Washington are the most involved in the policy-making process when compared to other developed nations' capitals. This is despite the Government Accountability Office's (GAO) admonition, in its 1992 report *Government Contractors: Are Service Contractors Performing Inherently Governmental Functions?* that functions which involve the direct responsibility of agency officials: namely, policy, decision-making or managerial-related work should not be performed by external consultants. A detailed exploration of the history and record of policy consulting – and its impact – in the USA is long overdue.

Fortunately, developments under the Obama administration in terms of improved reporting of service contracts allow such a study to be undertaken. This chapter provides insights into data culled from these sources on the general picture in the USA over the past decade. Determining these trends is not an unproblematic process, however, and this study also reports on some of the choices and limitations remaining with existing data sources which affect the robustness of these findings.

3.3 Policy Consulting in US Government: Growth and Status

Several jurisdictions now clearly acknowledge the policy-related nature of consulting activity in their definitions of the subject. The Dutch Government, for example, categorizes policy activities as either 'policy sensitive' (interim management, organization advice, policy advice and communication advice), 'policy support' (legal advice, ICT and accounting, finance and administrative organization – see Chapter 5 on the Netherlands) or 'non-policy support' (Van den Berg 2017). The USA has been the focus of studies examining the expansion of public demand for consultancy services, not only as a consumer of such services, but also as the world's main supplier and industry leader, for at least two decades, if not longer. Saint-Martin in particular has noted how the very scope and size of the US government, combined with the openness of its policy advisory system, allowed the consulting industry to grow rapidly in the areas of public administration and public management (Saint-Martin 2012).

Continued efforts to control the growth and size of government in the USA, especially at the federal level, involved increased contracting out of both 'core' and peripheral government services to a ready and willing set of private sector actors. Saint-Martin (2006) has noted how much of the shift from a 'Weberian model of public administration' towards an 'entrepreneurial state' in the US could be attributed to the fashionable idea of 'reinventing government' (Osborne and Gaebler 1992), a process which gained support and credibility from Bill Clinton, an adherent of contracting out both before and after his election. Under his presidency, policy impact could be seen through various bodies such as the National Performance Review Commission, reinvention teams, laboratories and summits, as well as a 'Reinventing Government Bill' (Saint-Martin 2006), all of which supported enhanced contracting out of internal government services, as well as various public service delivery activities.

Policy consulting was among these activities. The end of the 1960s had given rise to the concurrent birth of the policy analysis industry and the era of public management. The two were joined together in the 'public contracting state' for the first time in the 1980s and 1990s, as the American government's contracting out of a variety of services reached the level of billions of dollars (Saint-Martin 2012). Many of these ideas were in turn exported to other democracies, such as the UK and Canada, which were similarly influenced by efforts to streamline the government's operations and control and constrain its growth.

The impact, or potential impact, of these developments on the nature of the civil service and traditional notions of government and government accountability were noted early in this growth cycle. Wilmer and Gutman's *The Shadow Government: The Government's Multi-Billion-Dollar Giveaway of Its Decision-Making Powers to Private Management Consultants, 'Experts,' and Think Tanks*, for example, had by 1976 asserted that the federal government's budgetary expansion and outsourcing of services to management consulting firms and think tanks had created a parallel system of actors mirroring and delivering government services outside the usual envelope of budgetary and legislative scrutiny. Implied here were potentially serious problems for legitimacy and accountability of government to the public, as well as potential problems of inefficiency, corruption and other administrative malaises.

Public institutions such as the Government Accountability Office (GAO, previously Government Accounting Office) and the Office of Management and Budget (OMB) have also increasingly reported to the Comptroller General and to Congressional and Senatorial Requesters on the impact of increased federal agency external contracting. Specifically, they have focused on how this activity has moved from peripheral areas, such as printing services, to the performance of 'inherently governmental functions', such as human resources management, policing and the military. This also included efforts to develop 'federal policy, issuing rules and regulations, or making best value determinations among contractors competing to provide needed goods or services', which were deemed most preferably executed by civil servants operating under traditional civil services codes of conduct and responsibility (GAO 2012: 1).

Ultimately, these calls for increased scrutiny led in 2010 to an Obama administration statutory requirement for civilian agencies to submit standardized annual inventories of their service contracts to government, and to make these publicly available along with data on contract duration and scope, as well as information on the contractee. This development allowed for easier access to better quality data, which in turn has resulted in recent GAO and Congressional Research Service (CRS) data providing the basis for high-quality empirical analyses of US government service contracting – including policy-related contracting – for the first time.

3.3.1 The Nature of Contract Reporting in the United States

There are many definitional and other nuances in classifying government activities and reporting on government contracting, which bedevil research on the subject (Howard 1996a; Howlett and Migone 2014). Several of these problems encountered in other countries have been alluded to earlier. Many of these – such as a lack of standardization, time lags and secrecy – have been dealt with in the USA through the imposition of standard reporting formats and the provision that data be made available promptly to the public via the internet. Other questions about the accuracy of the data reported and its meaning, however, remain significant in the US case.

The Federal Acquisition Regulation (FAR) is the primary legislation directing all federal executive agencies' acquisition of supplies and services with appropriations funding, and has been in effect since 1984 (FAR 2005). It highlights a vision for the Federal Acquisition System to 'deliver on a timely basis the best value product or service to the customer, while maintaining the public's trust and fulfilling public policy objectives' (FAR 2005: 1.1-1).

Subpart 4.6 of the FAR prescribes uniform reporting requirements through the system-wide Federal Procurement Data System – Next Generation (FPDS), which, under the terms of the Federal Funding Accountability and Transparency Act of 2006, requires all unclassified federal award data to be accessible to the public. Contract information must be available in the FPDS when contract actions are above a 'micro-purchase threshold'. This threshold is held at $3,500, except for specific cases subject to legislation external to the FAR, in which the thresholds are:

(i) $20,000 in the case of any contract to be awarded and performed, or purchase to be made, inside the United States;

(ii) $30,000 in the case of any contract to be awarded and performed, or purchase to be made, outside the United States. (FAR 2005: Subpart 2.1)

In comparison to other nations, where the limit on contract reporting is often as high as $100,000, these are quite low limits and help capture aspects of smaller policy-related contracts, which higher cut-off levels miss (Howlett and Migone 2013a).

Reported data should also include any modifications to those actions that change previously reported contract action report data, regardless of dollar value (FAR 2005). This addresses a second concern existing in many countries: that initial contract values often change – both in a negative and a positive way – and that these changes are not reflected in accounts which provide only budgeted amounts rather than actual expenditures (Howard 1996a). Many contracts will be modified several times across their lifespan, sometimes with increases or decreases to the original contract value, which can lead to accounting discrepancies from one year to the next.

The USASpending.gov website further expands on this subject, specifically by explaining the presence of contracts with negative values obligations: 'The agency made a modification to an award but there was no additional funding. The agency reduced or rescinded more than the original award amount; there is a negative subsidy on a loan and the funds are being returned to the Treasury; duplicate corrections reports have been submitted by the agency' (USASpending.gov 2016).

This online portal provides data on all agencies and departments dating back to 2000, including information about the contract, except what work was actually done. For many policy functions, this final level detail is needed, meaning the data provided on the website is insufficient to determine what activities are covered by the contract. The website does, however, provide a great deal of information on the kind of organization that conducted the work, where they are based, and the size and duration of the contract. Each contract has 201 columns of information, though most are binary 'yes or no' fields.[1]

---

[1]   See www.fpds.gov/fpdsng_cms/index.php/en.

In addition, each contract is identified with a standardized Procurement Instrument Identifier (PIID), which agencies must ensure is unique across the government, where one contract may deliver a service to several departments. Again, this addresses another issue often faced by researchers: that the purpose of contracts is unclear, and the same contract may be attributed different purposes by different agencies (Howard 1996a).

In general (and notwithstanding these caveats), the USA thus has recently developed a system for service contract reporting, which is of a very high standard of transparency and accuracy relative to those found in many other countries.

3.3.2 Specific Service Contract Inventories (FAIR Act) and the Treatment of Defense, 'Other Fair Act' and 'CFO' Agencies

With the help of service codes from the FPDS database, agencies subject to the Chief Financial Officers (CFO) Act – except the Department of Defense (DoD) – and agencies outside the core group covered by the Federal Activities Inventory Reform (FAIR) Act agencies) are required to organize inventories of contract activity by function. The Office of Management and Budget's (OMB) Office of Federal Procurement Policy (OFPP) provides guidance to agency management as to the specifics of reporting on their service contracts.

In addition to providing service contract inventories, agencies are required to conduct analyses of their inventories in terms of 'inherently governmental' functions, 'critical' functions and 'other' functions. Specifically, agencies are directed to focus on functions where they 'may be at increased risk of losing control of their operations in this area due to overreliance on contractors', as well as service codes where they have observed an above-average growth in activities in the past ten years (OFPP 2011). Notably, the guidance establishes a threshold of $25,000 in obligations for contracts. This covers most contracts, since 'well over 95 percent of civilian agencies' total service contract obligations for FY 2010 ... [are] ... above $25,000' (OFPP 2011).

These inventories thus now provide researchers with an easily accessible and user-friendly source to analyse the American federal agencies' service contracting on a yearly basis. Agency inventories are classified in two categories (CFO Act agencies – excluding DoD and 'other FAIR

Act Agencies') and data is provided through hyperlinks to agency websites.[2]

CFO Act agencies include: Department of Agriculture, Department of Commerce, Department of Education, Department of Energy, Department of Health and Human Services, Department of Homeland Security, Department of Housing and Urban Development, Department of the Interior, Department of Justice, Department of Labor, Department of State, Department of Transportation, Department of Treasury, Department of Veterans Affairs, Agency for International Development, Environmental Protection Agency, General Services Administration, National Aeronautics and Space Administration, National Science Foundation, Nuclear Regulatory Commission, Office of Personnel Management, Small Business Administration, Social Security Administration.

Other FAIR Act agencies include: Broadcasting Board of Governors, Commodity Futures Trading Commission, Consumer Financial Protection Bureau, Consumer Product Safety Commission, Court Services and Offender Supervision Agency for the District of Columbia, Defense Nuclear Facilities Safety Board, Equal Employment Opportunity Commission, Federal Communications Commission, Federal Election Commission, Federal Energy Regulatory Commission, Federal Labor Relations Authority, Federal Maritime Commission, Federal Mediation and Conciliation Service, Federal Trade Commission, Merit Systems Protection Board, National Archives and Records Administration, National Endowment for the Arts, National Endowment for the Humanities, National Labor Relations Board, National Transportation Safety Board, Office of Special Counsel, Peace Corps, Railroad Retirement Board, Securities and Exchange Commission, Selective Service System, US International Trade Commission.

3.3.3 The Situation of the Department of Defense

While the DoD is excluded from the list of agencies covered by the CFO Act, it still has to comply with the aforementioned guidance when reporting contract awards predominantly funded by civilian agencies (Office of the Under Secretary of Defense 2013). In addition, in accordance with title 10 of the United States Code *Procurement of Services: Tracking of Purchases*, the Secretary of Defense is required to submit

---

[2] Accessible at www.whitehouse.gov/omb/management/office-federal-procurement-policy/.

an annual inventory of the activities performed, pursuant to contracts for services to Congress.

Hence, the Department has decided to collect the function indicators for DoD funded actions as well, while complying with the OFPP guidance for reporting on their service contracts using data from the FPDS (Office of the Under Secretary of Defense 2013). The DoD thus provides the public with service contract inventories in essentially the same format as the aforementioned FAIR Act agencies. It should be noted, however, that the FPDS excludes data from certain DoD components due to national security procurement exceptions (CRS 2015; GAO 2012).[3]

3.4 Examining the US Case

As stated above, the availability of data in the USA is very good by international standards – which, unfortunately, are quite poor. Several sources of data are available on contracts, with a high degree of correspondence between the datasets. The data covers many smaller contracts, with a wide range of information generally available on contractee size and location, as well as contracted activities. Although this standardized and internet-available data only goes back a decade or so, this is sufficient to establish the nature of contemporary trends in this area of government activity.

In compiling this data, however, it is necessary to first determine which federal procurement codes cover policy-related consulting and contracting activity. This raises the issue of the selection of which FPDS codes to use for analysis.

3.4.1 Selection of Service Codes

As set out above, the FPDS database of procurement codes lies behind the classification of contracts found in agency SCIs. Some service contract codes are specifically policy-related, but other categories also may contain a policy aspect and should also be included in the dataset. Choosing which codes will be used to aggregate policy-related services

---

[3] Inventories are accessible at www.acq.osd.mil/dpap/cpic/cp/ and contracts are subdivided according to contracting by *Air Force, Army, Navy* and *Other DoD agencies.*

is a careful process, because while there may be a very low proportion of contracts in certain service categories, excluding them means dropping valuable data points.

Ultimately, after careful examination of the contents of contracts in many codes, the list of codes shown in Table 3.1 were used for the preliminary selection of contracts relevant to the analysis.

Table 3.1 *List of FPDS codes for policy consulting*

Code	Description	Support – Professional	
B505	Cost Benefit	R405	Operations research / quantitative analysis
B506	Data (other than scientific)	R406	Policy review/ development
B507	Economic	R407	Programme evaluation services
B510	Environmental Assessments	R408	Programme mgmt. / support
B513	Feasibility (non-construction)	R409	Programme review/ development services
B522	Legal	R410	Program evaluation/ review/ development
B524	Mathematical / Statistical	R413	Specifications development
B528	Regulatory	R429	Emergency response, disaster planning, etc.
B541	Defense	R499	Other
B542	Educational	R707	Management services/ contract & procurement support
B545	Housing/ Community dev.		
B546	Security (physical/ personal)		
B547	Accounting/ Financial mgmt.	D307	IT and telecom – IT strategy and architecture
B548	Trade Issue		
B549	Foreign/ National Security Policy		
B550	Organization / Administrative / Personnel		
B553	Communications		
B554	Acquisition Policy/ Procedures		
B555	Elderly/ Handicapped		
B599	Other		

3.4.2 Limitations of the FPDS Database and Choices Made in How to Deal with Them

The GAO (2012) has also highlighted the limited accuracy, utility and completeness of some aspects of the FPDS data. Specifically, it does not provide the number of contractor FTEs performing each service, identify the requiring activity, or allow for the identification of all services being procured (GAO 2012).

This can be illustrated by the high number of both contracts and obligated dollars attached to the codes B599 and R499, both of which are 'Other' categories. For instance, the Department of Labor's 1,255 R499 contracts during 2015 constituted 15.7 per cent of contracts, and 10.5 per cent of the total contract budget, which reached $231 million. Another serious concern is the reliability of the data itself; the GAO has consistently found inaccuracies in FPDS data in their work. Notably, DoD officials reported that 'the obligations for FY 2008 are "artificially higher by $13B and the FY09 number is artificially lower by $13B" due to over-obligation on a single contract', showing how a single error can strongly skew analyses (CRS 2015).[4]

Similarly, some problems persist with the thresholds of reporting. While the FPDS reports on contracts 'whose estimated value is $3,000 or more' (FPDS FAQs, CRS 2015), the 2010 OFPP guidance instructs agencies to focus on actions in excess of $25,000. Although some databases do include a significant number of contracts below this latter cut-off, especially in data from the DoD, we focused our analysis on data in excess of $25,000 to avoid skewing our data on the number of contracts, as well as to ensure data comparability between the different groups of agencies. The downside of using this threshold is that the analysis is less representative of policy-related contracting, since it

---

[4] Other issues were faced when compiling information from service contracts. First, many contracts have a value of zero or below. Second, the same PIID number (contract identification number) may appear several times across years; it is indeed required that 'every modification to that contract, regardless of dollar value must be reported to FPDS' (FPDS FAQs, CRS 2015: 22). However, there are duplicate PIID numbers for the same year with contract obligations for the same dollar amount. We assume this means that the information was incorrectly entered twice or more, and because of the volume of contracts it is not something we have been able to address systematically.

excludes many modifications to contracts of $25,000 or less, as well as a non-negligible amount of smaller contracts which, taken altogether, skew obligated dollar values.[5]

The service contract inventories of the different government bodies are theoretically available from fiscal year 2010 onwards. The OFPP Service Contract Inventories provide hyperlinks for each agency's website, where their Service Contract Inventories for a certain year can be downloaded by year. In general, the Service Contract Inventories are provided either as Excel (.xls) or PDF files and are organized according to the specific FPDS codes (see Table 3.2), containing information such as the service obligation (the amount of the contract) and the city and country of the contractor, in addition to short descriptions of the purpose of the contract. Within the service inventory, the FPDS code is represented by the Product Service Code (PSC) column. To illustrate the different data columns of a service inventory, the following table presents the available data from the Department of Commerce, which was also the most complete service inventory data source.

Most of the columns are reflected in every service inventory, but some columns are included only in selected ministries. The PIID and DUNS numbers in particular seem to be 'additional' data information, since they were not recorded in some of the other service inventories. Moreover, some departments had other additional data which was more or less unique to that specific department (e.g. the Department of State). That implies that the data disclosure guidelines for the FAIR Act are not consistent and that the institutions are free to add additional data in their publications.

---

[5] The summaries of the service inventories – one-pagers in PDF format showing statistics about codes selected as interesting by agencies because of possible interference with inherently governmental functions or because of a large share of obligated dollars – are almost always available. However, the complete excel file of detailed service inventories identifying all service contracts obligated by the agency for a given fiscal year are not consistently available. When working with the PDF summary only, it is impossible to sort out if negative- and zero-dollar contracts have been properly accounted for, as well as if contracts below the $25,000 threshold have been included in the analysis. Additionally, some agencies have not published the service inventories for selected years mostly until 2012. Corrupted or too large data files that are impossible to open or work with were also an issue.

Table 3.2 *Example for the data columns of the service inventory from*
the Department of Commerce (DoC)

Inventory Item	Comment
Year	Fiscal Year
PSC	Service Code
Code Check	Control query if the PSC code belongs to the list of codes of interest
Product or Service Code (PSC) Description	Description of the Service Code
Contracting Agency	
Contracting Department	
Funding Agency	
Place of Performance City	
State	
Country	
Date Signed	
Extent Competed	
Fair Opportunity / Limited Sources	
Type of Contract	
Description of Requirement	
Vendor Name	
Action Obligation	
PIID	Procurement Instrument Identifier
Referenced IDV PIID	
DUNS Number	https://en.wikipedia.org/wiki/Data_Universal_ Numbering_System.

3.4.3 Detailed Analysis of Contracts' Description of Requirements

The Product and Service codes (PSC) offer a broad overview of the type of services performed; however, this may not be the most precise estimate of the policy work contracted by departments and agencies. Indeed, a closer look at the information available in the Service Contract Inventories (SCIs) indicates that a relatively small share of obligations contracted under our codes of interest (COI) is in fact policy-related. In order to analyse the type of work performed for each individual contract, we investigated the

Description of Requirements section of each contract for two CFO Act agencies' SCIs.

The *Description of Requirements* entry offers the most detailed account of the work performed in the contract. Although the length of the description greatly varies from contract to contract, it usually includes a brief description of the tasks required, with varying degrees of specificity and quality. In some instances there is simply no description, and in others a high number of acronyms are used. Yet, for most of the contracts, the *Description of Requirements* entry is enough to allow us to understand the general essence of the work performed.

In order to verify how precisely our COIs identified policy work, we used the Department of Interior (DoI)'s and the Department of Education (DoEdu)'s SCIs for FY 2014 as samples. The two agencies were chosen according to the size of their contracting for the COI: the DoI contracted the highest amount, while the DoEdu was among the smallest consumers of these contracts among agencies. Each contract was recoded according to the nature of the work done (policy, IT, environmental, financial, administrative, technical, data engineering, maintenance, etc.), after which the proportion of policy work for each COI was examined (see Table 3.3). Overall, we found that the proportion of policy work, both in terms of number of contracts and obligations contracted, constitutes a minority. For the DoI, 36 contracts out of the 1,383 selected included policy-related work, which translated into only 2.1 per cent of the obligations contracted. For the DoEdu, the proportion was higher, with 92 out of 233 contracts, encompassing 44 per cent of the obligations contracted.

So, for example:

Codes which included obligations for policy-related contracts accounting for more than 10 per cent of contracts, in both agencies surveyed, were:

– B505 Special Studies/Analysis Cost Benefit;
– B506 Special Studies/ Analysis – Data (other than scientific);
– B507 Economic;
– R410 Program evaluation/review/development.

On the other hand, some of our COIs did not include any policy-related contracts in either of the two departments, which may point to a need to exclude them from the selection. These were:

– B545 Housing/Community Development;

Table 3.3 *Analysis of two CFO act contracts according to description of requirements*

COI	Department	Number of Contracts	Total Obligations	Number of Policy-Related Contracts	Policy-Related Contract Obligations	% of Total Obligations Spent on Policy-Related Contracts
B505	DoI	1	$ 627,00.00	1	$ 627,00.00	100
	DoEdu	1	$ 1,000,000.00	1	$ 1,000,000.00	100
B506	DoI	6	$ 729,608.11	2	$ 284,485.19	39
	DoEdu	11	$ 75,637,807.30	10	$ 48,975,989.10	65
B507	DoI	17	$ 3,085,828.92	9	$ 2,336,783.72	76
	DoEdu	4	$ 17,267,984.30	1	$ 1,700,000.00	10
B510	DoI	130	$ 33,899,483.85	8	$ 905,719.63	3
	DoEdu	0	$ –	0	$ –	0
B513	DoI	3	$ 1,025,667.00	0	$ –	0
	DoEdu	0	$ –	0	$ –	0
B522	DoI	0	$ –	0	$ –	0
	DoEdu	0	$ –	0	$ –	0
B524	DoI	2	$ 213,234.27	1	$ 115,514.27	54
	DoEdu	0	$ –	0	$ –	0
B528	DoI	0	$ –	0	$ –	0
	DoEdu	0	$ –	0	$ –	0
B541	DoI	0	$ –	0	$ –	0
	DoEdu	0	$ –	0	$ –	0
B542	DoI	2	$ 245,000.00	0	$ –	0

Table 3.3 (*cont.*)

COI	Department	Number of Contracts	Total Obligations	Number of Policy-Related Contracts	Policy-Related Contract Obligations	% of Total Obligations Spent on Policy-Related Contracts
B545	DoEdu	70	$ 79,617,633.00	43	$ 43,019,162.00	54
	DoI	1	$ 187,949.45	0	$ –	0
	DoEdu	0	$ –	0	$ –	0
B546	DoI	1	$ 98,736.00	0	$ –	0
	DoEdu	0	$ –	0	$ –	0
B547	DoI	0	$ –	0	$ –	0
	DoEdu	0	$ –	0	$ –	0
B548	DoI	0	$ –	0	$ –	0
	DoEdu	0	$ –	0	$ –	0
B549	DoI	0	$ –	0	$ –	0
	DoEdu	0	$ –	0	$ –	0
B550	DoI	2	$ 113,261.00	1	$ 75,000.00	66
	DoEdu	0	$ –	0	$ –	0
B553	DoI	2	$ 174,724.00	0	$ –	0
	DoEdu	2	$ 231,324.10	0	$ –	0
B554	DoI	0	$ –	0	$ –	0
	DoEdu	0	$ –	0	$ –	0
B555	DoI	0	$ –	0	$ –	0
	DoEdu	0	$ –	0	$ –	0
B599	DoI	5	$ 5,826,127.11	0	$ –	0
	DoEdu	2	$ 1,675,201.00	2	$ 1,675,201.00	100

R405	DoI	23	$ 1,910,854.53	0	$ –	0
	DoEdu	2	$ 646,162.20	1	$ 453,584.00	70
R406	DoI	3	$ 258,197.07	1	$ 51,376.07	20
	DoEdu	5	$ 4,315,543.00	0	$ –	0
R407	DoI	0	$ –	0	$ –	0
	DoEdu	0	$ –	0	$ –	0
R408	DoI	9	$ 35,913,407.97	0	$ –	0
	DoEdu	27	$ 8,949,932.40	5	$ 1,489,975.10	17
R409	DoI	2	$ 102,259.72	0	$ –	0
	DoEdu	0	$ –	0	$ –	0
R410	DoI	76	$ 7,748,667.02	7	$ 1,569,921.96	23
	DoEdu	51	$ 25,969,355.00	19	$ 12,624,485.00	49
R413	DoI	4	$ 464,712.00	0	$ –	0
	DoEdu	1	$ 500,000.00	1	$ 500,000.00	100
R429	DoI	0	$ –	0	$ –	0
	DoEdu	0	$ –	0	$ –	0
R499	DoI	1050	$ 187,517,528.30	6	$ 834,281.45	0.4
	DoEdu	57	$ 50,959,288.00	9	$ 5,271,370.00	10
R707	DoI	44	$ 11,818,871.52	0	$ –	0
	DoEdu	0	$ –	0	$ –	0
ALL COIsDoI		1383	$ 291,396,817.84	36	$ 6,235,782.29	2.1
	DoEdu	233	$ 266,770,230.30	92	$ 116,709,766.20	44%

– B546 Security (physical/personal);
– B547 Accounting/Financial management;
– B548 Trade Issue;
– B553 Communications;
– B554 Acquisition Policy/Procedures;
– B555 Elderly/handicapped.

Another finding of this study relates to one of the challenges mentioned earlier with the *Other* codes (B599 Other and R499 Other Support/Professional), which constitute a large share of the contracting. Contracts coded as R499 drove the decrease in contracting over the years 2012–2015 (see 'General Findings' section in this chapter). For the DoEdu, 9 contracts out of 57 in the R499 category are related to policy work, and these constitute 10 per cent of the obligations contracted under this code. Yet, these obligations represent only 0.04 per cent of the total policy-related obligations contracted by the DoEdu. For the DoI, the proportion is even smaller, with 6 contracts out of 1,050, representing 0.4 per cent of obligations, related to policy in R499. However, the policy-related contracts in the R499 category represented 13.4 per cent of the total policy-related obligations contracted by the DoI that year, which is non-negligible. The B599 code represented a smaller number of contracts, yet there is a stark difference in the policy content of contracts in this category between the two agencies studied. The DoEdu had two contracts coded as B599, which were both related to policy. The DoI commissioned five contracts under this code, of which none had to do with policy (see Table 3.3 for an example of these entries).

This exercise was repeated with a sample of two FAIR Act agencies' contract inventories for fiscal year 2014: the US Securities and Exchange Commission (SEC) and the Consumer Financial Protection Bureau (CFPB) (see Table 3.4). Codes which included obligations for policy-related contracts for the CFPB were B507 (Economic), R408 (Program management and Support services), R410 (Program evaluation/review/development) and R499 (Other – Support / Professional). Over all the COIs, 13.9 per cent of obligations were policy-related. Of note, the three contracts identified as policy-related for code B507 in the CFPB sample referred to 'analysis of credit-card data' which could either be part of an investigation or

Table 3.4 *Analysis of 2 FAIR act agency contracts according to description of requirements*

COI	Agency	Number of Contracts	Total Obligations	Number of Policy-Related Contracts	Policy-Related Contract Obligations	% of Total Obligations Spent on Policy-Related Contracts
B506	CFPB	0	$ –	0	$ –	0
	SEC	3	$ 777,926	0	$ –	0
B507	CFPB	4	$ 3,395,000	3	$ 3,335,000	98.2
	SEC	0	$ –	0	$ –	0
B599	CFPB	0	$ –	0	$ –	0
	SEC	1	$ 48,258	0	$ –	0
R405	CFPB	0	$ –	0	$ –	0
	SEC	2	$ 321,735	1	$ 28,610	8.9
R408	CFPB	20	$ 1,239,976	1	$ 554,472	2.6
	SEC	46	$ 7,443,835	0	$ –	0
R410	CFPB	6	$ 7,691,131	1	$ 449,997	5.9
	SEC	2	$ 785,984	1	$ 632,776	80.5
R413	CFPB	0	$ –	0	$ –	0
	SEC	1	$ 795,496	0	$ –	0.0
R499	CFPB	5	$ 5,362,968	2	$ 936,842	17.5
	SEC	47	$ 8,316,681	0	$ –	0.0
R707	CFPB	3	$ 165,270	0	$ –	0.0
	SEC	5	$ 1,083,163	0	$ –	0.0
ALL COIS	CFPB	38	$ 7,854,345	7	$ 5,276,312	13.9
	SEC	107	$ 9,573,078	2	$ 661,386	1.1

aiming more generally to gather information for educational or policy means. If the former, these contracts may not be considered to be policy related, which would significantly lower the total value of policy-related obligations. Codes which included obligations for policy-related contracts for the SEC were R405 (Operations Research / Quantitative Analysis) and R410 (Program evaluation/review/development), for a smaller total share of policy-related obligations of 1.1 per cent. Consistent with earlier research, the SEC spends a lot on contracts compared to other FAIR agencies, but very little of this is policy related, most likely because of its independent commission status and enforcement as well as regulatory functions.

Overall, this analysis points to the major trade-off of different methodologies utilizing the PSC codes to identify policy work contracted by the US government. Examining each contract individually requires a significant amount of time, but yields more precision regarding which contracts and their associated obligations had some policy contents. This may be especially relevant given the heterogeneity of policy contracting among departments and FAIR Act agencies, which ranges from 1.1 per cent to 44 per cent among the four SCIs surveyed. Using aggregate PSC data, on the other hand, is less time consuming but does not give the exact amounts of policy-related contracts and obligations. Rather, it gives an overview of the general trends in contracting, which include but are not restricted to policy work.

Future research should thus enlarge the sample of agencies and departments for which this analysis was conducted, in order to underline which codes do not include any policy contracting, which codes consistently include a majority of policy-related work and how the proportion varies for the *Other* codes, with the objective of refining the COI selection. Nevertheless, it is possible to make some observations about the general nature of US consulting based upon these figures.

3.5 General Findings

The GAO (2011) compiled comparable data on procurement spending at civilian agencies for fiscal years 2005–2010. It looked specifically at contracts described as professional and management support services in the databases cited earlier. They found a 44 per cent increase in civilian agency obligations on these contracts over this time period, which grew from $22 billion to $32 billion (according to 2010 USD currency), or more than twice the rate of increase for other services.[6] In keeping with its main concern about retaining 'core' services in-house, the GAO also analysed a sample of 235 contracts selected from 5 civilian agencies (the Departments of Homeland Security (DHS), Transportation (DOT), Housing and Urban Development (HUD), the US Agency for International Development (USAID), and the National Science Foundation (NSF)). It found that 'more than half of the 230 statements of work for professional and management support service contracts requested services that closely support the performance of inherently governmental functions' (GAO 2011: ii).

While this reflects the concern in the United States, which has mainly been about protecting and retaining 'inherently governmental' functions in public hands, most GAO reviews do not make an explicit distinction for policy consulting services. Most of the research has either looked at consulting services generally, or at management consulting specifically, as well as its effects on the organization and administration of government.

Of course, defining policy consulting is not easy. Management consultancy firms often offer policy-related services, and it is debatable whether the administrative reforms often performed by management consultants constitute policy. In a study of the Australian government's use of consultancy services, however, Howard (2006) highlights that consultants aim to provide expert advice, offered for a fee. He criticized the categorization of consultants on the basis of whether they perform policy or management work, because it leaves the question of 'how much influence over policy is entailed by management and indeed implementation?' unanswered (2006: 54). Instead, he suggests distinguishing between 'programme content' and 'corporate services'.

While recognizing the difficulty of defining and separating such functions, the GAO report stated that 'administration begins when the contractor's involvement in basic management functions is so extensive that an agency's ability to develop options other than those

---

[6] Garrett and Beatty (2011) had however forecasted decreasing government spending levels in the following years (2011 and 2012) in an article outlining the impacts of this prognostic on government prime contractors and subcontractors.

proposed by the contractor is limited' (GAO 1991). In reaction to this publication, agency officials contended that contractors only advise on governmental functions and do not administer them.

3.5.1 The Picture by Different Units of Government

In what follows, these activities are separated out and reported for the three categories of agencies – regular, CFO and DoD – over the period 2010–2015. The methodology used to identify policy consulting activity is detailed in Appendix C.

3.5.1.1 CFO Act Agencies, Excluding DoD

The situation with respect to service contracting for our COI (see Table 3.1) in the US government since 2010 can be found in Figure 3.1 for departments with available data.

As this shows, contrary to much anecdotal evidence, policy services contracting in most main line ministries of US government has stagnated since 2012, peaking in 2014 for most agencies and dropping in 2015. With respect to policy-related consulting, an analysis of the 31 codes mentioned in Appendix C revealed the situation in Table 3.5 for 2015, for those five national departments that had accessible and

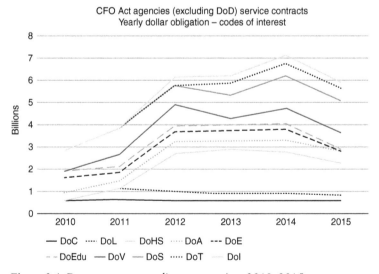

Figure 3.1 Department expenditures over time 2010–2015

Table 3.5 *Five major policy-related service contract agencies 2015*

Department	Fiscal Year	Observations	Total $ Obligated	$ Obligated to 'codes of interest' (COI)	COI / Total Contracts
Health	2015	90,000	$21,810,688,797	$4,168,089,707	19.11%
Labour	2015	7,998	$2,197,748,606	$302,211,769	13.75%
Agriculture	2015	68,462	$6,116,601,246	$339,766,014	5.55%
Vet's Affairs	2015	214,397	$20,067,991,564	$691,730,680	3.45%
Interior (Land and Resources)	2015	71,527	$4,154,804,799	$783,716,999	18.86%

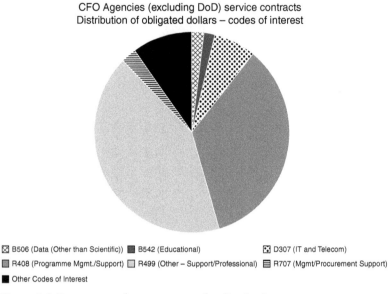

CFO Agencies (excluding DoD) service contracts
Distribution of obligated dollars – codes of interest

⊠ B506 (Data (Other than Scientific))   ■ B542 (Educational)   ⊡ D307 (IT and Telecom)
▦ R408 (Programme Mgmt./Support)   ☐ R499 (Other – Support/Professional)   ☰ R707 (Mgmt/Procurement Support)
■ Other Codes of Interest

Figure 3.2 Departments key contract codes distribution

readable datasets for the six-year period.[7] This reveals that the weight of consulting for policy services – as identified through our code selection – varies from agency to agency but remains below 20 per cent of the services listed in the inventories.

Considering the service inventories' distribution by COI (see Figures 3.2 and 3.3), it is obvious that the service codes R499 (Other – Support/Professional) and R408 (Program management/ support) dominate the datasets in terms of the value of contracts. These proportions vary across departments: the Department of Labor has extensively used services within the R499 framework, and between 80 per cent and 90 per cent of their budget was spent on this category. The Department of Commerce also shows values of

---

[7] The service contract inventories of the national departments of the USA can be acquired via a list from the White House which refers to the particular department. However, despite the fact that the departments are obliged to publish their service contract inventories, the publications are far from consistent and uniform. Some departments publish the data in relatively convenient Excel files which can be easily analysed, but other departments publish only pdf files and summaries of the contract inventories rather than data about every single contract. Moreover, some of the departments have already archived (or not even published) data for some fiscal years. Therefore, the following discussion only considers departments with accessible and readable datasets.

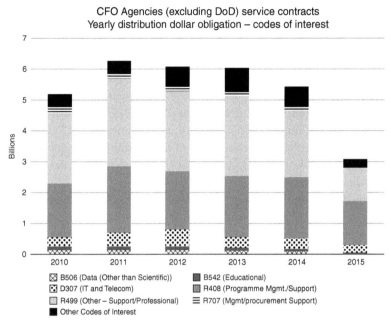

Figure 3.3 Departments key contract codes yearly distribution

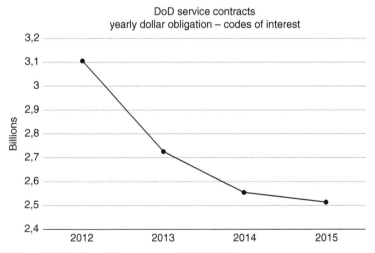

Figure 3.4 DoD service contracts 2012–2015

around 70–80 per cent for R499 contracts. On the other hand, the Department of State has invested heavily in R408 contracts, accounting for up to 90 per cent. A relatively balanced share can be found in the Department of Homeland Security and the Department of Energy. There are also departments which do show a relatively diversified service contract inventory, such as the Department of Education and the Department of Agriculture. The Department of Agriculture shows investments within the D307 category, which belongs to IT management and support. The Department of Education has procured contracts under B542 (educational services) to more than 40 per cent of the value of contracts.

The decrease in the amount of dollars obligated between 2012 and 2015 is mostly due to a reduction of obligations coded as R499 (Other – Support/Professional). The share and absolute value of contracts coded as 'other codes of interest' is also shrinking over time. In contrast to the two other categories of departments examined, the CFO Act agencies (excluding DoD) show a significant amount of contracts coded as R707 (Management Services/ Contract & Procurement support), B506 (Data (other than scientific)) and B542 (Educational), in all of which the share of contracting has declined over time.

3.5.1.2 Department of Defense

Civilian component contract data for the DoD was compiled for each service for the years 2012–2015 – that is, not including intra-service military contracting. The data is divided into four files per year for the following military agency categories: Air Force, Navy, Army and 'Other DoD Agencies'. Data from these four sources was combined to obtain a global picture of DoD spending. Interestingly, total obligated USD by the DoD on selected codes has also decreased every year from 2012 to 2015.

The most expensive types of services are the ones attached to codes D307 (IT and Telecom), R499 (Other – Support / Professional), B541 (Defense) and R408 (Program management and support).[8] The large share of USD obligated to code R499 should be noted – amounting to more than 50 per cent of obligated dollars for the years 2013–2015 – since the contracts categorized as such may refer to services that do not

[8] See Figures 3.4, 3.5 and 3.6.

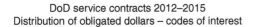

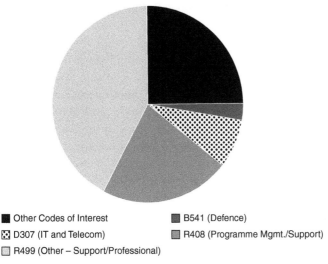

Figure 3.5 DoD key contract codes distribution

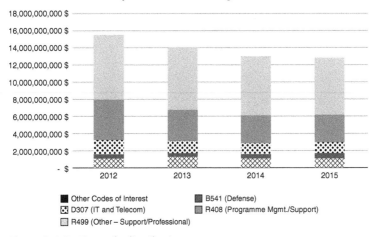

Figure 3.6 DoD yearly distribution

include any policy aspect. Notably, the drop in total USD obligated for the contracts coded seems to be mostly driven by a decrease in Program management and Support services (code R408).

3.5.1.3 Other FAIR Act Agencies

As listed earlier, 28 agencies, boards and commissions make up the 'Other FAIR Act agencies'.

The total amount of spending over five years in these agencies is dominated by three service codes (R408, R499 and D307), which comprise 89 per cent of the COI spending. Two of these are management/IT consulting-related, while R499 is a miscellaneous category (see Figures 3.7 and 3.8).

The 2011–2015 COI trend is upward, growing 58 per cent in that time, although declining in 2015. Individually and as a group, the service codes are highly volatile. If we remove the three large service codes, and all those without contracts across the five years of study, we can compare how service code obligations changed over time. The figures are too volatile to show any real trend, with a standard deviation of 228 per cent among service-code index values. Yet, most often

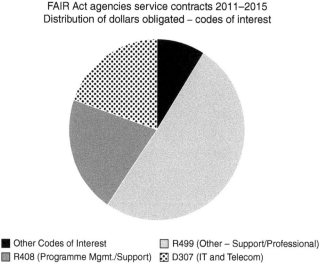

FAIR Act agencies service contracts 2011–2015
Distribution of dollars obligated – codes of interest

■ Other Codes of Interest   ☐ R499 (Other – Support/Professional)
▨ R408 (Programme Mgmt./Support)   ⊡ D307 (IT and Telecom)

Figure 3.7 Key contract codes distribution 2011–2015, FAIR Act agencies

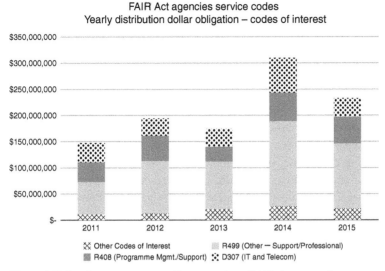

Figure 3.8 Service contract spending over time, FAIR Act agencies

these figures increased by more than 100 per cent – sometimes due to the presence of abnormally large contracts.

3.6 Conclusion

This study has shown that the US federal government is a major purchaser of services via contracts, and this trend has attracted the notice of government budgetary and accounting agencies. Increased scrutiny from the public, elected officials and academia has led to the creation of a new reporting regime, through the creation of the FPDS database, as well as a 2010 statutory requirement for agencies to publicly report on their service contracts. While the resulting data is relatively precise, consistent and complete compared to other countries, the issue of reporting and analysing policy contracting in the US is not without its problems. This is not only to do with the definition of policy consulting itself, but also the many caveats and criteria set out herein with respect to the nature, and limitations, of official reporting on the subject.

This study provides overall results in this area of government activity for three different components of government: CFO Act agencies, FAIR act agencies and the DoD. It found both overarching and diverging trends between the three types of departments.

As expected, the DoD is by far the largest purchaser, while FAIR is the smallest, confirming that it is preferable to disaggregate data so as not to lose the smaller patterns in the overall analysis of DoD trends. Significantly, with respect to overall expenditures and popular opinion, while secondary data from the GAO (2011) indicates an increase from 2005 to 2010, in the years where more precise data was available for analysis (2010 to 2015), all these units saw relative declines, not increases, in their purchasing of such services.

Some other trends are also similar to those found in other countries, including the finding that a small number of units are responsible for most of the spending: the DoD, DoI, Department of Transportation, Department of State and Department of Veterans Affairs. The recent decline in contracting can also be found in the studies of other jurisdictions. In Canada (see Chapter 6), the federal government's expenditures in management consulting peaked in 2009–2010 before dropping (Howlett and Migone 2013a). In Sweden (see Chapter 7), spending on management consultants dropped in 2008 and growth resumed, albeit at a much slower pace, until 2011 (Pemer, Börjesson and Werr 2014). Finally, the UK's ANAO (2016) also found that departments have substantially reduced their spending on consultants and temporary staff since 2009–2010, but saw an increase in reported spending since 2011–2012.

4 Entrenched and Escalating: Policy-Relevant Consulting and Contracting in Australia, 1987–2017

4.1 The Political, Public Policy and Management Context

This chapter seeks to contribute to knowledge about the activities and significance of external consultants and other service contractors within the policy process in Australia. In keeping with the quantitative, empirical orientation of this book, it seeks to do so through an analysis of the summary details of consultancies and other contracts with the national government, as publicly listed in official reporting systems since the mid-1980s. As a first step in this task it is appropriate to briefly sketch the political and public policy context of the period.

Historically, the liberal democratic political system in Australia developed as an amalgam of, first, a parliamentary system of executive government inherited from the United Kingdom and, second, mechanisms of federalism from 1901, influenced by the United States. By the mid-1980s the Commonwealth (national) government based in Canberra had become the dominant revenue-raiser within the federal system and had demonstrated an ability to lever this financial power to control or influence policy in many areas beyond those listed as its remit in the formal Constitution. Thirty years later, the Commonwealth's expenditure and revenue position, relative to that of the states, had further strengthened, though state governments did benefit from receipt of Commonwealth GST tax revenue, and they remain an important arena for decision-making and delivery of many services.

At both levels of the federal system, governments are formed by the party or parties forming a majority in the lower houses of Parliament, where voting is conducted by a modified majoritarian procedure in single-member electorates. For more than a century, the lower-house contest for executive government has been fought out between the Coalition (Liberal and a rural-based National Party) and the Australian Labor Party (ALP). The upper houses of Parliament have retained the constitutional right to veto lower house legislation. In the second half of the twentieth century the electoral systems for the upper houses have moved to proportional representation. This has resulted in minor parties usually holding the balance of power and exercising this to significantly constrain or influence government legislation. The partial independence of the upper houses has also tended to strengthen the parliamentary committee system, which in turn, at least in the national Parliament, has played a significant role in the introduction of public reporting on external consultants and contractors.

Historically, the political system in Australia was characterized by a relatively strong 'career service' bureaucracy. Although most aspects of the institutional architecture of the political system in Australia have not fundamentally changed since the early 1980s, one significant change has been the assertion by the major parties of greater leverage by the political executive over the appointed bureaucracy. This 'political management' has been achieved by expansion in the numbers of political staff of ministers (the 'Ministerial minders') and changes to legislation governing the appointment and tenure of the top echelons of the bureaucracy. The extent of this politicization has received considerable attention from political scientists (e.g. Halligan and Power 1992; Maley 2012).

While the formal architecture of the political system in place at the beginning of the 1980s remained largely stable, the broad public-policy orientation of the major parties – and indeed of the bureaucracy – did undergo a paradigm shift in the first half of the period, which has had lasting consequences for the significance of consultants and contractors. The decade from the mid-1970s had seen a tumultuous debate about appropriate policy responses to adverse economic trends, and this bipartisan anxiety continued through to the end of the 1990s. From the mid-1980s, both the ALP and the Coalition presided over a major shift from a 'protectionist state' to a 'competition-espousing' state. Concepts and programmes that had shaped the expansion of the public sector in the previous eight decades were progressively rolled back in favour of strategies to reduce or constrain the size of the public sector and to stimulate competition within the public and, supposedly, the private sector. Although distinct differences in emphasis persisted, both the major parties at Commonwealth and State level took action to sell off many profitable government-owned businesses and to halt the post-1945 trajectory of increase in the level of tax revenue, and spending from tax revenue, relative to the size of the economy. From around 2000, the context that had spurred the reform programme shifted for a combination of reasons – notably, improved economic fortunes and a preoccupation with counter-terrorism. Despite this, the reform trajectory from the mid-1980s, while seemingly slowed, has not been halted or reversed. In part, this continuation is due to the fact that the reform programme has been seen as the key factor in prolonged economic growth, a view which underplays other contributing factors such as rising demand from China for Australian mineral resources (Carson and Kerr 2017; Meagher and Goodwin 2015; Miller and Orchard 2014). The marketization reform programme has had diverse agents: particular business 'peak' organizations, business-funded think tanks, pragmatic ALP leaders, micro-economists within and outside the bureaucracies and public administrators funnelled through MBA programmes.

Within this context at the Commonwealth level, the discourse within and around the Australian Public Service (APS) developed in successive stages. With its antipathy to stereotypes of proceduralist public administration, 'managerialism' in the mid-1980s ushered in flexibility for managers in the allocation of 'running costs' between in-house staff and outside procurement. The mantra to 'do more with less' quickly moved to 'commercialization' and the use of agency devolution, competitive tendering and 'contracting out'. In the post-2000 era, the conceptual challenge for the APS commentariat has been to deal with the organizational and cultural legacy of managerialism and commercialization – i.e. with a field of implementation and service delivery marked by heterogeneous mixes of not-for-profit, for-profit and in-house operators. Concepts of 'contract governance', 'network governance', 'integrative governance' and 'collaborative governance' have come to the fore, aimed at repairing adverse effects of market competition, such as fragmentation and loss of collaboration (Dickinson 2016; Edwards et al. 2012). Yet even proponents of these concepts are hesitant to claim pronounced success in practice (Shergold 2013).

As this governance discourse developed, debate intensified regarding the extent to which the in-house bureaucracy has been weakened by the combination of ministerial minder interference and increased reliance on outside service providers. Over the past decade, academics and practitioners have frequently characterized a shift in the APS since the mid-1980s, from 'monopolist' to 'competitor' in policy-making

(Halligan 2000: 57; Wanna, Butcher and Freyens 2010: 28; Moran 2013; Miragliotta, Errington and Barry 2014: 121). These commentators assert that in the past three decades the official paper trail leading up to Cabinet decisions has involved a widening range of non-APS authors; not only reports of official advisory bodies, but commissioned consultancy reports as well (Ayres 2001; Banks 2009; Head 2015a). By 2007, a concurrent serious decline in APS policy and strategy capability had been identified within the APS itself (Halligan 2008), while by 2010 it had been officially confirmed by the Rudd government's review of the APS (Halligan 2011). Since then, a rising chorus of veteran senior journalists, outgoing senior public servants, shadow ministers and even Malcolm Turnbull (shortly before becoming prime minister in 2015) have bemoaned a run-down in APS corporate memory, skills and confidence with regard to strategic policy development and operational responsibilities. Excessive reliance on consultants has been part of this critique, seen as both the result of caps on in-house staff and, in turn, the accentuator of loss of capacity (e.g. Tingle 2015; Thomson 2015; Donaldson 2018).

The emergence of 'consultants' on the public radar from the mid-1980s – especially 'commercial consultants' wholly reliant on fee-for-service income – brought with it sharp public comment about the motives, merits and impact of these new players. This stakeholder and popular conversation has waxed and waned ever since. Very early in the period, 'expensive consultants' were apt to join 'lazy bureaucrats' as objects of tabloid derision and even broadsheet notice. Media coverage of the 'cost of consultants' fluctuated, but a sharp increase in a particular year, or reflex Opposition pledges to 'rein in' spending, usually triggered media attention. High fees paid to consultants was but one of a host of concerns articulated periodically. These concerns mirror those reported in other chapters of this book: lack of competition in selection of consultants; pressure on 'fee-for-service' firms to please the client and 'legitimize' in-house preferences; secrecy of reports achieved through abuse of 'commercial-in-confidence'; uncertain quality of work; and lack of knowledge transfer and deskilling of in-house staff (e.g. Ranald 1997; Jardine 1997; Banks 2009; Gittins 2016). While use of external consultants to provide specialist advice not required on a regular basis (supplementation) was supported, use of consultants as an alternative to in-house staff (substitution) was not. In the early years of media publicity, it was easy for those resentful of the new prominence of commercial consultants to assume they were, or might be, 'taking over' policy – an idea that consulting firms disavowed (Mewett 1997; Howard 1997).

While the push for market reforms opened up the possibility of encroachment by external, commercial consultants, developments in this regard received quite limited academic attention from political scientists. In his 1998 book *Re-orienting a Nation: Consultants and Australian Public Policy*, John Martin did argue that 'consultants' played a key role as legitimators of radical policy change in the 1980s. In four of his five case studies, however, Martin's consultant was an individual expert whose primary employment background was that of a salaried academic. The hiring of such academic experts for advisory reports had many precedents historically. In other words, despite its title and its insights, Martin's work did not examine the new phenomenon of commercial consultants, working as sole traders or members of firms, and primarily reliant on consulting fees.

Other academic commentary recognized a difference between commercial consulting firms marketing themselves as boutique 'policy-oriented' consultancies and those marketing themselves as 'management' consultants. Helen Dent (2002), John Hamilton-Howard (2000), Russell Ayres (2001) and Geoff Hawker (2001) pointed to firms such as Allen Consulting, Access Economics and ACIL as firms specializing in broad policy advice (in these cases, micro-economic policy advice). None of these authors argued that such firms had overtaken in-house policy staff as sources of advice. Ayres (2001), who in his PhD thesis paid the closest attention to this issue, presented three case studies that pointed to varying degrees of significance in the role played by consulting firms with a 'policy' bent. His conclusion was that while some 'partial' markets for policy input had opened up in piecemeal fashion, they were still quite secondary to bureaucratic and network modes of policy-making.

As for the influence of 'management consultants' on the policy process, in interviews for a Radio National *Background Briefing* programme on *The Consultocracy* in 1999, leading public policy scholars Mark Considine and John Warhurst both acknowledged the growing profile of the large management consulting firms. On the one hand, both held that these firms had not yet become part of the traditional 'A team' of actors shaping policy (i.e. politicians, top business leaders and media barons). However, both did see potential for increasing indirect influence on policy through their role as advisers on techniques of implementation of ideas in 'good standing'. In his thesis, Ayres (2001: 111) also pointed to the potential for management and technical analysis to develop into policy advice:

Indeed, according to several consultants interviewed for this study, contracts that are ostensibly let to address fairly 'standard' managerial issues, such as information technology, business planning, performance auditing, legal considerations or accounting practice, often evolve into projects where the consultant is expected to respond to questions of policy. . . . These (policy) problems can then become the central concern of the consultancy.

Since 2000, there have been brief references in academic textbooks on Australian politics to a claimed greater role of consultants in public policy-making (Stewart and Maley 2013: 82; Miragliotta, Errington and Barry 2014: 121). Vromen and Hurley (2015: 175–178) assert that 'it is well-known that governments increasingly turn to private sector consultants for policy advice, to undertake programme reviews and increasingly to manage public consultations'. They emphasize, however, that 'in-depth research on the use of consultants as policy experts ... has been negligible': 'concrete data on the use of policy consultants by Australian governments are difficult to locate', so much so that there is 'a black box for researchers wishing to examine the extent to which governments hire and then implement the recommendations of private sector consultants'. In recent years, some case studies have begun to appear on aspects of policy-related consultancies, notably methodology and compromises on objectivity to please the client (Dollery and Drew 2017; Drew, Kortt and Dollery 2013; Drew and Grant 2017; Dollery, Fiorelli and Burton 2012). On the other hand, detailed assessments of the importance of external (especially commercial) consultants relative to other policy actors have not been forthcoming. Much more attention has focused on other factors associated with the posited decline of in-house policy capacity, such as the role of political staff in the Minister's office appointed directly by the Minister (Edwards et al. 2017).

In contrast, over the course of the past three decades the overall programme of market reform has received sustained stakeholder and academic critique, though with arguably marginal effect. The success or otherwise of reform instruments such as user pays, corporatization, competitive tendering, contracting-out, privatization and public–private partnerships has been the subject of a significant number of qualitative case studies. However, it remains the case that quantitative mapping of the scale of contracting, and the implications for the public policy process, has lagged. In particular, almost no scholars have made use of official sources of data on consultancies and contracts, seemingly because of the difficulties (until recently) of collating this material.

Collation and analysis of this data is the focus of this chapter. The chapter will examine trends in spending on consultancies and contracts, both overall and on those ostensibly most relevant to policy, before analysing the degree of concentration on both the supply side and the demand side of these policy-relevant engagements. The premise will be that the more dominant the corporate end of the supply market and the broader the number of departments involved, the more likely that successful consultants and contractors will have influence in the policy process across the government overall.

4.2 Official Data Sources

This chapter utilizes two official data sources for the tax-funded 'General Government' sector of the national government.[1] The first is the Annual Reports of Commonwealth Departments, used mainly for the period 1987–1994 for data on use of 'consultants'. In response to a succession of reports from the Joint Parliamentary Committee on Public Accounts during 1986–1989, central executive requirements were introduced (1987), and then elaborated upon (1991), for departments to provide summary information on their use of 'consultants' in annual reports. The basic components of summary information required for each consultancy have remained in place ever since. For most of this period, however, department listings have seldom been readily available in easily manipulable form. Moreover, the government has not been required to collate and analyse the information provided by departments, and has not done so (e.g. SSCFPA 2003).

---

[1] The Australian Bureau of Statistics and the Commonwealth Treasury draw a distinction between the 'General Government' and the 'Government Business Enterprise' (or 'Public Trading Enterprise') components of the public sector. Agencies primarily funded via taxation are assigned to the former; agencies primarily funded via user charges to the latter. Agencies in the latter are not required to publish summary details of consultancies or contracts.

The second source used in the chapter is the published summary details of contracts for the procurement of goods and services, covering the period 1997–2017. A *Commonwealth Gazette*, publishing various decisions of the executive arm of government, had commenced at Federation in 1901; a separate weekly, *Purchasing and Disposals Gazette*, was launched in 1985, specializing in procurement information. Although weekly listings went online in 1997 on the *Gazette Publishing System (GaPS)* website,[2] efficient aggregate searching of post-1997 data was not possible until 2015. Throughout the period, this inventory of summary information has encompassed contracts for capital as well as recurrent purposes.[3]

For the researcher, the Gazette reporting system has a number of advantages over departmental annual reports. It was comprised of a much larger number of data fields; the format of these fields was uniform across agencies, both in nomenclature and in electronic format (Excel); and the information submitted was published through a central location. In addition, it encompassed statutory authorities as well as departments, together with all contracts of purchase, not only contracts deemed to be 'consultancies'. Finally, with the move from the *GaPS* to an amended *AusTender* reporting website in July 2007, it became mandatory to indicate whether or not a contract was considered to be a 'consultancy'. For the first decade from the mid-1980s, however, annual reporting by departments was the only source available for mapping 'consultancies'.

4.2.1 Consultants and Contractors: The Scope for Autonomy

Over the course of the past thirty years, Commonwealth *Procurement Guidelines* have attempted to provide a basis for public servants to decide if a particular contract constituted a consultancy or not. Two hallmarks of the concept of consultancy are professional/technical expertise and independence in the application of that expertise in the

---

[2] The *GaPS* website during 1997–2007 was www.contracts.gov.au. Enquiries to this web address are now redirected to the *AusTender* website: www.tenders.gov.au.

[3] The Gazettal regime has not encompassed 'non-procurement contracts' which refer to government 'grants' to external organizations for purposes such as community services. As these grants become subject to increasing specification, there has been debate as to whether they should be brought within the Gazettal reporting regime.

framing of advice. Early in the period the *Guidelines* succeeded in differentiating consultants from temporary employees (Howard 1996a: 63–65); in the latter part of the period, the *Guidelines* have similarly succeeded in differentiating consultants from personnel working in APS agencies who have been supplied by labour hire firms under contract (DoF 2017c: 'Practice'). These differences are said to pertain to the level of autonomy in hours and place of work and in decision-making, with autonomy very high for consultants and low or non-existent for temporary and labour hire personnel. However, a major problem has not been addressed satisfactorily: how to identify contracts in which the contractor is likely to enjoy opportunity for consultancy-like autonomy in the interpretation and performance of their responsibilities under the contract.

Current DoF Procurement Guidelines seek to use the distinction in level of autonomy in regard to the end product to differentiate 'consultancy contracts' from 'general contracting services'. With consultancies, a high level of control over both process and end product is attributed to the consultant: 'Performance of the services is left largely up to the discretion and professional expertise of the consultant. ... [and] The output reflects the independent views or findings of the individual or organisation.' In contrast, with 'general contracting services', while a level of autonomy might also apply to process 'Professional or expert services provided under non-consultancy contracts are generally delivered without a high level of supervision and direction from the [APS] entity', the Guidelines posit that 'the output produced will not necessarily represent the independent views of the service provider – i.e. the (APS) entity controls the form of the output', with the service provider implementing 'an existing (APS) proposal or strategy' (DoF 2017c: 'Practice').

The premise that an APS agency can control the form and content of outputs in contracts in the services area is highly contestable, especially with regard to large contracts common in the era of outsourcing. The Guidelines acknowledge that general contracts might involve 'consultancy elements' where the 'intellectual output (does) represent the independent views of the service provider'; however, unless this output is the 'sole or major element of the contract', it need not be separately reported. The Guidelines go on to give sixteen examples of general contracts, but without getting to grips with this issue. Fourteen of these examples refer to more mechanistic activities (e.g. 'provision of travel services'), while only two ('conducting a recruitment activity'; 'project management') pertain to activities of a more complex nature where policy significance is more likely (DoF 2017c: 'Tips'). The result is that the delegation involved in large-scale contracting for management and related services remains unexplored. This is further highlighted by the comparison with the use of 'Product and Service' (P&S) codes reported on in Section 4.4. As one example, in the decade to 2017 only one-third of contracts given the P&S code *'8010 000 – Management Advisory Services'* were also flagged as consultancies. For this reason, it is much more appropriate to analyse spending on contracts in general, not just those identified as consultancies, in *AusTender* since 2007.

4.3 Growth in Spending on Consultancies and Contracts

Figure 4.1 provides an overview of reported spending on consultants by Commonwealth departments.[4] Figure 4.1 establishes that the level of spending reported in *AusTender* for the years since 2007 is much higher than that reported in Department Annual Reports up until 1999; on a per annum basis, the increase is from $142.635 million

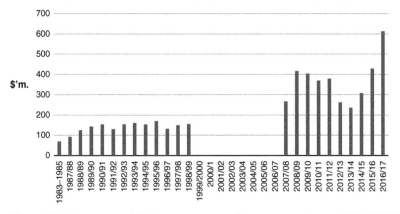

Figure 4.1 Commonwealth department expenditure on consultants, 1983–2017 (AUD$ million)

---

[4] The data for 1983–1994 has been taken from Howard (1996a), and for 1994–1999 from Hawker (2001). No data has been collated for the 1999–2007 period, while the totals for 2007–2017 have been derived from *AusTender* (DoFb). Spending on foreign aid consultancies has been excluded for all years.

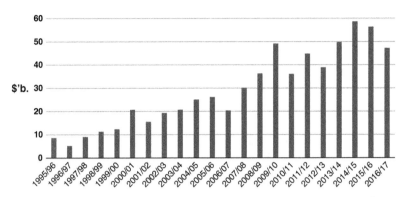

Figure 4.2 Commonwealth department and statutory authority expenditure on contracts for goods and services, 1995–2017 (AUD$ billion)

for the 1987–1999 period, to AUD$ 368.331 million for the post-2007 period. That said, the trend is far from a linear rise within either period. Moreover, the fluctuations in spending do not correspond with party in office. Incoming governments on either side would be expected to trim or curtail spending, given the ritualistic promises by opposition parties, but the timing of elections cut across financial year reporting and makes proof of post-election cutbacks difficult.

Consultancies being but a subset of contracts, Figure 4.2 displays the level of annual spending by Commonwealth departments and statutory authorities on gazetted contracts for all goods and services during the period 1995–2017.[5] Like Figure 4.1, it shows a much higher level of reported spending after 2000 than in the mid-to-late 1990s. The average annual expenditure in the five years leading up to June 2000 was AUD$ 9.229 billion; in the seven years before June 2007, it rose to $22.791 billion, while over the next ten years, up until June 2017, it almost doubled again, rising to $42.835 billion. The level of spending in 2017 was 451.4 per cent, or 5.51 times, higher than during the 1995–1996 period.

For the years 1995–1999 and 2007–2017, the Department of Finance (DoF) has provided an overall categorization of contracts into 'Goods' and 'Services', based on a grouping of more detailed industry classifications. In all but one of these years (1997/98), spending on 'Services'

---

[5] Sources are as follows: for 1995–1997, DOFA (1999); for 1997–2005, DoF (2017a); and, for 2005–2017, DoF (2017d) and corresponding back-years.

exceeded spending on 'Goods'. In the four years leading up to June 1999, the annual ratio of services/total spending averaged 52.5 per cent; in the ten years leading up to June 2017, it averaged 60 per cent.[6] There was no smooth year-to-year increase in the ratio during this later period but the figures point to a long-term increase in the relative importance of services. This reflects long-term trends in the wider economy but is nonetheless relevant for assessing the significance of contracts for policy and management. Moreover, there is extensive evidence, illustrated in Section 4.4, that some contracts given a 'goods' code should have been given one of the service categories.

Although the growth in reported spending on consultancies and contractors displayed in Figures 4.1 and 4.2 is in nominal terms, comparison with the movement in inflation, in numbers of in-house staff and in cost of in-house staff leaves no doubt that the pattern of growth was highly significant. Adjusted for inflation (using the appropriate price deflator for government spending), the reported spending on consultants in 2016/17 was 2.68 times higher than in 1988/89; more striking, the reported spending on all contracts in 2016/17 was 3.59 times higher in real terms than in 1995/96 (ABS 2017).[7] These increases in real spending contrast with long-term decline in the level of in-house staffing in the APS. One indicator is the 'headcount' of employees of agencies covered by the APS Act in June each year. For the years after 1990, the peak level was reached in 1993 (165,529). The level dropped in each of the next seven years, then rose during 2001–2012, before falling back to 152,095 in June 2017; a level 5.5 per cent below the 1990 level (Simon-Davies 2010; APSC 2017).[8] This APSC headcount does not adjust for part-time employees (who are counted as full-time). However, a second indicator compiled by the Treasury (Average Staffing Level in the General Government sector) is based on 'full time equivalent'; for the period 1998–2017 (the time series available), its movements are closely in line with the APS headcount.

---

[6] Figures for 1995–1997 are from DoFA(1999); figures for 2007–2017 are from back-years of DoF (2017d).

[7] See 'General Government – National – Final Consumption Expenditure: Chain Price Indexes', Series ID A2304688T in ABS 5206.0 *Australian National Accounts* (2017), Ausstats.

[8] These figures were not adjusted for what the APSC says were 'minor changes' that occurred in this period in the range of agencies covered by the Australian Public Service Act.

The evidence suggests that the trend in in-house staff 'running costs' (which take account of salary levels) was also in sharp contrast to the increase in real spending on consultants and contractors. Without further recourse to Treasury clarification, difficulties arise in compiling a consistent 'running costs' time series for the 1987–2017 period. Reference, however, is made in Section 4.5 to the rise in spending on external consultants, relative to in-housestaff running costs for the 1988–1994 period. In addition, figures for 'total departmental expenses' (encompassing spending on contracts and in-house staff costs) for the period 2007–2017 were provided by the DoF in its submission to a 2018 parliamentary enquiry into procurement reporting by the Joint Committee on Public Accounts and Audit (JCPAA). The DoF emphasized that the growth in total department expenses had been very modest (33.6 per cent in nominal terms for the decade to 2017) – indicating that the trend in in-house staff expenses had offset the trend in contract spending.[9] The DoF also pointed out that total operating expenses had consistently fallen as a percentage of total department expenditure (DoF 2018: 4–5).

4.4 Identifying Policy-Relevant Contracts

Documenting the quantum increase in spending on consultants and wider contracting is one thing; demonstrating a commensurate increase in consultancies and contracting that are policy-oriented or policy-related is quite another. The question of how to identify 'policy' decisions and documents, as distinct from decisions and documents of lesser significance, has been the subject of long-standing debate within the academic fields of public policy and public administration. By the 1980s, the emerging field of public policy had come to recognize that policy decisions (however initially identified) were often not put into effect as intended by their designers. As a result, the way decisions were implemented or administered had a major bearing on what policy 'meant' in practice (e.g. Howlett, Ramesh and Perl 2009; Hudson and Lowe 2009). Likewise, the academic field of public administration had come to acknowledge that notions of a clear separation of policy and administration were often difficult to maintain in practice (e.g. Davis et al. 1993: 7). Even where management and administration might be separated from 'Big P' policy, authors might speak of

---

[9] The DoF conveniently excluded the Department of Defence from these calculations.

'management policy', 'administrative policy' or 'operational policy'. For this reason, an influential school developed, which conceived of a 'policy process' or a 'programme development process', encompassing several 'stages' – most commonly, agenda-setting, policy-formulation, decision-making, implementation and evaluation.

Within this intellectual context, in seeking to ascertain the extent to which consultants and contractors influence the policy process, it is appropriate to cast the net broadly rather than narrowly. Fortuitously, the official listings of summary details of consultancies and contracts enable a broad catchment, as they offer comprehensive coverage of this activity across the range of agency operations. For analysts seeking to gain an indication of the type of service provided via a consultancy or other contract, there are two fields in official reporting that are potentially most useful.

The first is the 'Description' field, providing textual information about the content of the job. The word counts of the descriptions have always been quite limited, but became markedly more so in the second half of the thirty-year period. In various searches of consultancies in the 1987–1993 period conducted by Howard (2004, 2006) the average word count ranged between 13.11 and 19.01 words. In a study of 590 consultancies awarded to the Big Four accountancy firms and listed in department annual reports during 2002–2007, the average was 9.88 words. For the pool of gazette contracts identified through searches 2–14 and 16 (see Section 4.5), the average was 7.36 for 1997–2007 and 7.46 for 2007–2017. The brevity of these gazette descriptions imposes significant constraints on a researcher seeking to use this field to gain insight into the nature of the work being purchased from the contractor.

The second field is the 'Product and Service Code'. This second field has only ever been provided via the gazetting of contracts; it has never been part of the summary details required of department annual reports. The level of detail of this classification field increased dramatically during the past two decades, as indicated in Table 4.1 (DoFA 2004: 30–38; DoF 2017e).

The problem facing the researcher seeking to use the 'product and service' classification systems is that these systems have remained primarily descriptive rather than conceptual. For the most part they have been geared to specifying the location within the economy (industry, sub-industry, particular commodity) to which the good or service provided under the contract relates, rather than the nature of the input provided. In

Table 4.1 *Product and service classification systems: no. of codes*

	System	1st Level	2nd Level	3rd Level
Pre-1997 (Gazette)	ASIC	3	31	
1997–2007 (*GaPS*)	ANZSCC	9	69	292
2007–2017	UNSPSC		53	575
(*AusTender*)	(customized)		(at 2014)	(at 2014)

the *GaPS* era, 92 of the 292 ANZSCC codes did combine mention of the industry or commodity with the term 'services' – e.g. 'Higher education services' and 'Taxation services' – but without any indication of the type of service provided (i.e. whether it was fundamental advice, management or routine delivery). Conceptual terms used by scholars to characterize aspects of the policy process – such as 'consultation', 'advice', 'planning', 'policy', 'strategy', 'review', 'evaluation' (or their word-stems) – were entirely absent from the wording of the ANZSCC line item lexicon. The terms that came closest to this purpose were 'research' (used in four codes) and 'management consulting' (codes 865 and 866) (DoFA 2004: 30–38). The proliferation of more detailed codes under *AusTender* only partly improved this situation. The main gain was the creation of at least 12 third-level codes relating to general management, with the term 'management' being included in 17 codes. In contrast, the term 'policy' was mentioned in only 3 codes (2 related to the trade portfolio), 'planning' in 5 codes, 'strategic' in 1 code, and 'evaluation/evaluate' in 2.

The dearth of 'analytical' codes meant it was very likely that public servants would use the descriptive industry/commodity codes when they could have used one of the analytical codes (almost all of which were in the '8000' and '9000' cluster of codes). See, for example, the case in Table 4.2. In this case, the code '80101504 – Strategic Planning Consultation Services' might have been equally appropriate, since the description indicated that the project involved advice on commercial strategies to support munitions manufacturing in Australia. For further evidence of the under-reporting of policy-relevant contracts, and related issues and recommendations in regard to the 'P&S' coding system, see Howard (2018). Because of the limitations of both the 'Description' and 'P&S' fields for purposes of identifying contracts at least potentially relevant to policy and programme content, the approach taken here has been to search both fields, as well as the Agency Branch and Divisions fields.

Table 4.2 *Example of contract entry*

Contract ID	Description	Code No.	Code Title
CN575932	Commercial support for Domestic Munitions Manufacturing Arrangements	12130000	Explosive materials

4.5 Evidence of the Growth in Procurement of Policy-Relevant Work

4.5.1 The 'Take-Off' Years: Consultancies Oriented to 'Programme Content'

As mentioned earlier, prior to 1997 the annual reports of departments were the only usable source for quantitative research on the type of work undertaken by entities identified as consultants. It is appropriate to cite past research from the late 1980s and early 1990s, not only because word counts of descriptions were longer, but also because patterns of policy significance that can be documented in this seminal, 'take-off' period have implications for likely patterns in the later years of much larger spending on consultancies and other contracting.

Howard (2006) presented the findings of a 2004 examination of the title/description of 3,538 consultancies, reported by three Commonwealth departments in the five years until 1992/93. The departments – Community Services and Health (DSCH), Employment, Education and Training (DEET) and Industry, Technology and Commerce (DITAC) – were chosen because they represented a mix of economic and social areas. Moreover, they were in the middle of the spectrum of the 17 Commonwealth departments with regard to spending on consultants in absolute terms and relative to spending on in-house staff. Each consultancy was manually coded twice and, in the process, a 12-part categorization was developed (see Table 4.3).

Categories 1.1 to 1.3 were designed to identify consultancies oriented to the purpose of programmes – that is, concerned with questions such as: who was to be assisted and/or regulated; with what types of assistance or regulation; and to what ends? Category 1.1 was for background research, such as changing demographic patterns relevant

Table 4.3 *Consultancy categorization*

1.1	Program Research: Background
1.2	Program Research
1.3	Program Review
2.1	Program Administration: Research
2.2	Program Administration: Review
2.3	Program Administration: Implementation
3	Training
4	Program Communication
5	Information Technology
6	Information Systems
7	Other (e.g. recruitment)
8	Not classified

Table 4.4 *Example category 1.3 consultancy entry*

KPMG Peat Marwick	DCSH	92/93	Examine the performance and achievement of the CRS since its reorientation to providing community based vocational and social rehabilitation. (2)	$200,000
Arthur Andersen	DITAC	89/90	To assist the Department in developing strategies for the advanced manufacturing technology equipment and services industry in Australia.	$158,457

to programmes. Category 1.2 was for consultancies oriented to research on more direct aspects of programme purpose, such as the characteristics of programme users. Category 1.3 was for consultancies oriented to some form of evaluation or planning with regards to the purpose or substance of programmes (see Table 4.4).

Whereas categories 1.2 and 1.3 were oriented to programme objectives, categories 2.1 to 2.3 were for consultancies more oriented to internal organizational structures and processes by which these wider objectives would be pursued. Category 2.2 ('Program Administration – Review')

Table 4.5 *Example category 2.2 consultancy entry*

Coopers & Lybrand	DITAC	92/93	Review of Departmental structure and activities.	$100,650

was for consultancies that appeared to require evaluation and recommendations for change to administration (see Table 4.5). Category 2.3 was reserved for projects that appeared to involve not advice on implementation, but the actual carrying out of implementation; the prime example was the provision of audit services. As such, these tasks should not have been listed as consultancies.

The finding was that, overall, the three type 1 categories constituted 46.7 per cent of the total number of consultancies commissioned by the departments, and 52.96 per cent of the amount spent on these consultancies. These were much higher proportions than for the type 2 categories (14.6 per cent of the number and 11.1 per cent of the value of consultancies), or for each of the remaining categories. The proportion of consultancies in category 1 was highest for DCSH, although even DEET, as the lowest of the three in this regard, had 35.8 per cent of the number of its consultancies, and 40.6 per cent of its spending, in this 'program content' category. These patterns were also relatively stable year to year and underlined the consistent way in which a significant proportion of consultancy activity appeared (on the basis of the description field) to be oriented to programme development rather than support structures.

Of the category 1 types, category 1.3 ('Program Review') was the one bearing most directly on programme development. Overall, type 1.3's share of the total across the period was 16.5 per cent for the number of consultancies and 19.75 per cent for value. Some of these category 1 consultancies dealt not with programmes as a whole, but major projects within programmes, or even minor projects. Nonetheless, they entailed creative influence on the purpose and substance of activity; they were relevant to 'program content'. Of course, the other categories – from 2 through to 6 – also had the potential to affect the delivery of programme content, but the category 1 consultancies, especially 1.2 and 1.3, unambiguously had this potential. Further evidence of a significant proportion of consultancies oriented to programme content emerged in a follow-up study of consultancies undertaken by the (then) Big Six accounting firms across 14 Commonwealth departments in the 1987–1993 period (Howard 2004).

4.5.2 *From the* GaPS *to the* AusTender *Decade: Evidence of Dramatic Escalation in Potentially Policy-Relevant Contracting, 1997–2017*

The research cited on the 'take-off' years was based on the 'manual' assessment of entries in the Description field. To take advantage of the availability of online centralized contract data for the years after 1997, an automated, rather than manual, keyword approach has been adopted. A set of 16 searches was undertaken to identify contracts within the *GaPS* and *AusTender* databases that had:

(1) Particular 'product and service' (P&S) classification codes;
(2) 'Policy' and related keywords in their 'Description';
(3) 'Policy' in the title of the Division or Branch of the agency letting the contract.

The tables that follow compare results for the *GaPS* (1997–2007) and *AusTender* (2007–2017) decades with regards to each of these 16 searches.

Methodologically, the first 6 of these searches (1–6) were not as rigorous in their *GaPS/AusTender* comparability as the other 10 searches (7–16). Search 1 involved 'management' codes. The 'P&S' codes selected for the *GaPS* era (1997–2007) were codes '865 – Management Consulting' and '866 – Services related to Management Consulting Services'. These two codes were selected because their wording was the closest of any *GaPS* ANZSCC codes to the notion of 'policy'. Of the two codes, 865 was much the larger (83.8 per cent of their combined total). As previously mentioned, by 2010 under *AusTender* there were at least twelve detailed codes related to management available, instead of the two (865/866) under *GaPS*. Thus, for the *AusTender* decade, the approach taken was to search for contracts given the following P&S codes:

80101505 – Corporate objectives or policy development
80101504 – Strategic planning consultation services
80111501 – Management development
80100000 – Management advisory services

80161500 – Management support services
80101500 – Business and corporate management consultation services
80101506 – Organizational structure consultation
80101600 – Project management
80101604 – Project administration or planning
80101601 – Feasibility studies or screening of project ideas
80101603 – Economic or financial evaluation of projects
80101702 – Productivity or efficiency studies or implementation

These are the codes referred to in Table 4.6, in the search 1 row, as '*AusTender* – Selected (12) 8000 Codes'. Using this comparison is far from perfect, but it is the best available approximation. Using the same search criteria, searches 2–6 examined subsets of the 865/866 *GaPS* codes and the 12 selected 8,000 *AusTender* codes.

In contrast, searches 7–14 involved 8 different keyword searches of the contract Description field, again using the same keywords for *GaPS* and *AusTender* contract descriptions. The keywords chosen were ones associated with key analytical tasks in the policy process. Finally, search 15 examined contracts let by agency Divisions or Branches that had the word 'policy' in their title, while search 16 examined a subset of search 15 contracts, namely those which also had the word 'policy' in their contract Description. Unlike searches 1–6, searches 7–16 had no comparability limitations.

Table 4.6 shows that for all searches except search 15, spending per annum during the *AusTender* decade was higher than during the *GaPS* decade. Average annual spending on search 1 contracts was 7.44 times higher in the *AusTender* era than in the *GaPS* era. Even if some of this increase might have been attributable to under-capturing of *GaPS* era contracts relevant to search 1, the fact that spending on searches 2, 3 and 4 was 38.35, 13.97 and 7.49 times higher respectively for *AusTender* than for *GaPS* is striking evidence of a growth in contracts possessing signs of policy relevance. Likewise, the fact that across all eight of the Description field searches (7–14), the *AusTender* annual spending rate was anywhere between 2.03 and 6.11 times higher than the *GaPS* rate is just as impressive or even more so, given no comparability limitations. Bucking the general pattern, *AusTender* spending on search 15 contracts was only 24 per cent of *GaPS* spending. This category saw the highest amount of spending across the searches in the *GaPS* decade, and by a huge margin; the decline in average annual spending from AUD\$ 781 million to

$191 million had to do with a collapse in spending by Branches of the Department of Defence that had 'policy' in their title; more will be said about this in Section 4.7. Intriguingly, even with the massive contraction in search 15 contract spending, a subset of this category of contracts – contracts that also had 'policy' in their Description field – saw *AusTender* spending running at 12.61 times the rate of *GaPS* spending.

The final two rows of Table 4.6 show the increase in spending when all contracts identified in the searches of *GaPS* and *AusTender* are pooled for analysis (with duplicates removed). Spending on the total pool (i.e. searches 1–16) is 2.80 times higher for 2007–2017 than for the previous decade. When the disproportionately large number of contracts from search 1 and search 15 are removed, the spending in the remaining pool is 3.26 times higher for the *AusTender* compared to the *GaPS* decade. This latter pool (i.e. searches 2–14, 16) contains the contracts most likely to be relevant to policy and programme development.

The spending comparisons in Table 4.6 are in nominal terms. Adjusting for inflation would modify, but not fundamentally erode, the pattern displayed in the table. For example, using the appropriate price deflator for government spending, the rate of inflation that occurred between the mid-points of the two decades – 2002 and 2012 – was 37.86 per cent (ABS 2017).[10] In other words, the 2002 dollar values would be 1.38 times higher in 'real' terms. All of the increased ratios in Table 4.6 exceed this. The lowest of the increased ratios was 1.62 for search 5 contracts; using the price deflator, this search 5 increase ratio would still be 1.18 (or 18 per cent) in real terms.

The increase in spending between the two decades was a product of two factors: an increase in the number of contracts (after adjusting for a rise in the reporting threshold from $2,000 to $10,000 in January 2005), and an increase in the average value of contracts (also after adjusting for inflation). Of these two factors, the latter was the larger in 13 of the 16 searches.

In absolute terms, the numbers in Table 4.6 are eye-catching, point-ing to the sizeable level of spending on contracts with external entities for work that is suggestive of a contribution to programme develop-ment. Spending of $4.149 billion across the *GaPS* decade on projects coded as management consulting does not look insignificant; spending of $30,890 billion on the twelve selected management codes across the

---

[10] For details, see footnote 6.

Table 4.6 *Total spending on policy-relevant contracts per annum: increase from GaPS to AusTender decade*

	Searches	GaPS 1997–2007 AUD$	AusTender 2007–2017 AUD$	Ratio AusTender/ GaPS
1	*GaPS – Codes 865+866 (Management Consulting)*	414,943,422	3,089,034,288	7.44
2–6:	*AusTender – Selected (12) 8000 Codes (General Management)* Subsets of Codes 865/866 (*GaPS*) + Selected (12) 8000 Codes			
2	: Description contains 'policy'	709,257	27,202,056	38.35
3	: Description contains 'strategy' or 'strategic'	5,321,970	74,351,916	13.97
4	: Description contains 'plan', 'planning' or 'planner'	3,908,067	29,281,343	7.49
5	: Division or Branch title contains 'policy'	10,180,790	16,518,193	1.62
6	: Division or Branch title contains 'strategy or 'strategic'	33,070,422	149,375,685	4.52
7–14:	(All Codes): Description column contains:			
7	– 'research' or 'researcher'	81,897,725	229,606,610	2.80
8	– 'analyse' or 'analysis'	28,110,836	70,905,485	2.52
9	– 'plan', 'planning' or 'planner'	57,366,836	116,443,510	2.03
10	– 'strategy' or 'strategic'	42,142,884	171,597,314	4.07
11	– 'policy'	14,470,234	88,460,021	6.11
12	– 'assess', 'assessment', 'appraise' or 'appraisal'	23,945,741	130,386,805	5.45
13	– 'review', 'reviewer' or 'reviewed'	31,184,433	100,331,991	3.22
14	– 'evaluate' or 'evaluation'	30,747,739	87,745,595	2.85
15	(All Codes) Agency 'Division' or 'Branch' column contains 'policy'	787,265,740	190,654,814	0.24
16	(All Codes) Division or Branch contains 'policy': also, Description contains 'policy'	167,231	2,109,332	12.61
1–16		1,434,974,280	4,023,568,092	2.80
2–14, 16		325,500,596	1,061,843,607	3.26

AusTender decade looks imposing. Ideally, these figures need to be put in context and compared to in-house spending on comparable projects. This would be a very demanding task and has not yet been attempted.

4.6 Distribution of Spending on the Supply Side

In seeking to gauge the likely influence of contractors on the policy and programme development process, one plausible indicator is the degree to which market share amongst contractors is highly concentrated or highly dispersed. If the corporate end of the supply side is highly dominant, it bodes for stronger policy influence; if the cottage industry end looks far more prevalent, then policy leverage arguably should be less likely.

4.6.1 The 'Take-Off' Years

Howard (1997a) reported on the supply-side characteristics of 7,466 consultancies listed in 8 Commonwealth departments for the six-year period of 1987–1993. He emphasized the methodological difficulties in working from the 'names' of consultants, as they were listed, to ascertain underlying discrete consulting entities, whether individuals, temporary consortia or formal organizations. Acknowledging the likelihood of some underestimation, his finding was that across the 7,466 consultancies, the average number of jobs per consultant was a mere 2.50. In the dataset, 63.12 per cent of consultants appeared only once, 17.62 per cent appeared only twice, while only 6.9 per cent undertook more than 6 consultancies, according to the listings. It was this 6.9 per cent that received a very disproportionate share of consultancy income from the departments. Across the 8 individual departments, the share of spending going to the top 1 per cent of consultants (ranked by income) ranged from a high of 38.99 per cent to a low of 18.7 per cent. For the 8 departments as one pool, the share of the top 1 per cent was 36.28 per cent of the total expenditure of $278.102 million. There were 2,983 consultant names in the dataset (after vetting for variations in the formatting of the same name); 1 per cent entailed 30 names. Of these, 11 (the Big Six accounting firms and 5 IT companies) received 15.46 per cent of total income. The shape of the supply side was summed up as follows:

The image of a 'comet-like' structure emerges from the data – a small 'head' of large firms and a long 'tail' of small partnerships or lone self-employed operators. (Howard 1997a: 86)

The 1997 analysis did not look at the supply-side distribution for different types of consultancies. However, Howard (2006) did attempt this task in relation to the 3,358 consultancies listed by 3 Commonwealth departments in the five years up to 1992/93. A list of 1,576 unique consultant names was identified (in part by drawing on the 1997 exercise) and then grouped in a rudimentary way as follows:

Non-commercial: academics; public sector (including TAFE); peak organizations (business, professional, NGOs); trade unions; other not-for-profit/community organizations.

   Commercial: names containing 'Pty Ltd'; other business-sounding names; names containing 'and Associates'; names of individual persons (other than 'Prof.' and 'Dr.').

The finding was that entities that appeared to be non-commercial received 25.53 per cent of department spending; of the 74.47 per cent going to ostensibly commercial entities, 4.72 per cent went to individual surnames. Interestingly, there was a distinct difference in this ratio regarding the typology of consultancies developed in this 2006 study and detailed above. The entities thought to be non-commercial made up a much larger chunk of Type 1 consultancies (programme research and review) than Types 2–7: 39 per cent of the total number and 37 per cent of the total value of Type 1 consultancies, compared to 11 per cent of the number and 12 per cent of the value of Types 2–7. Within the 'non-commercial' sector, by far the main contributor to Type 1 consultancies was the 'Academics' groupings – not surprising, given the research orientation of Types 1.1 and 1.2. The entities that uniquely stood out for gaining a spread of work across almost all the categories were the Big Six accountancy firms; their share was 7.4 per cent of the number and 10.39 per cent of the total value of all consultancies (Howard 2006: 58–62).

4.6.2 *From the GaPS to the AusTender Decade*

Unlike the foregoing research on the 'take-off' years, Tables 4.7–4.10 are not based on 'Supplier Name'; instead, they are based on the supplier 'ABN' field in *GaPS* and *AusTender*. The requirement for suppliers to have a registered ABN (Australian Business Number) was introduced in 2000 as part of the implementation of the new Goods and Services Tax (GST). Since then, the supplier ABN has been part of the summary detail required to be submitted for Gazettal. Tables 4.7–4.10 apply to the years since 2000; they also, however, encompass the three preceding years.[11]

Reference to the ABN facilitates research into the composition of the supplier market because a single ABN can encompass a number of distinct supplier names and thus help to better identify the number of underlying supplier entities. In all searches undertaken so far, the number of ABNs has been found to be significantly lower than the number of supplier names. For example, for contracts coded 865 or 866 in *GaPS*, the number of ABNs was 74 per cent of the number of distinct supplier names (as they were recorded by public servants). It was also the case, however, that some firms that appeared to be the same or closely related (judging by their 'Supplier Name' field), were liable to have more than one ABN. The extent of this multiple-ABN phenomenon has not been quantified, but it was visible in the case of universities, for example. Some universities used only one ABN, others a handful and two a larger number. The multiple-ABN phenomenon was also visible in the case of three of the Big Four accounting–consulting firms. For the *GaPS* decade, 69 per cent of the total value of contracts identified through the 16 searches went to firms with an ABN in their contract record (almost all the other 31 per cent went to contracts during 1997–2000 with no ABN retrospectively assigned). For the *AusTender* decade, 98% of the total value of Search 1–16 contracts went to firms with an ABN, the other 2 per cent going to 'ABN-exempt' firms overseas.

One guide to the structure of the supply side of government contracting is the average number of contracts per ABN. However, a much better indication of the huge cottage industry sector of the supply side is the distribution of ABNs by number of contracts received, especially when viewed over a longer period. In Table 4.7, the first search (1–16) involved the pooling of all contracts identified in the 16 separate searches of the 1997–2017 period and the elimination of duplicate contracts. Because of the standout number of contracts captured in

---

[11] The reason for inclusion of 1997–2000 is that agencies had the option of entering ABN numbers into *GaPS* retrospectively. Virtually all agencies did this to some extent, presumably where other firm details matched. As a result, 45% of contracts let during 1997–2000 and identified through Searches 1–16 also displayed an ABN number. In a sample check, for Search 1 contracts the share of the top 10 and top 1% of ABNs altered only very slightly when the period of analysis was restricted to 2000–2007.

Table 4.7 *Distribution of contracts across ABNs: 1997–2017*

	No. of ABNs	No. of Contracts	Av. No. Contracts per ABN	No. of Contracts Received × % of ABNs						
				1	2	3–5	6–10	11–20	20+	
Searches 1–16	20,627	233,866	11.34	43.97	16.90	18.01	8.68	5.54	6.90	100
Search 1	12,432	102,495	8.24	47.31	16.88	17.25	7.87	5.13	5.56	100
Search 15	6,713	79,684	11.87	45.24	16.13	17.37	8.36	6.27	6.63	100
Search 2–14 +16	11,236	78,188	6.96	50.13	16.73	16.70	7.26	4.47	4.41	100
Search 11	1,042	2,942	2.82	65.90	15.47	12.30	3.55	1.44	1.34	100
Search 14	1,666	6,315	3.79	58.82	15.61	13.93	6.18	2.88	2.58	100

searches 1 and 15, the table analyses these separately. To complement this, the pool of contracts in the other 14 searches (i.e. 2–14, plus 16) is also analysed. Finally, results are also shown for searches 11 and 14, on the grounds that these have a particular resonance for the task of identifying contracts potentially significant for policy. The averages shown in the table are quite low, considering the 20-year time span. Strikingly, in all searches shown, the percentage of ABNs receiving just 1 contract over the 20-year period is higher than 44 per cent, while the percentage of ABNs receiving 10 or fewer contracts is above 87 per cent. For the individual and composite searches reported here, only between 1.34 per cent and 6.90 per cent of ABNs receive more than 20 contracts over the period.

Building on this finding, Tables 4.8 and 4.9 show that the distribution of income from contract spending on policy-relevant contracts was heavily concentrated. Table 4.8 shows the consistently high market share, across the 16 *GaPS* searches, of the top 1 per cent of ABNs, ranked by income. In 4 searches, the percentage is between 65 per cent and 70 per cent; in another 4, it is between 40 per cent and 50 per cent, while in 5 searches, it is between 30 per cent and 38 per cent. This pattern of market concentration was even more marked in the *AusTender* decade, with the table showing that in 10 of the 16 searches, the share of the top 1 per cent of ABNs increased over the *GaPS* figure.

Another perspective on market concentration is to look at the share of the top 10 ABNs, ranked by income. In 9 of the searches for the *GaPS* decade, the share of total contract income going to the top 10 ABNs was between 42 per cent and 75 per cent, while in a further 5 searches it was between 29 per cent and 33 per cent. In 11 of the searches, the share of the top 10 ABNs was higher in the *AusTender* decade than in the previous decade. In 5 of the searches, the increase was more than 20 percentage points.[12]

An even starker picture of market concentration emerges when all contracts identified in the 16 searches of *GaPS* and *AusTender* are pooled for analysis (with duplicates removed). Table 4.9 shows that the share of the top 1 per cent of ABNs was 62.38 per cent for the *GaPS* decade, 74.71 per cent for *AusTender* and 76.22 per cent for the

---

[12]   In 8 of both the *GaPS* searches and the *AusTender* searches, the share of the top 10 ABNs was higher than the share of the top 1 per cent. This occurred where the number of ABNs identified in a search was less than 1,000.

Table 4.8 *Income received by top 1 per cent of ABNs as % of total spending on policy-relevant contracts, 1997–2017*

	1997–2007		2007–2017		% of Total $ % Points
	Top 1 per cent of ABNs		Top 1 per cent of ABNs		
Searches	No. of ABNs	% of Total $*	No. of ABNs	% of Total $	AusT – GaPS
1 GaPS – Codes 865+866 (Management Consulting)	69	48.98	73	78.11	29.13
2–6: AusTender – Selected (12) 8000 Codes (General Management) Subsets of Codes 865/866 (GaPS) + Selected (12) 8000 Codes					
2 : Description contains 'policy'	1	12.93	3	40.79	27.86
3 : Description contains 'strategy' or 'strategic'	3	33.91	7	69.74	35.83
4 : Description contains 'plan', 'planning' or 'planner'	4	19.61	7	43.7	24.09
5 : Division or Branch title contains 'policy'	4	34.11	4	22.96	–11.15
6 : Division or Branch title contains 'strategy' or 'strategic'	7	68.96	5	62.02	–6.94
7–14: (All Codes): Description column contains:					
7 – 'research' or 'researcher'	11	32.14	16	58.99	26.85
8 – 'analyse' or 'analysis'	11	43.9	14	31.45	–12.45
9 – 'plan', 'planning' or 'planner'	16	70.25	16	41.52	–28.73
10 – 'strategy' or 'strategic'	11	65.59	15	75.1	9.51
11 – 'policy'	5	49.74	7	50.63	0.89
12 – 'assess', 'assessment', 'appraise' or 'appraisal'	13	37.39	20	61.48	24.09
13 – 'review', 'reviewer' or 'reviewed'	19	30.19	28	42	11.81
14 – 'evaluate' or 'evaluation'	9	28.44	10	33.46	5.02
15 (All Codes): Agency 'Division' or 'Branch' column contains 'policy'	51	65.3	23	43.02	–22.28
16 (All Codes) Division or Branch contains 'policy'; also, Description contains 'policy'	1	40.85	1	13.21	–27.64

* All figures in Table 4.8 are based on exclusion of contracts with no ABN.

Table 4.9 *Income received by top 1 per cent of ABNs and top 10 ABNs as %*
of total spending on policy-relevant contracts: pooled searches, 1997–2017

	Total Spending All Contracts AUD$	Total Spending Contracts with ABNs AUD$	Share of Top 1 per cent of ABNs %	Share of Top 10 ABNs %
	1997–2007			
Searches 1–16	14,349,742,799	10,519,990,361	62.38	17.91
Searches 2–14,16	3,255,005,960	2,556,852,308	53.59	30.03
	2007–2017			
Searches 1–16	40,235,680,916	39,285,681,987	74.71	33.81
Searches 2–14,16	10,618,436,068	10,099,491,752	61.42	29.10
	1997–2017			
Searches 1–16	54,585,423,715	49,805,672,348	76.22	28.04
Searches 2–14,16	13,873,442,029	12,656,344,060	64.24	24.44

combined pool of these contracts for the 1997–2017 period. Excluding
searches 1 and 15, to avoid any distorting effects of these two large sets
and the possibility that they were less relevant to policy, the share of the
top 1 per cent of ABNs decreases somewhat: 53.59 per cent for the *GaPS*
decade, 61.42 per cent for *AusTender* and 64.24 per cent for the 1997–
2017 period. The fact that the share of the top 1 per cent was higher for
the 1997–2017 period than for either decade, and regardless of whether
searches 1 and 15 were included or not, indicates that at least some of the
leading ABNs were prominent throughout the twenty-year period.

The share of the top 10 across these pools is similarly eye-catching,
though the pattern is slightly different. The share of the top 10 is less
than the share of the top 1 per cent across Table 4.9 (reflecting the large
number of ABNs involved). There is also evidence of greater turnover
in the composition of the top 10, given the lower percentage for the
1997–2017 period than for the two decades separately.

Market concentration would look even more radical when account is
taken of the limitations of the ABN as an indicator of underlying
commercial identity. For instance, one of the top 10 ABNs belonged
to Serco Pty Ltd, yet Serco had other ABNs, including one ranked 14th

in contract income and another ranked 31st. In a further sign of some strengthening at the 'top' end of the spectrum, there was also strong evidence of the market share of the Big Four accounting–consulting firms (PwC, KPMG, Ernst & Young and Deloitte) becoming more conspicuous in the post-2007 era. With regard to total value of contracts, the share of the Big Four was higher across all 16 searches for the *AusTender* decade than it was for the *GaPS* decade, and by big margins. For composite search 2–14 and 16, covering 1997–2017, these 4 firms were in the top 7 spots for number of contracts and the top 11 spots for income. There is not the space here to further analyse the identities of the top income-earning ABNs. However, in one glimpse, an interesting contrast can be drawn in relation to the results for the composite search 2–14 and 16 for 1997–2017: universities occupy 6 of the top 20 ABNs, ranked by number of contracts, but none of the top 20 ABNs, ranked by income.

The ABN system can be used to reveal other significant patterns in the gazetted contract data. Two of these offer some consolation for those fearful of a complete takeover by commercial firms of public policy contract inputs, in that they reveal that government and non-government not-for-profit organizations gained at least some minor share of contract expenditure. Under the Australian Business Register administered by the Australian Securities and Investment Commission (ASIC), the supplier's ABN is linked to other information about the supplier, notably their 'entity type' and 'charity' status. Use of the entity field reveals that of the $50 billion awarded to suppliers with ABNs across the pool of contracts identified in the 16 searches for 1997–2017, 8.30 per cent of this total was awarded to Commonwealth, State and Local Government entities. The proportion of spending going to these government entities exceeded 8% in 14 of the 32 searches of the two decades before and after 2007; interestingly, of these 14 searches, 8 involved the term 'policy' in either the Description or Division/Branch field'.

Of the remaining $45 billion awarded to non-government entities with ABNs in the same pool of contracts for 1997–2017, 7.41 per cent went to entities classified by the Australian Taxation Office as having 'charity' or 'public benevolent' status, meaning that $41.95 billion went to entities with no such ATO status. (To gain charity status the supplier organization has to satisfy the ATO, in conjunction with the Australian Charities Commission, that it is 'not-for-profit' and 'has

Table 4.10 *Percentage of total spending received by not-for-profit ABNs, 1997–2017**

Searches	1997–2007		2007–2017		% Points Difference *AusT* – *GaPS*
	Non-Charity %	Not-for-Profit Charity %	Non-Charity %	Not-for-Profit Charity %	Not-for-Profit Charity
2–6: Subsets of Codes 865/866 (*GaPS*) + Selected (12) 8000 Codes					
2 : Description contains 'policy'	99.4	0.6	28.29	71.61	71.01
5 : Division or Branch title contains 'policy'	96.43	3.57	81.12	18.88	15.31
7–14: (All Codes): Description column contains:					
7 – 'research' or 'researcher'	69.38	30.6	73.54	26.46	–4.14
11 – 'policy'	85.68	14.32	33.97	66.03	51.71
12 – 'assess', 'assessment', 'appraise' or 'appraisal'	80.6	19.4	75.74	24.26	4.86
14 – 'evaluate' or 'evaluation'	76.39	23.61	64.62	35.38	11.77
16 (All Codes) Division or Branch contains 'policy'; also, Description contains 'policy'	88.92	11.08	47.82	52.18	41.1

* Public sector ABNs are excluded.

only charitable purposes that are for the public benefit'.) When search 1 and 15 contracts are excluded from the $45 billion pool, the proportion going to ABNs with charity status rises to 13.43 per cent – or $1.70 billion out of $12.66 billion. Furthermore, the share going to ABNs with non-profit status rises sharply for searches featuring the term 'policy', as well as some other keywords, as Table 4.10 illustrates. To the extent that these keywords are a reliable indicator, then not-for-profit organizations were at least gaining a significant share of contracts most oriented to policy.

The entity types with significant rates of charity status were 'Australian Public Company', 'Other Incorporated Entity' and 'Other Unincorporated Entity'. At the same time, charity status was enjoyed by no more than half, and often much less, of these entity types. The entity types 'Australian Private Company', 'Other Partnership' (into which the Big Four accounting–consulting firms were placed) and 'Sole Trader' had virtually zero rates of charity status. While identification of charity status is useful, it would be even more useful to obtain a breakdown of different types of 'Public Company'. The suppliers that fell within this category ranged from large publicly listed share companies to the commercial units of larger organizations which historically had not been associated with the concept of a for-profit company and where the purpose of these 'public company' units might well have been to cross-subsidise wider, non-profitable operations. An example of the latter was the Public Company status of many contracting units within Australian universities. Further research is needed to ascertain whether the possession of charity status is a key indicator of 'values' and behavioural differences within public company suppliers. The same can be said for the broader distinction between public and private company suppliers.

4.7 Distribution of Spending amongst Departments and Other Agencies

So far, this chapter has focused on the supply side of the contracting relationship: the distribution of contracts amongst suppliers. What of the demand side? That is, the extent to which contract spending was concentrated in a few agencies or dispersed amongst many?

4.7.1 The 'Take-Off' Years

Howard (1996a) analysed spending on 'consultancies' reported in the Annual Reports of all 17 Commonwealth ministerial departments in the six years until 1993/94, and found 2 significant patterns. The first was marked differences in the level of spending amongst departments. In terms of aggregate spending, the departments fell into 3 groups. Three departments spent in excess of $167 million over the period: the Department of Foreign Affairs and Trade (DFAT) – entirely because of its AIDAB foreign aid branch; the Department of Administrative Services (DAS); and the Department of Defence (DoD). Eight departments spent between $29 million and $73 million, while 7 spent between $5 million and $17 million.

The second finding was of a 'consistent and pervasive long-term upward trend in the reported number and aggregate cost of consultancies across departments'. The 7 departments in the lowest of the 3 spending bands increased their spending year-to-year on 76 per cent of possible occasions; the departments in the middle band did so on 61 per cent of possible occasions, while Defence increased its spending in each of 5 possible occasions across the six-year period. This second finding was evidence that increasing use of external consultants was an APS-wide phenomenon (Howard 1996a: 68–71). The only exceptions to a general trend for increased expenditure in most years were DAS, where spending declined, and the huge AIDAB component of DFAT, where spending fluctuated.

Assessment of the significance of an increase in spending on external consultants and contractors ideally requires reference to the context, especially trends in spending on in-house staff. Howard (1996b) did construct such a time series for individual departments for the six years to 1993/94. His finding was that, excluding DAS and DFAT, as well as 2 social welfare departments (DSS and DEET) who took on extra in-house staff in response to the severe 1991 recession, the ratio of spending on consultants compared to in-house staff across the other 13 departments more than doubled, from 2.7 per cent to 5.82 per cent. At first glance, the level of this ratio during 1993/94 might have looked modest, but a doubling in six years presaged a longer-term and more far-reaching structural shift. Moreover, the ratio understated the significance of the shift in human resources, in that the in-house expenditure numbers included all staff, including clerical staff, not only staff with the professional and technical skills associated with the engagement of consultants. Accepted measures of in-house spending specifically devoted to policy work were not available; however, the estimates cited by Ayres (2001: 107–109) further underline the significance of the increase in the consultant/in-house ratio.

4.7.2 *From the* GaPS *to the* AusTender *Decade*

To ascertain patterns that emerge in relation to the two decades from 1997, a two-step analysis was undertaken. The first step was to rank the share of spending going to each 'agency' appearing in each of the 16 searches of *GaPS* and *AusTender*. To get a better grip on the underlying distribution of spending, the second step was to group particular agencies initially identified through this computer searching.

In all, 141 differently named agencies were computer-identified in the 16 searches of the 1997–2007 period. In 11 of the searches, the number of agencies identified exceeded 60. Of the total pool of 141 agencies, 38 were 'departments' operating under the direct, day-to-day control of a minister; 97 were 'statutory authorities' ultimately responsible to a minister, but operating on a more arms-length basis; and 6 were small departments of the parliament. Despite being outnumbered by statutory authorities, ministerial departments generated 89.73 per cent of overall agency spending on contracts identified through the 16 searches (duplicates removed). As an analytical tool, statutory authorities could have been grouped with ministerial departments under their mutual ministers/portfolios, but its marginal utility did not warrant this time-consuming exercise.

Instead, attention was focused on the 38 ministerial department 'names' identified through computer searching. Whereas statutory authorities were established under separate Acts of Parliament, and as a result very seldom underwent a name change, ministerial departments did not require legislation for their creation, abolition and restructuring. Accordingly, marginal changes in their name occurred much more frequently, as governments chose to move some functions from one department to another or to simply rebrand the same department. In the *GaPS* decade, the names of only 5 departments remained unchanged: Prime Minister and Cabinet, Treasury, Foreign Affairs and Trade, Defence and

Veterans Affairs. Of the other 33 department names identified through the searches, an exercise was undertaken to group these entities on the basis of their similarity of names. This rationalization yielded 10 groupings, which are displayed in Table 4.12 along with the 5 departments with unchanged names.

Within each of the 15 groupings set out in Table 4.12, some functions would have been moved between departments within the grouping. Such moves do not affect the statistics for the grouping as a whole. Some functions, however, would have been moved in such a way that their location would have crossed a grouping. One example in Table 4.12 was policy responsibility for some working-age income support payments (unemployment, sole parent and disability payments), which shifted in the period between the 'employment' and 'family and community services' grouping. Other income support payments (such as the Age Pension) remained in the 'family and community services' grouping. The other main examples in regards to the 1997–2007 period were in 1998/99 when 'Resources', 'Energy' and 'Family Services' moved to departments that were in a different grouping.

The labels for the 15 groupings are taken from actual names used for departments; the exception is 'Income Support', which has been added to 'Family and Community Services' to indicate that this grouping covered this major area of government expenditure. As mentioned, the groupings in Table 4.12, and also Table 4.14, do not take account of statutory authorities. The sole exception is AusAID, an exceptionally high spender on contracts identified through the searches. Throughout the 1997–2007 period AusAID remained an autonomous agency outside the Department of Foreign Affairs (DFAT), but it has been grouped with DFAT to facilitate comparison with the *AusTender* era, when it was brought under DFAT. Overall, the 15 groupings are not completely consistent in their coverage across the period. On the other hand, they are a reasonable guide to trends in the major areas of Commonwealth responsibility, designed to give a broad indication of the distribution of contract spending on the demand side.

Table 4.12 sets out the distribution of contract spending during 1997–2007 across the 15 groupings for particular searches, while Table 4.11 displays the total value of spending associated with these searches. The rationale for featuring the 2 composite searches and the 4 individual searches is the same as that set out in relation to Tables 4.7 and 4.9.

Table 4.11 *Ministerial departments: contracts, 1997–2007*

		No. of Contracts	AUD$
Searches 1–16	See Table 4.6 for titles of searches	121,064	12,901,632,058
Search 1	Codes 865 + 866 ('Management Consulting')	36,899	3,296,172,802
Search 15	(All Codes): Agency 'Division' or 'Branch' column contains 'policy'	66,854	7,649,621,328
Search 2–14 +16	(n.b. See Table 4.6 for titles of searches)	27,245	2,773,027,383
Search 11	(All Codes): Description column contains 'policy'	880	135,459,611
Search 14	(All Codes): Description column contains 'evaluate' or 'evaluation'	2,387	274,532,197

Two patterns emerge from Table 4.12. The first is that across 5 of the 6 searches shown, the biggest share of spending was that of the DoD, and by large margins. At the same time, its share did vary significantly across these searches. Defence was responsible for 66.07 per cent of spending by ministerial departments on the contracts identified through all the searches (1–16). This figure was significantly shaped by the department's high share of search 1 and, especially, search 15 contracts. Within search 15 contracts, $1.851 billion worth of contracts were let by departments with 'Divisions' whose title included the word 'policy'. These contracts were distributed across 9 of the 15 department groupings shown in the table, but 2 groupings were responsible for almost all of this spending: DFAT/ AusAID (62.36 per cent) and Attorney-General's (34.46 per cent). A further $5.813 billion worth of contracts were led by departments with 'Branches' whose titles included the word 'policy'. These contracts were distributed across 8 of the 15 department groupings, but 1 grouping/department (i.e. Defence), was responsible for 97.85 per cent of this expenditure. These search 15 patterns would appear to reflect not only a difference in propensity to spend on contracts, but also a difference in propensity to use the term 'policy' in the titles of Division and Branches across the groupings.

Table 4.12 *Department groupings: % share of spending on policy-related contracts, 1997–2007*

	Search 1–16	Search 1	Search 15	Search 2–14, 16	Search 11	Search 14
Department groupings						
Defence	66.07	57.74	74.36	44.33	39.35	31.26
Foreign Affairs and Trade (incl. AusAID)	11.65	3.43	15.07	10.18	17.03	6.59
Attorney-General's	5.02	0.56	8.33	0.80	0.08	1.13
Immigration and Multicultural Affairs	3.22	9.17	0.73	11.87	0.75	0.52
Health	3.72	6.28	0	12.37	3.32	36.29
Education, Training, Employment and Workplace Relations	2.13	3.99	0.66	5.03	1.01	6.87
Veterans Affairs	1.28	0.37	0.24	5.12	4.55	0.95
Income Support, Family and Community Services	0.98	1.59	0	2.83	30.16	11.78
Environment	0.67	0.95	0	2.22	0.7	1.62
Transport and Regional Services	0.93	2.29	0.34	0.96	0.12	0.68
Finance, Administration and Treasury	1.59	5.12	0.15	1.22	0.91	0.32
Industry, Science and Resources	0.50	1.09	0	1.16	1.35	0.77
Prime Minister and Cabinet	0.39	0.73	0.11	0.80	0.13	0.16
Communications, Information Technology and the Arts	0.60	2.08	0	0.66	0.36	0.63
Agriculture	1.25	4.59	0	0.46	0.18	0.43
	100	100	100	100	100	100

When the two big 'catchments' of contracts – search 1 and search 15 – are excluded, the share of the DoD drops to 44.33 per cent of the total value of contracts identified through the other 14 searches. Of particular interest, the share of Defence drops further in the two searches (11 and 14) perhaps most germane to the task of identifying policy-relevant contracts. For contracts where 'policy' was mentioned in the 'Contract Description' field (search 11), the share of Defence was 39.35 per cent, while for searches where 'evaluation' or 'evaluate' were similarly mentioned (search 14), its share was 31.26 per cent.

The second pattern emerging from Table 4.12 is that, notwithstanding the dominant place of the DoD, the table does provide some evidence for the view that a structural shift in governance across the APS was underway. The 'Income Support, Family and Community Services' grouping of departments was responsible for 30.16 per cent of total department spending on search 11 contracts and 11.78 per cent of spending on search 14 contracts. Likewise, the 'Health' grouping was responsible for 36.29 per cent of spending on search 14 contracts. Due to AusAID, the 'Foreign Affairs and Trade' grouping was also more broadly prominent across the searches in Table 4.12. Moreover, the only instances in Table 4.12 where a department grouping failed to register any spending was in relation to search 15 and, as mentioned, this was likely attributable to a propensity not to use the term 'policy' in naming Divisions and Branches.

Turning to the *AusTender* decade, the same two-step analysis was performed as for the *GaPS* decade. The first step yielded 158 differently named agencies as funding the contracts identified in the 16 searches of the 2007–2017 period. Of these, 36 ministerial departments were responsible for 89.73 per cent of total agency funding. As with *GaPS*, these ministerial departments were rationalized into 10 groupings, with the 5 departments whose name remained unchanged during 2007–2017 (the same 5 'stayers' from 1997 to 2017) making up the other 5 'groupings'. Table 4.14 displays these groupings: all but 3 of the 15 have the same 'title' as the *GaPS* groupings. The same caveats apply as for the *GaPS* procedure: grouping of similarly named departments are likely to conceal some shifts in functions, not only within but across the groupings. The major 'visible' shifts across the groupings were 'Energy', 'Water', 'Arts' and 'Tourism', which all straddled 2 groupings over the course of the ten years to 2017. 'Resources' was also a separate department to 'Industry' during

Table 4.13 *Ministerial departments: contracts, 2007–2017*

		No. of Contracts	AUD$
Searches 1–16	See Table 4.6 for titles of searches	64,803	35,202,856,178
Search 1	**Selected 8000 Codes (General Management)**	35,774	27,780,384,751
Search 15	**(All Codes): Agency 'Division' or 'Branch' column contains 'policy'**	8,661	1,884,763,217
Search 2–14 +16	(n.b. See Table 4.6 for titles of searches)	29,441	8,453,637,812
Search 11	**(All Codes): Description column contains 'policy'**	1,371	820,913,912
Search 1	**(All Codes): Description column contains – 'evaluate' or 'evaluation'**	2,527	761,158,337

2007–2014, but not for all years, hence it remains here in the 'Industry, Science and Resources' grouping. Table 4.13 sets out details of the searches that were covered in Table 4.14 – the same as those covered in Table 4.12.

Table 4.14 documents a wider distribution of spending across the groupings, as compared to the *GaPS* era. The share of the DoD of contracts identified through all the searches (1–16, duplicates removed) was 35.55 per cent, compared to 66.07 per cent in the 1997–2007 period. The main factor in this was the huge reduction in spending by Branches of Defence with 'policy' in their title: a reduction from $5,687 million in the *GaPS* era, to $175 million in the *AusTender* era. However, even for search 1 contracts, the reduction in Defence's share was from 57.74 per cent to 39 per cent, while for all searches, excluding searches 1 and 15, it was from 44.33 per cent to 28.06 per cent. For the 2 searches arguably most relevant to policy, the Defence reductions were even larger: for search 11 it was from 39.35 per cent to 15.43 per cent, while for search 14 it was from 31.26 per cent to 14.09 per cent. Notwithstanding these reductions, Defence was still the leading presence, outspending all the other groupings in searches 1–16, search 1 and searches 2–14 and 16, while being the third highest spending grouping in searches 11 and 14. Also, part of the reason for the lower Defence shares was the hive-off from the Department of the Defence Materiel Organisation (DMO), which became a statutory authority in 2007/08. Inclusion of the DMO would have lifted the 'defence' share of spending on search 1–16 contracts in the *AusTender* decade from 35.55 per cent to 41.91 per cent. The effect of DMO inclusion on other searches would have varied above and below this difference, but without altering the basic pattern of decline.

Table 4.14 therefore provides further evidence of a structural shift in governance on the demand side of the contracting relationship, with several groupings being responsible for standout shares of spending with regard to particular searches. The 'Immigration and Border Protection' grouping generated 31.01 per cent of spending on search 1 contracts (the 12 'General Management' codes selected as possibly most relevant to policy). The 'Education, Training, Employment and Workplace Relations' grouping was responsible for 39.89 per cent of spending on search 11 contracts. The 'Income Support, Family and Community Services' grouping generated 38.41 per cent of spending on search 14 contracts, while the 'Health' grouping made up a further 21.04 per cent. As with Table 4.12, the only instances in Table 4.14 where a departmental grouping failed to register any spending was in relation to search 15.

Further evidence that the increase in spending on policy-relevant contracts was broadly based on the demand side can be gained by examining year-to-year changes in spending levels. In regard to contracts identified through the composite search 2–14 and 16, spending increased more often than it decreased for all but 2 of the 15 department groupings in both the *GaPS* and *AusTender* decades. Where decreases occurred, it often reflected the effect of an abnormally high multi-year contract having been awarded in the previous year.

Table 4.15 restates and compares the percentage share of the groupings for the decade before and after 2007, in relation to contracts identified through the composite search 2–14 and 16; groupings are listed in order of total income for the 1997–2017 period as a whole. For the entire period, there are three bands: Defence, six groupings generating between 6 per cent and 15 per cent of total departmental

Table 4.14 *Department groupings: % share of spending on policy-related contracts, 2007–2017*

Department groupings	Search 1–16	Search 1	Search 15	Search 2–14, 16	Search 11	Search 14
Department groupings						
Defence	35.55	39	9.27	28.06	15.43	14.09
Immigration and Border Protection	25.1	31.01	0.45	15.97	0.8	0.74
Foreign Affairs and Trade (incl. AusAID)	11.42	12.72	3.4	8.38	17.95	11.79
Education, Training, Employment and Workplace Relations	5.72	3.64	2.19	11.80	39.89	5.13
Environment	4.27	1.76	0	12.41	0.5	1.61
Health	3.91	3.26	0.1	6.06	1.64	21.04
Income Support, Family and Community Services	3.08	1.56	9.54	7.18	9.1	38.41
Finance, Administration and Treasury	2.76	1.6	25.14	1.82	0.27	0.16
Industry, Science and Resources	1.74	1.56	0	2.61	9.39	0.8
Infrastructure, Transport and Regional Development	1.78	1.37	10.45	1.19	0.48	0.6
Attorney-General's	1.78	0.26	28.05	0.89	0.18	1.98
Prime Minister and Cabinet	0.85	0.62	5.02	0.55	2.14	1.3
Agriculture and Water Resources	0.7	0.69	0.01	1.37	1.11	1.06
Veterans' Affairs	0.68	0.24	6.38	1.16	1.05	1.12
Communications, Information Technology and the Arts	0.66	0.71	0	0.55	0.07	0.15
	100	100	100	100	100	100

Table 4.15 *Department groupings: % share of spending on searches 2–14 and 16 contracts, 1997–2017*

Department Groupings	1997–2007	2007–2017	1997–2017
Defence	44.33	28.06	32.08
Immigration and Multicultural Affairs*	11.87	15.97	14.96
Education, Training, Employment + Workplace Relations	5.03	11.8	10.13
Environment	2.22	12.41	9.9
Foreign Affairs and Trade (incl. AusAID)	10.18	8.38	8.82
Health	12.37	6.06	7.62
Income Support, Family and Community Services	2.83	7.18	6.11
Industry, Science and Resources	1.16	2.61	2.25
Veterans Affairs	5.12	1.16	2.13
Finance, Administration and Treasury	1.22	1.82	1.67
Agriculture*	0.46	1.37	1.14
Transport and Regional Services*	0.96	1.19	1.13
Attorney-General's	0.8	0.89	0.87
Prime Minister and Cabinet	0.8	0.55	0.61
Communications, Information Technology and the Arts	0.66	0.55	0.57
	100	100	100

* For titles of these groupings for 2007–2017, see Table 4.12.

spending, and eight groupings generating between 0.57 per cent and 2.25 per cent of this spending.

Ideally, the spending levels of each department grouping should be compared to that grouping's spending on in-house staff. Such an exercise spanning the two decades would be immensely complicated and has not been attempted. If it was to be undertaken, it might indicate a somewhat different pattern, with the third band of department groupings, displaying low shares of contract spending, possibly revealing a higher propensity to spend on contracts, if calculated relative to lower in-house running costs.

4.8 Conclusion

The preceding quantitative analysis of the official summary details of consultancies and contacts at the national level in Australia over the past three decades has established some clear patterns. It has confirmed the massive contrast in the neo-liberal era between growth in spending on consultants and contractors and stagnant levels of in-house staffing. It has also built a compelling case that this long-term major growth in spending extended to consultancies and contracts that represented significant action in the policy and programme development process. It has done this via two methods. The first was manual classification of types of consultancies in the 'take-off' years of the late-1980s and early-1990s, when the word lengths of consultancy descriptions were longer. This analysis argued that a significant proportion of all consultancies examined were oriented to programme content, not simply 'management' or areas of corporate services. The second method was keyword searches of contract descriptions and Agency/Branch titles, together with selections of P&S codes for the 1997–2017 period. This analysis demonstrated that the level of spending on contracts meeting criteria oriented to policy relevance was far greater during 2007–2017 than during 1997–2007, which in turn was much greater than the rate of spending on consultants in the 'take-off' years.

The analysis also demonstrated the extremely uneven share of spending amongst suppliers. It reported on searches of eight departments for 1987–1993 and sixteen searches of all department and statutory authority contracts for 1997–2017. It found that the share of total spending received by the top 1 per cent of consultants in the 1987–1993 period (ranked by income received), and the top 1 per cent of contractors with ABNs, with very few exceptions, fell in the range of 30–70 per cent. For the same searches, the share of the top 1 per cent of ABNs was generally and markedly higher for the decade after 2007 than for the decade prior. The collective pool of contracts identified by the 16 policy-oriented searches that went to suppliers with ABNs during 1997–2017 was worth $50 billion; the share of this spending received by the top 1 per cent highest-earning ABNs was 76 per cent.

The analysis also reported on the share of spending received by 'the top 10' in these data sets, and the results were equally, or more, striking. For the eight departments examined for 1987–1993, 10 firms earned 15 per cent of total spending on consultants. For the $50 billion spent on

ABNs during 1997–2017, as identified via the 16 searches, the 10 highest earners constituted 28 per cent of total supplier income. For the subset of this pool – $13 billion worth of contacts identified by the 14 searches with indubitable policy relevance credentials – the share of the top 10 was 24 per cent. The analysis has not reported on the identity of the major players, but it can be noted that Broadspectrum Pty Ltd and Serco Pty Ltd, two infrastructure and services management firms, were the two highest-earning ABNs across the 1–16 pool of contracts. While their profile, and those of similar firms, might not suggest 'leadership' on substantive policy issues, the scale of their engagements, and the intimate involvement in programme management and delivery these potentially represent, do raise questions about their indirect policy influence and potential political leverage. The multi-billion contracts awarded to Broadspectrum and Serco to run asylum-seeker detention centres are emblematic here. The analysis has also pointed to the prominence of the Big Four accounting–consulting firms.

Furthermore, the analysis documented the other side of the supplier market: the huge number of operators who received tiny amounts of Commonwealth agency contract income. In the study of eight Commonwealth departments for the 1987–1993 period, 80 per cent of entities supplying consultancies were engaged only once or twice. Even more remarkably, of the 21,627 ABNs recorded as suppliers for the 233,866 contracts identified via the 16 searches for the 1997–2017 period, 87 per cent received fewer than six contracts in this period. These entities likely ranged from sole operators, perhaps former public servants, to small consortia or organizations, presumably picking up work from other levels of government or the non-government sector. Trawling through this roll-call of multitudinous suppliers across the various searches is apt to leave a positive as well as a sceptical impression: that government agencies might well be tapping into rich sources of outside expertise that potentially enrich, as well as fragment the policy and programme development process.

In addition to the corporate and cottage industry face of the supplier market, the analysis pointed to a third, intriguing feature. In an analysis of consultants engaged by three departments during 1988–1993, a rudimentary categorization of 'commercial' and 'non-commercial' was developed. For contracts identified through the 16 searches for 1997–2017, the Australian Business Register was used to identify recipient ABNs with 'not-for-profit'/'charity' status and those without.

Although the non-commercial entities received less income than the commercial entities across all types of consultancies and almost all searches, their share of spending was distinctly higher for contracts most explicitly oriented to policy: more than a third for 'programme content' consultancies (1988–1994), and higher still for contracts whose description included the terms 'policy' and 'evaluation' in the 2007–2017 period. This is heartening for those fearful of contracts for policy inputs being captured entirely by commercial firms.

Regarding the demand side of the relationship, three patterns emerged from the preceding analysis. First, in both the 'take-off' years and the two decades since 1997, there was a very broad base of department participation in the growth in spending on consultancies and service contracts. Second, in terms of absolute amounts of spending, in both the earlier and the later periods departments tended to fall into three bands of spending, with Defence occupying the top band throughout. Third, in the 'take-off' years the ratio of spending on external consultants to in-house staff rose for most departments. Given the evidence provided by DoF to the 2018 JCPAA enquiry in relation to the past decade, it is highly likely that this ratio also continued to rise for most, if not all, departments in the second half of the period. In the preceding discussion, it was suggested that the influence of contractors on the policy process was likely to be greater if supply across the national government was concentrated but demand was dispersed. Concentration on the supply side has been amply documented; a significant dispersal – i.e. broad involvement across departments – has also been recorded, though the pattern is not as striking as on the supply side, given the disproportionate size of Defence's share of total spending.

What are the implications of the foregoing Australian case for the notions of *consultocracy* and the 'contractor state'? The literal interpretation of 'consultocracy' – rule by consultants – would require Australian evidence to show that the power of consultants now rivals or exceeds the power of policy actors long-held to be most influential in the policy process: i.e. the appointed executive, external business peaks, media organizations and so on. This chapter has not addressed this question, though it has referred to claims of in-house capacity decline. At least going by publicly available sources, students of fundamental economic and social policy in Australia in the neo-liberal era should be struck less by the influence of external consultants, working on a fee-for-service project basis, than by the continuing power of industry peak organizations, business-funded think tanks, the Murdoch media empire and orthodox economists in bureaucratic institutions such as the Treasury and the Productivity Commission. The influence of these forces is often facilitated, but also potentially modified, by poll-driven ministerial minders and party officials. In other words, these traditional quarters seem to remain the seminal ones for setting broad policy directions. That said, ideologues and sectional lobbies increasingly require technical research to validate or operationalize their positions; it is here that consultants are now ubiquitous and essential.

The notion of the 'contractor state' is more open-ended than 'consultocracy'. It might be taken to mean a long-term increase in contracting relative to in-house resourcing. More fundamentally, it could mean the replacement of in-house service provision by external contracting. Even more radically, it could signify the ability of contractors to use their market position to bend government policy-makers and contractees to their interests. The evidence presented in this chapter certainly fits the first interpretation of 'contractor state'; it also suggests that the second and third interpretations, while not fitting the present situation, are not implausible scenarios for the medium-term future.

Although they might not be the source of basic ideology or sectional interest formation, fee-for-service consultants and large firms receiving huge contracts undoubtedly have a significant role to play in facilitating and shaping the detailed formulation and implementation of broad policy directions set by others; consultants projecting expertise in financial accounting have enjoyed especially high status. Moreover, assessment of the cumulative significance of these firms has to take account of their overall interaction with the political and wider social system through mechanisms such as donations, lobbying, recruitment of elected and appointed state executives and public relations/'thought leadership' (M. Howard 2005).

From Corporatist to Contractor State? Policy Consulting in the Netherlands

5.1 Introduction

The externalization and politicization of policy advice has received an increasing amount of scholarly attention in recent years (see Bakvis 1997; Macdonald 2011; Craft and Howlett 2013). Existing research focusses mainly on the visible actors, such as political advisers (Shaw and Eichbaum 2018), advisory committees (Siefken and Schulz 2013), knowledge institutions (Blum et al. 2017) and lobbyists (Fraussen and Halpin 2017). These actors are interesting because of their potential influence on the policy process in their respective roles as agenda-setters, framers, policy entrepreneurs or legitimizers. They are also important in the sense that they can strengthen or weaken the role and position of traditional political-administrative actors (such as legislators, ministers, civil servants and regulators). However, theoretically and empirically very little is known about the role and influence of the less visible type of actors: external personnel who are hired on a temporary basis as policy or management consultants (but see Howlett and Migone 2013a; Van den Berg et al. 2015). They too are in a position to influence policies and to strengthen or weaken the role of traditional actors, but who these external advisers are, what they do, where and for what reasons they are hired, let alone how and to what extent they exert influence on politics and policies, is still a blind spot in the political science and policy science literature.

This chapter delves into the use of external policy personnel in the Netherlands, which can serve as an example of the dynamics in the policy advisory systems of consensus-driven, neo-corporatist polities as described by Lijphart (1999) and Daalder (2011), as a separate category of countries from more majoritarian and public-interest-driven Anglophone countries. Previous studies have found that, as a result of depillarization in the 1960s and 1970s and NPM-type reforms in the 1980s and 1990s, the volume and role of external personnel increased in those decades (Van den Berg 2017). However, few systematic insights are thus far available as to the patterns of use of external personnel during the most recent decade, which has been characterized by fiscal austerity (Hammerschmid et al. 2016) and political fragmentation (SCP 2017).

Therefore, this chapter aims to give a systematic overview of the use of external personnel in the policy process for the period 2007 (just before the start of the economic crisis) up to 2016 (the latest available data). In doing so, own survey data and official government statistics are used, broken down in types of activities following the reporting and accounting logic of the central government itself. Also, a systematic analysis is made of the volume of external personnel relative to the number of permanent civil servants, and relative to the apparatus-spending of the various ministries. Lastly, we will take into account the political context of hiring external personnel as this has – unlike in previous time periods – played a role of significance in the recent decade.

This chapter is organized as follows. First, the background of the Dutch political and administrative system, as well as its policy advisory system will be set out (5.2), followed by the main developments in the policy advisory system of the last decades (5.3). Section 5.4 provides a description of the present policy consultancy landscape in the Netherlands, after which the various types of activities in which external personnel is involved will be addressed, as well as the differences across ministries in the distribution of these activities (5.5). Section 5.6 delves into the scale of external hiring across the past ten years, while in 5.7 the differences in volumes of external hiring across ministries is analysed. Section 5.8 focusses on the motivations for hiring external staff, and on the explanations for the large cross-time and cross-departmental variations. Also, the political context of external hiring and the creation of a budget cap on externally hired personnel will be addressed, followed by a number of concluding remarks (5.9).

5.2 The Dutch Political, Administrative and Policy Advisory System

The Netherlands' political and administrative system can be summarized as a constitutional monarchy, governed by means of a parliamentary democracy and structured as a decentralized unitary state. First, constitutional monarchy entails that the King is the head of state, but that political power rests with the government, headed by the prime minister. Second, the government is formed after parliamentary elections based on a system of proportional representation. Combined with a very low electoral threshold, this has historically led to a) a fairly fragmented party-political landscape (13 parties in parliament at present), b) multi-party coalition governments (four parties are presently necessary to form a parliamentary majority), and c) a highly consensus-oriented decision-making and policy-making style (Bovens et al. 2017).

Third, the decentralized unitary state connotes a state structure in which provincial and local authorities are subject to the authority of the political and administrative centre in The Hague, but where provinces and municipalities enjoy a fair amount of autonomy in carrying out their tasks and responsibilities (Heringa et al. 2015).

The Dutch political-administrative system is based on the European Continental *Rechtsstaat* model, in which, unlike most Anglo-Saxon systems, law is seen as the primary source of authority. Yet, the Dutch version of the *Rechtsstaat* diverges from the more closed *Rechtsstaat* regimes in France and Germany, for instance, in the sense that the Dutch government has traditionally been relatively open to external ideas, expertise and interest representation (Van den Berg 2011; Pollitt and Bouckaert 2017).

The Dutch central civil service consists of all organizations and officials subject to the political executive – i.e. ministerial departments, agencies, independent administrative bodies and state-owned enterprises. Other institutions with a public legal basis, such as public health care institutions, public schools and subnational authorities, are part of the public sector but not of the central civil service. The central civil service is for the most part a departmentalized civil service, meaning that each ministerial department is responsible for its own budget and its own personnel. Only the top ranks (director level and upwards) form an integrated senior civil service (Van der Meer et al. 2012). In recent years the organization of the central civil service has become somewhat more integrated, with a unified logo and shared service centres for a limited number of organizational and facility tasks. Also, in recent years first moves have been made to create system-wide personnel pools of, for instance, interim managers that can be insourced by individual departments.

In order to understand the nature of the Dutch policy advisory system, it is important to note that 'deliberation, consultation, and pursuit of compromise and consensus from the deeply rooted basic traits of Dutch political culture' (Kickert and In 't Veld 1995: 53). These principles and their according institutions and practices have developed in the light of historical cleavages along the lines of politics, religion and geography. The modern institutionalized system of consensus politics assumed its shape during the power struggles between the Catholics, Protestants, socialists and, albeit reluctantly, Liberals in the late nineteenth century (Rihoux et al. 2015). The system emerged to accommodate potentially disruptive tensions between religious and socio-economic subcultures by means of cooperating according to informal diplomacy-like rules of the game. As such, there were various subcultural segments, or pillars, in which the associated political parties defended the pillars' interests.

In addition, and most interestingly from the perspective of policy advisory systems, an elaborate system of ancillary non-state organizations (such as trade unions and interest organizations of different types) played a leading role in the policy-making process, as sources of policy advice and as venues of cross-pillar elite accommodation. The pillarized structures reflected a representative and democratically legitimizing system of policy-making and service delivery, and explain why the central civil service has historically been small and reliant on external sources of policy input and external bodies of public service delivery (Van der Meer et al. 2012). In the mid-1960s a process of depillarization and a connected erosion of the pillarized intermediary organizations set in, which impacted both the policy advisory system and the service-delivery landscape in a similar way: fragmentation and a loss of legitimacy.

5.3 Continuity and Change in the Dutch Policy Advisory System since the 1980s

In response to the fiscal crisis of the late 1970s and early 1980s, and in order to counter the alleged overstretching and overburdening of the government apparatus in that time, attempts were made to reduce the size of the government. While the Netherlands was not among the first countries to embrace the principles of NPM, from the late 1980s onwards most of its ideas were turned into reform policies (Pollitt and Bouckaert 2017). Halligan notes that in the Anglophone countries at the time, where New Public Management caught on before it did elsewhere, governments sought 'to incorporate special skills by the use of external advisers and as an alternative source to the public service', and that '[p]rivate sector consultants have also flourished in the age of privatization'. 'More generally', Halligan contends, 'under fiscal austerity, governments have sought to reduce staff and functions. Often this has involved the substitution of consultants for public servants because it has been more politically (and managerially) acceptable. As a result, external organizations have been increasingly used for policy design and development' (1995: 154–155).

It has to be noted that in the case of the Netherlands, as well as in other consensual systems, externalization of policy advice has been less straightforward than it was in many more centralized and majoritarian systems, as the traditional system of advisory bodies and councils was already largely external to the permanent departmental civil service. However, that does not mean that *further* externalization, understood as the outward shift of policy advice, did not take place (Van den Berg et al. 2015).

Based on a cross-time comparative survey study conducted among senior civil servants and external policy advisers, Van den Berg reported evidence of three trends in the Dutch policy advisory system: depillarization, politicization and externalization (2017). First, *depillarization* occurred in the sense that the traditional representative-and-expertise-providing bodies and councils lost part of their legitimacy due to the eroding pillar structure, and because they were seen as costly and standing in the way of the implementation of austerity policies in the 1980s.

Second, *politicization* of the policy advisory system took place through a) an increase in the degree to which political–strategic insight is seen as relevant for the toolbox of the civil service in conjunction with a decrease in the relevance of substantive expertise, and b) an increase in the role of politically appointed ministerial advisers in policy advice (Van den Berg 2018).

Lastly, *externalization* took place in the sense that there was a focus shift from the village-like corporatist policy advisory system to the idea of 'independent expertise'. This shift needs to be seen in the broader context of reforms of the public sector in the 1990s, including privatization of state-owned enterprises, the creation of executive agencies at arm's length from the smaller central ministries and a focus shift towards regulatory governance (Pollitt and Bouckaert 2017). The dominant function of the advisory system soon became the provision of expertise, rather than the channelling and voicing of pillarized societal interests. Thus, members of advisory committees were increasingly selected by politicians and civil servants because of their expertise rather than their representative function for a given interest group or constituency (Oldersma et al. 1999).

In short, the already large degree of external policy advising in the Netherlands was further extended through NPM-style reforms in the 1980s and 1990s (Woldendorp 1995; Halffman and Hoppe 2005; Van der Meer et al. 2012; Dijkstra et al. 2015; Pollitt and Bouckaert 2017). In addition, previous studies have pointed to an ongoing decrease in the policy advising capacity of the core civil service since 2003 (Van der Meer et al. 2012; Dijkstra et al. 2015), which has gone hand in hand with an increase in the use of external councils and institutes in the period 2007–2013. In particular, external research institutes, ad hoc committees and external consultants seem to have become increasingly prominent sources of policy advice (Van den Berg 2017).

Therefore, in line with Halligan's general 1995 expectations, for the policy advisory system it seems that, on the whole, NPM-style reforms in the Netherlands have led to cutbacks for internal advising capacity and to a preference for hiring external consultation on short-term contracts instead. What has been specific for the Netherlands is that externalization entailed an outward shift not only from the central civil service, but also from the manifold permanent advisory councils to temporary external personnel (TEP).

In the remainder of this chapter we will go deeper into the specifics of the use of TEP in the Netherlands. Our analysis is structured along the lines of the who? (5.4), what? (5.5), how much? (5.6), where? (5.7) and why? (5.8) questions. As an empirical basis for this analysis, a combination of primary survey data, government statistics and official documents is used.

5.4 Who? A Description of the Policy Consultancy Landscape in the Netherlands

The Netherlands has for a long time been claimed to have, together with the USA, the highest density of management and policy consulting firms in the world (Rosenthal 1996: 111). Who are the people that work for these firms, to what extent are they active in the public sector and to what extent do they contribute to policy-making? In order to answer these questions, we first need to understand the central government personnel system.

Dutch central government organizations have four main ways in which they can deploy personnel. The first, and by far the most important way is by means of its own administrative staff with temporary or permanent appointments (type I). To the extent that the departmental annual budget allows it, individual departments have a high degree of discretion in formulating their personnel policies and hiring and retaining internal staff. For an overview of general staffing principles, and the size and composition of the Dutch central civil service, see Van der Meer and Roborgh (1993), Van der Meer and Dijkstra (2017) and Toshkov et al. (2018).

The second way of deploying personnel is by means of *insourcing* from a) other government organizations at the central, regional or local level, including educational institutions, or b) general personnel pools that are at the service of all central government organizations, such as the so-called interim-pool of the Senior Civil Service, project pools and shared service organizations (type II). For the Netherlands the latter is a relatively new, and compared to the United Kingdom, for instance, a little developed staffing instrument (Van den Berg 2011). The third way is to *outsource* activities to a private sector party (type III). Outsourcing is when an external party produces a product on a contract basis. Prior to the start of the activities, the commissioning party and the supplier agree on the terms of the product to be delivered, where subsequently the commissioning party does not direct or control the specific personnel or other means that the supplier uses. Examples of outsourcing therefore are: facility services (cleaning, catering, security, etc.); the development, construction, maintenance and exploitation of public works; and maintenance of ICT systems. Lastly, organizations can make use of *external hiring*, which is often referred to as the 'flexible shell' surrounding the core of internal staff (type IV). Formally, this flexible shell is meant to absorb peak loads in administrative work, such as when sick leave needs to be covered, when specific job openings cannot be filled by means of the internal hiring procedure and in case of highly specialist or innovative activities, which would be too costly or otherwise undesirable to internalize.

The essential difference between outsourcing and external hiring, therefore, is the nature of the supervisory relationship between the government organization and the contractor. In contrast to outsourcing, in the case of external hiring, activities are being carried out within the commissioning organization, and the commissioning organization has considerable control over the deployment of personnel capacity and expertise.

From a budgeting and accounting point of view, there is a relevant difference between type III (outsourcing) and type IV deployment (external hiring), too. Spending on external hiring is accounted for as part of the departmental personnel costs, while outsourcing is accounted for as general procurement. In addition, while the central-government-wide total for external hiring is annually reported to parliament through the Annual Report on Central Government Management (JBR), no annual comprehensive overview of outsourcing is provided (MinFin 2013/ 2017). Table 5.1 summarizes the four types of government personnel deployment, and the definition and demarcation of each type.

In addition, we can profile externally hired personnel in terms of their educational background and their professional focus. Virtually without exception, externally hired personnel are highly educated, as most have an academic (84 per cent) or college (9 per cent) background. Table 5.2 shows the distribution across the field of education of

Table 5.1 *Types of government personnel deployment*

Type	Definition
I: Internal staff	Personnel in the service of the state, appointed temporarily or permanently, by the government organization in question
II: Insourcing	The temporary deployment of personnel from other government organizations
III: Outsourcing, external procurement	The carrying out of activities, commissioned by a central government official, by a for-profit or not-for-profit organization, which leads to the delivery of a given product, the terms of which have been contractually agreed on, with no involvement of the commissioning official in the production of the product
IV: External hiring	The carrying out of activities, commissioned by a central government official, by a for-profit private organization, through the deployment of personnel capacity and expertise, which is co-supervised by the commissioning official

Table 5.2 *Field of education of externally hired*
personnel by Dutch central government organizations

Field of Education	%
Law	21
Public administration	12
Finance/economics/business	12
Engineering	11
Social sciences	11
Communication and media studies	10
Sciences	6
Geography	6
Humanities	6
Other	5
Total (N = 378)	100

Source: Van den Berg (2017).

external consultants. Of these consultants, 22 per cent had previously been employed as a national civil servant, while 20 per cent had previously been employed as a civil servant at the local level.

In the Netherlands, it seems that working as an external government consultant can be regarded as a profession in and of itself. About 50 per cent of external advisers spend more than 70 per cent of their working time on contracted assignments for the government, while a little over 20 per cent spend less than 30 per cent of their working time on government assignments. Unsurprisingly, the specialization of working for government organizations is strongest amongst those advisers who are mostly involved in formulating and evaluating policies (see Figure 5.1).

5.5 What Do Policy Consultants Do?

As set out earlier, external consultants can either be deployed based on a contract for a project that is carried out externally (type III deployment), or they can be temporarily hired to carry out activities internally (type IV deployment). As the two types are different in both a legal and an accounting sense, to gain more insights into the nature of the activities of policy consultants we have to rely on two separate routes: for type III deployment we use survey responses of policy consultants themselves; for type IV deployment we use government statistics on external hiring.

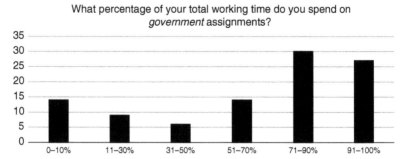

Figure 5.1 Share of externally hired personnel's working time spent on government assignments
Source: Van den Berg et al. (2015).

First, we look at our survey data. In order to determine the degree to which the work of externally deployed personnel is process-driven (see Howlett and Migone 2013), respondents were asked about the nature of their activities. The respondents cited 22 different activities in total, and these were clustered into four categories: policy advice, policy implementation, policy evaluation and process support activities (see Table 5.3).

The results indicate that externally deployed personnel are mostly employed to provide policy advice and process support, and that they are to a lesser degree involved in policy implementation and policy evaluation. The ministries in which the highest percentage of external consultants is employed to supply policy advice are Social Affairs and Employment (89 per cent), Infrastructure and Environment (85 per cent) and Public Health, Wellbeing and Sports (84 per cent). The ministries in which external consultants were least often used as policy advisers are Defence (67 per cent) and Economic Affairs (73 per cent). Also as regards staff roles in ministries across the board, external consultants are hired relatively less for the purpose of giving policy advice (73 %). This contrasts to some extent with the findings of Howlett and Migone (2013) for Canada. They found that external consultants are mostly used in process support, while the question of their input in terms of substance remains to some degree unanswered.

For three out of the four types of activities, the Ministry of Defence scores lowest of all ministries. For policy evaluation and process support in particular, the Ministry of Defence is an outlier on the low end of the distribution. Leaving the Ministry of Defense aside, the cross-ministerial

Table 5.3 *Involvement of external consultants in various policy- and process-related activities, per ministry*

Ministry	Regularly Involved in … (%)[1]			
	Policy Advice[2]	Policy Implementation[3]	Policy Evaluation[4]	Process Support[5]
Foreign Affairs	76	61	46	77
Defence	67	43	25	56
Economic Affairs	73	59	41	78
Finance	80	41	46	79
Social Affairs, Employment	89	45	62	85
Home Affairs	82	43	52	82
Security, Justice	79	29	43	71
Public Health, Wellbeing, Sports	84	42	57	82
Education, Culture, Science	77	35	53	74
Infrastructure, Environment	85	43	42	84
Staff Roles	73	27	39	72
Unweighed Average	79	43	46	77

Source: Van den Berg et al. (2015).

variation for process support is relatively small: between 71 per cent (Security and Justice) and 85 per cent (Social Affairs and Employment).

[1] 'Regularly involved in' is the percentage of respondents that indicated carrying out one or more of the presented tasks under each heading every three months, every month, every week or every day. As respondents were asked to answer for as many of the activities that applied, percentages add up to more than 100 per ministry.

[2] 'Policy advice' denotes one or more of the following tasks: a) gathering policy-related data or information; b) carrying out policy-related research and analysis; c) identifying policy options; d) supplying and/or assessing policy options; e) carrying out a field analysis; f) issue tracking; g) carrying out a legal analysis; h) preparing briefing notes or position papers; i) giving ministerial briefings; j) formulating policies; k) drafting reports, presentations or markers for decision-makers; l) consulting decision-makers about policy issues.

[3] 'Policy implementation' denotes the implementation of policies or policy programmes.

[4] 'Policy evaluation' denotes one or both of the following tasks: a) evaluating policy outcomes and results; b) evaluating policy processes and procedures.

[5] 'Process support' denotes one or more of the following tasks: a) drafting a departmental planning; b) preparing budget proposals; c) negotiating with relevant stakeholders on behalf of clients; d) consulting citizens about policy issues; e) informing departmental management; f) informing policy advisers; g) informing external stakeholders.

We now turn to the perspective of the receiving end of temporarily hired personnel. As regards the question of what work the consultants do, the Dutch central government makes a clear distinction between the various types of activities externally hired personnel may be contracted to do, based on a functional classification. The first rough distinction is made between a) policy-sensitive activities, b) policy support activities, and c) non-policy-related support activities, hired through generic employment agencies.

The first category, policy-sensitive activities, is further broken down into 'interim-management' (managers who temporarily fill up internal openings), 'organizational advice' (advice on organizational change and staffing policies), 'communication advice' (advice on public information, communication, policy campaigns and suchlike) and 'policy advice' (advice for the purpose of new policies, or the adjustment of existing policies). Official documents explain that policy advice in the case of external hiring can take multiple forms:

- policy-substantiating advice, i.e. advice that is used to shape and substantiate new or adjusted policies;
- policy support, i.e. the provision of workshops, brainstorm session, expert meetings, etc., for the purpose of new or adjusted policies;
- specific policy expertise, including cost–benefit analysis or other types of ex-ante evaluations. Ex-post evaluations are not part of this category, as they fall under outsourcing (type III, described above).

The second category, policy support activities, involves 'legal advice' (advice on new and existing legislation), 'ICT advice' (advice on the procurement and development of ICT products, prior to decision-making concerning ICT projects) and 'accountancy, financial and administrative advice' (support of the internal audits and financial expertise).

Lastly, the third category, referring to non-policy-related support, denotes operational capacity for (seasonal) peaks, hired through employment agencies. In addition, according to official guidelines, any other type of external hiring should be accounted for under category C.

At first sight this might seem to be a clear-cut categorization, but it soon becomes apparent that in practice confusion may arise on various points, leading to less than precise accounting. Some examples are i) that policy support is the label of first-tier category B, but also pops up in the third-tier under category A, ii) that it only becomes clear from the more detailed explanation that actual ICT projects should not fall under the category which has the label ICT in it, and iii) that rather than there being a separate category 'other', additional types of external hiring are counted together with the specific category of operational capacity.

Figure 5.2 shows that overall, roughly two-thirds of type IV external hiring in the past decade has been of the category 'operational capacity and other'. For all ministries, this is by far the largest category. The second largest category for all ministries is ICT advice, with the ministries of Home Affairs, Finance, and Security and Justice showing the relatively largest users of this kind of external personnel. These three ministries have invested great sums of money in automation and digitalization in recent years for the national police force, the tax service and the judiciary, respectively.

For the other activity types, the cross-sectoral variation is greater. 'Accounting and financial advice' has a remarkably large share with the

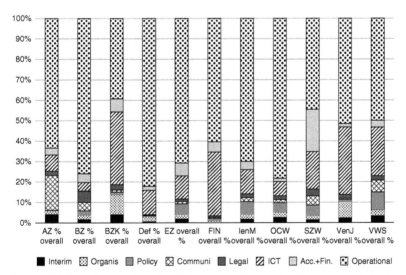

Figure 5.2 The distribution of activities as carried out in the various ministries 2007–2016
Source: MinBZK.

Ministry of Social Affairs and Employment, while 'Organizational advice' has been particularly large within the ministries of Home Affairs and Security and Justice. This can be explained by the fact that up until 2010, the Ministry of Home Affairs was the home of a large government-wide modernization programme, serving all ministries, and by the fact that the Ministry of Security and Justice underwent a large-scale reorganization when the security domain (which was previously part of the Ministry of Home Affairs) was added to it in 2010. The Ministry of General Affairs (i.e. the Prime Minister's Office) has the highest relative share of externally hired communication advisers, which is explained by the fact that the Government Information Service (the government's central communications service) resorts under this ministry. Actual policy-making advice, defined in its narrow sense as discussed under Section 5.3, takes up a surprisingly low average share of 3.5 per cent, varying across ministries from 0.4 per cent within the Ministry of General Affairs to 8.8 per cent within the Ministry of Health.

The above analysis shows that ministries can deploy external consultants either on a project that is externally procured or by staff externally hired to work inside of the organization. The data show that most policy-related activities are carried out based on externally procurement contracts, and that for most support and operational activities consultants are hired to work temporarily inside of the organization.

5.6 The Scale of Policy Consultancy

The available cross-time data for type IV personnel deployment is shown in Table 5.3. It demonstrates some interesting differences in pre- and post-economic crisis patterns of external hiring. First, external hiring rose steadily in the years 2007–2009, but showed a substantial decrease after the effectuation of austerity measures beginning in 2009. After 2012, as the economy picked up and austerity measures were relaxed, total volumes of external hiring increased again. However, the pre- and post-crisis patterns of external hiring are markedly different. The so-called policy-sensitive activities, which made up 15–18 per cent pre-crisis, decreased both in absolute and in relative terms to a stable 5 per cent after the crisis. It is also notable that despite the austerity measures, the external hiring for operational capacity decreased only

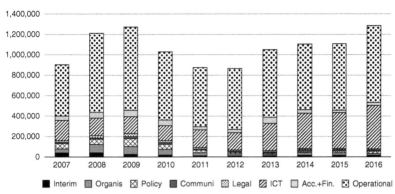

Figure 5.3 Volume of externally hired staff per year in absolute figures (×1000 Euro), split for activity categories
Source: MinBZK (2008/2017).

slightly, returning to pre-crisis levels by 2013. The largest growth during the period 2007–2016 appears to be relatively unrelated to the financial and economic crisis, as it is in the field of ICT consultancy, explained by the increasing priority in the automatization and the general digital turn in policy-making and service delivery across government departments (see Figure 5.3).

5.7 Where? Cross-Sectoral and Cross-Organization Type Variation

Which are the ministries that rely more on externally hired staff than others, and why? Table 5.4 shows that in terms of their deployment of external staff, Dutch ministerial departments can be divided into three groups: the big users, the medium users and the small users. The group of big users consists of the Ministry of Security and Justice, the Ministry of Infrastructure and the Environment, and the Ministry of Finance. What these three ministries have in common is that they each have large operational services and executive agencies resorting under them. For instance, for the Ministry of Security and Justice, this is the national prison system and the police; for the Ministry of Infrastructure and the Environment this is the central service responsible for the design, construction, management and maintenance of the main infrastructure facilities, including the main road network, the main waterway

Table 5.4 *A categorization of activities carried out by externally hired personnel as used by the Netherlands central government*

	Activity Category A	Activity Category B	Activity Category C
Main Category	Policy-sensitive	Policy support	Non-policy-related support
Subcategories	• Interim management • Organizational advice • Policy advice • Communication advice	• Legal advice • ICT advice • Accountancy, finance and administrative organization	• Operational capacity for (seasonal) peaks, hired through employment agencies • Any other types of TEP

Source: MinFIN (2010/2017).

network and water systems; and for the Ministry of Finance this is the tax service. Then there is a group of middle users, consisting of the Ministry of Defense, the Ministry of the Interior and the Ministry of Economic Affairs. The small users are the Ministry of Health, the Ministry of Education, the Ministry of Foreign Affairs, the Ministry of Social Affairs and Employment and the Ministry of General Affairs (Prime Minister's Office). Of this group, the Ministries of Health, Education and Social Affairs are the largest-spending departments, but they have relatively small own operational or implementation services, where large volumes of externally hired staff would be necessary. By contrast, Foreign Affairs and General Affairs are departments with relatively small budgets, and they also lack large-scale operational activities. Interestingly, the three large users show a clear pattern that is aligned with the conjunctural economic cycle: the crisis was followed by a decrease in externally hired staff, followed by an increase when the economy was recovering. The middle group does not conform to this pattern: for Defence and Economic Affairs the highs of the late 2000s were never reached again after the crisis, while for the Ministry of the Interior the volumes increased all the way though, regardless of the austerity of the crisis years. A final interesting spike is seen for the Ministry of Education, which is explained by the specific conditions of the implementation agency DUO, which had an extraordinary

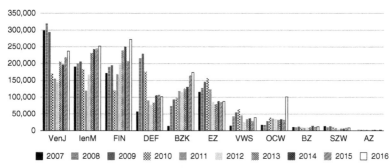

Figure 5.4 Volumes of policy consulting per ministry (×1000 Euro)
Source: MinBZK (2008/2017).

peak year in activities that year and exceptionally high costs for externally hired ICT consultants (see Figure 5.4).

5.8 Why? Patterns and Time-Dynamics of Reasons Why Government Hires Consultants

In the Introduction we identified a number of potential reasons why government organizations may wish to deploy external consultants. This can be because of the temporary character of a project or activity, the specificity of necessary knowledge and expertise, or the fact that a given organization is under construction and as soon as service delivery is stable enough, internal appointments will be made. The above analysis has already shown that in the Netherlands, the largest volumes of externally hired staff are used for operational purposes, to absorb seasonal peaks in the organization's activities (e.g. the Tax Service), policy changes or sudden additional tasks for which there is no internal staff available (e.g. DUO) and labour market shortages for ICT staff (across the board).

One question that still requires our attention here is the rival hypotheses of the 'communicating vessels' versus the 'co-varying volumes'. This speaks to the question of whether increases in the deployment of external staff are related to decreases in the volumes of internally appointed personnel (compensation) or whether a rise in externally hired personnel is actually the result of an increased need for staff generally for a given purpose (caused by a higher political priority, societal developments or chance events), where the volume of both internally appointed staff and externally deployed staff are on the rise simultaneously.

In order to explore which of the two hypotheses would be most plausible for the Netherlands, we compare the volumes of internally appointed staff per year per ministry for the period 2007–2016, see Table 5.5. The data have been indexed at 100 for the year 2007. The only ministry for which the communication vessels hypothesis seems to hold is the Ministry of Defense. There, the steady decrease in internally appointed staff has gone hand in hand with a steadily larger volume of externally hired staff. For the other departments, the volumes of externally hired staff have sometimes shown exceptional fluctuations, but the volumes of internally hired staff have been relatively stable for the most part, therefore not giving support to either the communicating vessels hypothesis or the co-varying volumes hypothesis. The large change in the volume of internally appointed staff between 2009 and 2010 for the ministries of the Interior and of Security and Justice is accounted for by the transfer of the police service from the Ministry of the Interior to the Ministry of Security and Justice. Here it seems to be the case that the loss of internal staff has indeed coincided with an increase in externally hired staff for the Ministry of the Interior, and that the increase of internally appointed staff for the Ministry of Security and Justice coincided with a decrease of externally hired staff, but given that the whole task of national police was shifted from the former to the latter, the theorized communicating vessels dynamic does not seem to be at play here.

5.8.1 Political Debate on the Scale of External Hired Staff

While the hiring of temporary external staff has not generally been a hot issue in Dutch politics or society, over the last decade there has been real parliamentary debate on the topic, stemming from a concern shared broadly among the various factions that hiring of external staff was taking place at too large a scale, and that in many cases hiring external staff is an ineffective way of spending public money. As a result of this debate, in 2008 the government agreed with parliament that the hiring of external personnel by ministries should not exceed 13 per cent of the total spending on personnel for that ministry. The norm has the character of 'comply-or-explain', meaning that if the norm is exceeded, the ministry in question justifies why the exceedance was necessary. In 2010 it turned out that in 2009 six ministries had spent more than 13 per cent of their total personnel spending on externally hired staff.

Table 5.5 *The relative development of internally appointed and externally hired staff across ministries (2007–2016)*

	2007		2008		2009		2010		2012		2016	
	Internal	TEP	Internal	TEP	Internal	TEP	Internal	TEP	Internal	TEP	Internal	TEP
AZ	100	100	103	496	103	598	102	542	97	448	97	444
BZ	100	100	103	101	103	116	102	95	97	92	97	115
BZK[6]	100	100	105	532	109	659	13	695	12	820	12	1,232
EZ	100	100	103	110	103	126	102	135	97	75	97	76
FIN	100	100	103	112	103	114	102	70	97	115	97	159
IenM	100	100	103	105	103	108	102	96	97	88	97	132
OCW	100	100	103	101	103	166	102	229	97	199	97	593
SZW	100	100	103	85	103	99	102	84	97	44	97	65
VenJ[7]	100	100	103	107	103	98	270	57	268	48	260	79
VWS	100	100	103	288	103	370	102	430	97	175	97	263
Def	100	100	95	377	98	399	97	306	87	135	80	177
Total	100	100	101		103		102		97		94	

[6] Up until and including 2009 the police fell under the Ministry of the Interior.
[7] As of 2010 the police have fallen under the Ministry of Security and Justice.

The explanation of the ministries included various policy intensifications and projects that had been decided prior with parliamentary consent. In other cases the explanation was that for certain service-delivery agencies, the demand for staff fluctuates to such an extent across the year that temporary external hiring is necessary for a proper and cost-efficient functioning of those agencies.

In response to the apparent difficulty in quickly decreasing the share of external hiring within government organizations, in 2010 a new norm was agreed between government and parliament, entailing that from 2011 onwards, individual ministries would not exceed 10 per cent of total personnel spending on external hiring, otherwise they would have to explain their exceedance. As part of the agreement, the government stressed that decreasing personnel capacity, whether internally appointed or externally hired, would by definition have consequences for the capacity to carry out tasks. While parliament pushed for an enforceable norm, the government resisted this based on the argumentation that an enforceable norm would not be appropriate for organizations that are expected to function flexibly: 'Having to respond quickly to current social problems or incidents does not sit well with a personnel system that is tied to a hard percentage of expenditure for external hiring (e.g. the measures taken in the context of the flu pandemic and the credit crisis)' (MinBZK 2010).

The cap on external hiring was the initiative of the leftist Socialist Party, mainly as a means to curtail the hiring of over-paid consultants, managers and advisers at the top of organizations at a time when members of the permanent civil service were being laid off due to austerity measures. As one Member of Parliament commented,

Within the ministries a culture of external hiring has developed. Overpaid external staff is hired, while at the same time ordinary civil servants are being laid off. In the past 8 years the amount of money that ministries have spent on externals has gone up by 80%, up to no less than 1,3 billion euros. If the [hiring cap] would be applied here, that would save hundreds of millions of euros.[8]

However, as was also demonstrated above, the measure that was enacted concerned not only the hiring of external consultants,

---

[8] www.sp.nl/nieuws/2010/11/roemernorm-voor-alle-ministeries

managers and advisers, but all forms of external personnel, including operational personnel hired through generic job agencies, which has consistently formed approximately two-thirds of the total externally hired personnel in central government organizations.

5.9 Conclusion

This chapter has explored the practice of deploying temporary external staff by central government. The main findings are summarized here. Characteristic of the Netherlands is its open policy system, in which societal interests and scientific knowledge find their way in relatively easily. In addition, the use of external staff has traditionally been high, in line with other countries in this study, such as the United States and Australia. Yet, the Netherlands differs starkly from these Anglo-Saxon countries in the sense that it generally uses a highly consensus-driven policy-making style and has a neo-corporatist policy advisory system.

The high levels of externally hired staff have long been regarded as a feature of strength, inferring positive qualities such as leanness and adaptability, and securing the capacity to let new ideas and practices from outside of the system in. However, the analysis shows that in recent years, public and parliamentary debate flared up a couple of times. Critics have pointed to an arguably disproportionate level of external staff compared to regular civil servants, to the high costs involved and to the long-term deterioration of knowledge and expertise within the public service itself.

Analysing the nature of external hiring in the Netherlands requires distinguishing between two types: a) outsourcing, or the external procurement of policy activities, leading up to the delivery of a given product; and b) external hiring, where external personnel capacity and expertise is deployed within the organization, under direct supervision of the commissioning public organization.

Cross-departmental and cross-time comparable data for *outsourcing* are not available, so we rely on original survey data. A few observations stand out. First, consultants delivering outsourced policy products have usually specialized in policy consultancy for the government. Second, most of the outsourced tasks involve policy advice and process support, where policy implementation and policy evaluation are also important but slightly less-sought activities.

For ***external hiring***, systematic data are available which indicate that the large majority of temporary staff are deployed for operational and implementation activities, and mostly in implementation agencies such as the tax service and public works. As to the distribution of external hiring across ministerial departments, the high-using category consists of the Ministry of Security and Justice, the Ministry of Infrastructure and the Environment and the Ministry of Finance. The moderate users are the Ministry of Defense and the Ministry of the Interior and of Economic Affairs, followed by a larger group of low-using departments: the Ministry of Health, the Ministry of Education, Foreign Affairs, Social Affairs and the Prime Minister's Office.

Over the period 2007–2016, the volume of externally hired personnel has remained stable at a high level, while organizational and policy advice, which was substantial before the crisis, dropped from 2010 and did not recover in the remainder of the period studied. In contrast, external hiring in the field of ICT support grew steadily in the period from 2007 and was therefore not affected by the crisis. A final finding of this exploration is that the volumes of external hiring per ministerial department seem to evolve over the years relatively independently from the changes in the size of the permanent civil service apparatus. No support was found for either the 'communicating vessels' or the 'co-varying volumes' hypothesis.

The findings in this chapter yield new and systematic insights into the Dutch practice of externally hired policy work. However, more research is needed in order to fill in important knowledge gaps, especially pertaining to the cross-time and cross-departmental volumes of outsourcing, the precise activities of external consultants and their impact on both policy decisions and on the overall success of policies in their implementation stages.

6 Policy Consultants for Substance and Process: A Review of the Supply and Demand for Canadian Policy Consulting

6.1 The Study of Government Procurement for Policy Advice in Canada: The Role of Policy and Management Consultants

The use of external consultants by the public sector has been an increasingly relevant area of focus for almost three decades, for both government bodies (ANAO 2001; House of Commons Committee of Public Accounts (UK) 2010) and academics (Bakvis 1997; Perl and White 2002; Saint-Martin 2005; Speers 2007; Howlett, Migone and Seck 2014; Howlett and Migone 2014). This is due to both the costs and the role of private sector entities in shaping policy capacity and policy choice. Aside from the most recent contributions, the main focus has been the financial impact of contracting out this function rather than on understanding how external sources have affected the capacity of departments and other government units (Riddell 2007). There are various reasons for this trend. At perhaps the broadest level, the ascendancy of New Public Management (NPM) injected strong elements of cost-accounting, efficiency and rationalization into government activity. In a sense, the idea of 'service' reflected these approaches towards the corporatization of the state (Freeman 2000; Vincent-Jones 2006; Bilodeau, Laurin and Vining 2007; Butcher et al. 2009).

Outsourcing itself can be broken down into various segments depending on what is outsourced (i.e. services vs. goods), but we can also attempt to analyse, often with less success, the 'use' of certain kinds of outsourcing, such as whether a certain contract is aimed at supporting policy advice or more general administrative support. In the Canadian academic landscape, an early set of primarily empirical works were written at the end of the 1990s. They mainly relied on anecdotal analysis and the authors had to mine highly aggregated and unspecific public accounts data to discern the pervasiveness of policy consultants at the federal and provincial levels (Bakvis 1997; Saint-

Martin 1998a, 1998b; Perl and White 2002). In the mid-2000s, a new wave of research looked at policy analysts and advisers at both the provincial and federal levels, using surveys and other data, but dealt with policy consulting only in passing (Howlett and Newman 2010; Howlett 2009a; Prince 2007; Saint-Martin 2005, 2006; Speers 2007). Since 2013, however, a more robust set of analyses regarding the quantitative data for the federal government has emerged (Howlett and Migone 2017, 2014a, 2014b, 2013a, 2013b, 2013c; Howlett, Migone and Tan 2014).

In terms of findings, in their 2002 study Perl and White found the 'evidence for a growing role played by policy consultants at the national government level is compelling in Canada', noting that annual government-wide expenditure on 'other professional services' reported in the Public Accounts of Canada for fiscal years 1981/82 to 2000/01 showed 'a continuous increase from C\$239 million[1] in 1981/82 to C\$1.55 billion in 2000/01' (2002: 52). This absolute growth was matched by the growth of consulting as a share of total government expenditures, as 'spending on external policy consultants increased steadily from 0.35 per cent of total government expenditures in 1981/82, to 0.97 per cent in 2000/01, almost tripling Ottawa's budgetary allocation to policy consulting' (Perl and White 2002: 53). However, they noted that the data was extremely highly aggregated, so very different types of professional services were lumped in the financial records, even if they effectively had little direct impact on public policy decision-making.

The policy analysis and advisory research at the turn of the decade (Howlett and Newman 2010; Howlett and Wellstead 2012; Howlett and Migone 2014a) did not focus on consulting, but was important because through a series of in-depth surveys it shed considerable light on the similarities and differences that existed among policy personnel: for example, the finding that many policy analysts could be more readily categorized as working as 'troubleshooters' – i.e. using a short-term project-oriented approach-rather than being long-term strategic 'planners'. The relevance of the governance model (whether policy workers operated in a multi-level system, for instance) for the nature of policy work and the predominance of 'firefighting' approaches and

---

[1] Please note that all Canadian procurement figures throughout the chapter are expressed in Canadian dollars.

of process expertise (as opposed to subject matter expertise) in provincial and territorial policy workers were also set out these analyses.

Finally, the analysis of contract data from the Government of Canada in the early 2010s (Howlett and Migone 2014b, 2013a, 2013b, 2013c; Howlett, Migone and Tan 2014) highlighted a strong imbalance in the Management Consulting category in favour of a small group of actors: finding about 5 per cent of companies accounted for 80 per cent of all contracts awarded. While Saint-Martin (1998a: 320) is correct in stating that 'there is no direct and simple causal link between increased spending and increased influence' of management consultants, this dominance was also married to a 'permanence' of consulting services, with many contracts extending over multiple years, and a select group of companies becoming long-standing partners in the activity of the state. In a sense, this could be defined as an 'invisible public service' (Howlett and Migone 2013a, 2014b).

6.2 Data Issues

We should note, at the outset that, to one degree or another, these studies, like those in other countries (e.g. Howard 2005 on Australia, and Boston 1994 on New Zealand), all confront limitations in the available data.

Until recently, it was the case in Canada that data problems, especially but not solely in the area of policy consulting, were acute and prevented serious evaluation of the subjects. There are long-standing problems in separating consultants hired to perform more rank-and-file jobs (such as information technology consulting or management consulting) and those classifiable as policy advisers or policy consultants. Other problems concern data collection techniques in government, which either did not cover relatively small contracts, or blended policy-related work together with other activities such as 'professional services' or 'temporary work'. What is more, decisions about these reporting matters were often left up to individual units, meaning that whatever data existed was often idiosyncratic and difficult to compare across units. In other words, it has been very difficult to arrive at an accurate assessment of the scope and use of any kind of consultants, including management and policy ones, across government.

Recently, both regulatory and institutional steps have been taken in Canada to deal with some of these issues, although often unintentionally and linked to government efforts aimed at further cost efficiency or to contracting scandals and their aftermath.[2] In particular, access to data about federal government contract expenditures, for example, has been improved due to two developments linked to the 2004 'Sponsorgate' scandal surrounding Quebec advertising contracts and the Liberal Party (Gomery 2005, 2006). First, on 23 March 2004, the federal government introduced rules of proactive disclosure so that, beginning in October 2004, all contracts above CAD$10,000 are published on government websites. This increased the number of contracts reported in detail, lowering the old limit of CAD$100,000.

Another tool is the Federal Accountability Act, which came into effect on 12 December 2006. The Act has legislative, procedural and institutional facets designed to increase the transparency and accountability of all government spending, including contracting; along with the new framework for procurement accounting procedures and the requirement to table an annual report for government agencies.

The Act also created the Office of the Procurement Ombudsman, which is tasked with addressing perceived business fairness and competitiveness issues in the procurement area, and reports regularly on policies and practices in this area. In 2003, the federal government also developed a Management Accountability Framework (MAF) laying out the Treasury Board's expectations of management best practices across all areas of government, including contracting.

The new data and enhanced clarity are useful to researchers inquiring into government contracting, including policy-related consulting. It remains the case, however, that published government data is not designed for or collected in a fashion that facilitates tasks such as separating consultancies focusing on non-strategic or policy-related tasks. Seldom does readily available contract data include much non-financial detail, and this creates various obstacles in the analysis of the activities involved.

---

[2] For example, to rationalize and streamline the process of government procuring between April 2008 and January 2009, Public Works and Government Services Canada (PWGSC) consulted on the scope of the *Task and Solutions Based Professional Services* (TSBPS) project to generate a better process of data collection on outside goods and services contracts. This helped develop a set of shared rules controlling reporting across government agencies. However, this was mostly a business-oriented exercise, intended to facilitate the relationship between contractors and government.

More recently, the Government of Canada also embarked on a widespread open data project, which has made available complete historical sets of contract data for all federal contracting for the past decade. Currently, open data for contracting is organized along Goods and Services Identification Number (GSIN) codes, which will shortly be replaced by the United Nations Standard Products and Services Code (UNSPSC). GSIN codes are more detailed than the proactive disclosure codes and are therefore utilized in this research. However, there remains a struggle with individuating policy-related contracts. For this reason, we have supplemented the GSIN contract history data with relevant keyword searches in the Buy and Sell Canada website.

6.3 Analysis: Data on the Development of Contracting in the Canadian Federal Policy Advisory System

Beyond a smattering of early pieces on the subject of contracting from the 1960s and 1970s (see Deutsch 1973; Meredith and Martin 1970), as we have seen studies of policy and management consultants' roles in Canada can be divided temporally into an initial set of primarily empirical works written at the end of the 1990s, and more conceptual discussions about policy advisers and their impact after 2000. The former tended to rely on anecdotal analysis and required the authors to mine relatively unspecified and undetailed public accounts for numbers on the cost and pervasiveness of policy consultants at both the federal and provincial levels (Bakvis 1997; Saint-Martin 1998a, 1998b). The more recent crop of research explores the role of policy analysts and advisers at the provincial and federal levels, using surveys and other data, but in more detail deals with policy consulting only in passing (Perl and White 2002; Howlett and Newman 2010; Howlett 2009c; Prince 2007; Saint-Martin 2005, 2006; Speers 2007).

6.3.1 Data on the Demand for Advice

Four broad categories of expenditures are found in the GSIN system: Services, Services related to Goods, Goods and Construction. In Figure 6.1 we separate the information on services from the rest of the expenditures for contracts awarded. The information in Figure 6.1 has various limitations. For example, the Service category is very broad and includes areas such as Studies and Analysis (rather than R&D), Custodial Operations and Related Services, and Lease and Rentals of

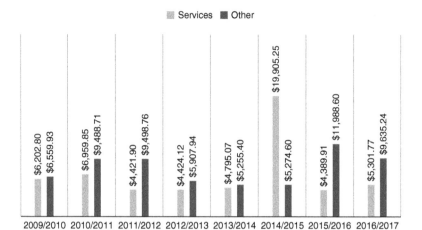

Figure 6.1 All GSIN categories: value of contracts awarded millions of dollars
Source: Open Data Canada; Contract History http://open.canada.ca/data/en/
dataset/53753f06-8b28-42d7-89f7-04cd014323b0   Contains   information
licensed under the Open Government Licence – Canada. https://open
.canada.ca/en/open-government-licence-canada

Facilities. Second, the value of the contract is recorded in full for
the year in which it was awarded (i.e. a contract awarded in 2014/15
but spanning the 2014/15 to 2017/18 period would be recorded in the
first year only).

Figure 6.1 provides us with a bird's eye view of contracting in the
federal government and – if we exclude the 2014/15 fiscal year, which
is an outlier – the average awarded amount of contracts is around
CAD$13.5 billion per year. Of this, an average of $5.2 billion is
allocated to services. Within these categories, Services is the most
relevant to this chapter. To begin, we develop a first subset of 180
GSIN codes that could potentially include work leading to policy
advice and calculated the total value of contracts awarded between
January 2009 and March 2017. It should be noted that this is a very
small percentage of all GSIN codes, which total 4,929. This resulted
in a total value of $6.6 billion (for a full list of the 180 codes, see
Appendix A).

As Table 6.1 shows, the distribution of these values is highly skewed.
On the one hand, 49 end users, representing 64.5 per cent of all entities,
have awarded contracts for a total combined value of less than
C$5 million in the subset of contracts, accounting for 0.68 per cent of

Table 6.1 *First subset – codes potentially relevant to policy advice (180 GSIN codes): entities × total expenditure, 2008–2017: distribution*

Value of the Contracts	# of End Users	% of End Users	Combined Value	Value %
Less than 500 K	30	39.5	$4,491,256	0.07
500 K to 1 M	6	7.9	$4,161,271	0.06
1 M to 5 M	13	17.1	$36,515,766	0.55
5 M to 10 M	4	5.3	$35,538,191	0.53
10 M to 25 M	4	5.3	$65,831,419	0.99
25 M to 50 M	8	10.5	$248,199,366	3.73
50 M to 100 M	4	5.3	$298,261,041	4.48
100 M to 500 M	3	3.9	$942,985,165	14.16
More than 500 M	4	5.3	$5,024,892,992	75.44
Total	76		$6,660,876,467	

the overall amounts awarded over time. On the other hand, 7 end users (9.2 per cent of total) account for 89.6 per cent of the amounts awarded.

The data distribution confirms previous patterns (Howlett and Migone 2014b, 2017), with a strong polarization in the size of the contracts awarded. In our sample, 19 out of 76 end users awarded more than $25 million in contracts over the whole period from this subset. The results are skewed by the awards of the Canadian Space Agency ($1.05 billion) and the Department of National Defence ($2.33 billion). For the former, most of the awards ($932,569,808) fall under the Astronautics Research and Development code. Similarly, Military Research and Development ($791,949,741) and a large award in the Program Management – Analysis/Control area for health procurement[3] account for most of the amounts (see Table 6.2).

Our next step was to analyse the distribution of GSIN codes by award size. In our subset of 180 codes, 128 codes have awards of less

---

[3] Contract W3931-030182/001/XF, which deals with health procurement with the Department of Defence, has a total noted value of $899,508,285. However, the contract is split between a R122A (Program Management – Analysis/Control) portion valued at $448,810,965 and a portion assigned as G009E (Medical/Dental Clinic Services). As reported under open data, the total value of the contract is the former, and we have used that amount in our calculations.

Table 6.2 *First subset (180 GSIN codes): major end user by value awarded*

End User Entity	Value Awarded
Correctional Service of Canada	$25,480,624
National Research Council Canada	$25,916,592
Agriculture and Agri-Food Canada	$26,042,669
Privy Council Office	$27,355,681
Veterans Affairs Canada	$31,183,498
Foreign Affairs, Trade and Development	$34,925,952
Fisheries and Oceans Canada	$37,026,003
Natural Resources Canada	$40,268,347
Public Health Agency of Canada	$58,649,741
Health Canada	$63,094,768
Transport Canada	$79,479,540
Royal Canadian Mounted Police	$97,036,992
Aboriginal Affairs & Northern Development Canada	$170,187,687
Treasury Board of Canada	$360,834,492
Canadian Commercial Corporation	$411,962,986
Employment and Social Development Canada	$749,851,654
Public Works and Government Services Canada	$878,765,686
Canadian Space Agency	$1,057,029,489
Department of National Defence	$2,339,246,163

than $10 million, and only 16 (8.8 per cent of all codes selected) have been awarded more than $50 million (see Table 6.3).

As shown, the top four GSIN codes account for 65.7 per cent of the total. Research and Development activities in the sciences are also very well represented in this top tier of contract awards. However, there is no immediately evident area of activity among these where we would expect to regularly find policy work, with the possible exceptions of consulting and business services (R019E; R019F; R199H). Some other codes are unlikely to provide any policy work, especially at the strategic level (e.g. Administrative Services or Spacecraft Instrumentation Development). To deal with this issue, a second subset of 14 GSIN codes that include the activities most likely to produce policy advice is shown in Table 6.4. It should be noted that a code is included in the GSIN system which would have been extremely useful for this analysis: R123AD *Policy Analysis/ Evaluation*. However, this code is inactive and we could find no contracts

Table 6.3 *First subset (180 GSIN codes): contract awarded 2009/10–2016/17 – over $50 million*

GSIN	Description	Total
AN117500	Medical (R&D)	$57,761,919
AZ110254	System Design, Development and Testing: Science and Technology Related (R&D)	$65,772,775
AZ110140	Product/Material – Design, Development, Formulation, Modification: Science and Technology Related (R&D)	$70,142,543
R019R	Professional Services / Financial Analysis	$71,225,761
AR210480	Spacecraft Instrumentation Development (R&D)	$73,096,823
R199J	Administrative Services	$74,164,119
B101A	Environmental Impact Studies	$115,564,223
T004K	Media Monitoring Services	$126,430,083
R199X	Adjudication Services	$147,879,665
R123AH	Project Management Services	$189,053,584
B219A	Other Engineering Studies	$252,410,299
R019F	Consulting Services	$369,254,093
AD917700	Military (R&D)	$845,308,359
R122A	Programme Management – Analysis/Control	$913,994,855
R199H	Consulting Services, Change Management / Organizational Development (CM/OD)	$989,504,605
AR910400	Astronautics (R&D)	$1,307,222,724

awarded under it. In the same vein, the code R107A *Library Services and Subscriptions*, which could be seen as supporting policy analysis, is also inactive. Moreover, it is interesting to note that this latter GSIN code falls under the Administrative and Management Support Services category of the code description. Included in this group are service categories such as Policy/Review and Development (R120), Program Evaluation Studies (R122) and Program Review and Development Services (R123); however, there is no useful GSIN code developed within these broader categories.

The R120A (Regulatory Analysis Professional Services) GSIN code group only appears to have been applied in two instances. The first is a request for a proposal from 2013 with a potential ceiling of $35,000 that is not matched with a contract number and therefore seems to not

Table 6.4 *Second subset – codes most likely relevant to policy advice: contract awarded 2009/10–2016/17*

GSIN	Description	Total
B506A	Economic Development Studies	$18,900
B506B	Socio-Economic Surveys	$29,925
B400A	Space Policy Studies	$63,000
T002AK	Research and Writing	$1,511,559
B506D	Economic Studies / Modelling and Analysis	$2,427,635
AZ110210	Research Project Management Services (R&D)	$2,520,915
AJ716500	Humanities and Social Sciences (R&D)	$6,176,646
AE913500	Economics (R&D)	$6,871,976
R123AQ	Evaluation & Performance Measurement Services	$8,990,994
T001B	Public Opinion Research – Qualitative	$13,091,796
T001A	Public Opinion Research – Quantitative	$22,149,736
R019U	Professional Services / Program Research Analysis	$28,299,063
R019E	Business Services	$43,893,389
R199H	Consulting Services, Change Management / Organizational Development	$ 989,504,605
	Total	$1,125,550,139

have been awarded. The intention was to commission a study on the costs of regulation of specific industries. The second instance is the public release of the Final Professional Services National Procurement Strategy. It should also be noted that the R120A GSIN categories are named along with Transcription Services (R104), Expert Witness (R101) and Data Collection Services (R113). Even aside from the marginal use of the R120A code group, placing policy analysis in the 'support' area is certainly an interesting choice. Table 6.4 highlights the value of contracts awarded to the areas that are most relevant to our analysis.

The analysis of these contracts is complex, however, because in many cases there is no indication in the published data of the contract deliverables. For example, the Humanities and Social Sciences (R&D) code would seem to be an interesting field for analysis. However, none of the twenty contracts (see Table 6.5) posted a breakdown of the activities, or a request for a proposal from which we could extract the contract content.

Table 6.5 *GSIN AJ716500 humanities and social sciences (R&D) contract history*

Contract Number	Fiscal Year	Supplier	Individual Contract Value	End User	Contracting Unit
0D160-073731/001/SS	2009/10	Alderson-Gill & Associates Consulting Inc.	$60,276	PSEPC	Contracting Division
23218–103997/001/SS	2009/10	Sikumiut Environmental Management Ltd	$188,439	NRC	Office of Energy Research & Dev.
EN579-162045/001/SC	2016/17	D2 L Corporation	$285,947	PWGSC	Canadian Innovation Commercial Program (CICP)
EN579-162046/001/SC	2015/16	Teknoscan Systems Inc.	$414,654	PWGSC	Canadian Innovation Commercial Program (CICP)
EN579-162835/001/SC	2016/17	The Pyxis Innovation	$293,761	PWGSC	Canadian Innovation Commercial Program (CICP)
EN579-170764/001/SC	2016/17	D2 l Corporation	$163,276	PWGSC	Canadian Innovation Commercial Program (CICP)
H4033-092104/001/SS	2011/12 & 2012/13	Mobile Detect Inc.	$2,260,000	Health Canada	HPB RPB Administration
HT175-091028/001/HAL	2010/11	Memorial University of Newfoundland Office of Research	$409,000	Health Canada	Health Program – Atlantic Region
M7594-120926/001/SS	2011/12	Serco Facilities Management Inc.	$221,480	RCMP	HQ Procurement & Contract Services
W7707-088145/001/HAL	2009/10	Memorial University of Newfoundland Fisheries and Marine Institute	$56,481	DND	Defence R&D Canada Atlantic

Table 6.5 (*cont.*)

Contract Number	Fiscal Year	Supplier	Individual Contract Value	End User	Contracting Unit
W7707-098232/001/HAL	2009/10	Dalhousie University	$14,690	DND	Defence R&D Canada Atlantic
W7714-083659/001/SV	2010/11	Université d'Ottawa Valorisation de la Recherche et Transfert De Technologie	$400,000	DND	Defence R&D Canada Ottawa
W7714-083660/001/SV	2011/12	University of Alberta Research Services	$196,756	DND	Defence R&D Canada Ottawa
W7714-083662/001/SS	2010/11	Educational Testing Service Canada Inc.	$505,995	DND	Defence R&D Canada Ottawa
W7714-115065/001/SS	2011/12	3DInternet Inc.	$67,212	DND	Defence R&D Canada Ottawa
W7714-115122/001/SS	2011/12	Premergency Inc.	$243,459	DND	Defence R&D Canada Ottawa
W7714-115148/001/SS	2012/13	Canadian Association of Fire Chiefs	$168,991	DND	Defence R&D Canada Ottawa
W7714-125477/001/SQ	2012/13	McMaster University Research Accounting	$91,120	DND	Defence R&D Canada Ottawa
W7714-125506/001/SS	2012/13	Corporation of The City Of Guelph	$85,070	DND	Centre for Security Science
W7719-115026/001/TOR	2010/11	Humansystems Inc.	$50,039	DND	Defence R&D Canada Toronto
			$6,176,646		

Table 6.6 *GSIN AJ716500 – distribution of contracts by end user*

	Total Amount	% of Total	# of Contracts
PSEPC	$60,276	1.0	1
NRC	$188,439	3.1	1
RCMP	$221,480	3.6	1
PWGSC	$1,157,638	18.7	4
DND	$1,879,813	30.4	11
Health Canada	$2,669,000	43.2	2

In terms of who won the Humanities and Social Sciences (R&D) contracts, it can be noted that there is an extreme fragmentation of the field, with each of the 20 contracts being awarded to a different provider, with the exception of the Memorial University of Newfoundland, which obtained two contracts. Hence, at least for this specific GSIN code, the supply side does not seem to suggest that there is a dominant player. Of interest is that universities have secured six of the contracts for a total of 18.9 per cent of the total value. Additionally, these contracts are limited in time to one fiscal year, with the exception of one instance, as shown in Table 6.5.

In terms of demand, the Department of National Defence (DND) has been the most prolific user, with 11 contracts awarded out of 20 (see Table 6.6).

The situation is similar regarding other relevant GSIN codes, with relatively few contract descriptions being available in the published data. Some exceptions exist, such as a contract with the University of Waterloo that developed GradeX, 'a one-of-a-kind, customized decision-support tool for railway safety inspectors to evaluate risks at grade crossings and identify cost-effective safety improvement strategies'.[4] The contract itself was worth $120,000 and was awarded by Transport Canada under the *Research Project Management Services (R&D)* GSIN code (AZ110210) between 10 January 2014 and 10 January 2016. Also found was a 2014 library subscription for reports and briefings on European Union fisheries and ecosystem issues (FP802-130367) for

---

[4] NA, 23 September, 2013: 'Ottawa asks Ontario university to find better rail crossing safety tools', *Maclean's Magazine*: www.macleans.ca/news/ottawa-asks -ontario-university-to-find-better-rail-crossing-safety-tools/

a value of $17,000, alongside standing offers for policy-related services regarding Indigenous research, for which we have no specific detail on the deliverables.

More descriptions can be found for the Professional Services/ Program Research Analysis GSIN code (R019 U). Here, contract descriptions vary from a market survey of underwater-warfare applied-research systems to investigation, research, analysis and writing services for the Office of the Veterans Ombudsman and the Office of the Department of National Defence and Canadian Forces Ombudsman. Of interest is a request for a proposal, indicating a contract for:

[The] provision of professional services to enhance the analytical foundation underlying Canada's evidence-based approach to decision-making under its Defence Procurement Strategy (DPS). The scope of work includes: identification of strategic national industrial priorities (Key Industrial Capabilities); articulation of a long-term vision for a sustainable Canadian defence sector; enhancement of Canada's capacity for defence sector research and analysis performed independently from the Government; and strategic information, intelligence, research, analysis and advice in support of Canada's development of approaches to leverage economic benefits from defence procurements.[5]

The contract was awarded by US-based PWGSC for the period between fiscal years 2015/16 and 2016/17, to US-based The Avascent Group Ltd. During that period, the contract grew from $1.5 million to $4.52 million, and an additional extension was agreed upon towards the end of March 2017, bringing the total value to $7.345 million.

As an additional step, all contracting entities within the second, policy-oriented subset that had the word 'policy' in their name were identified. This third subset yielded slightly more than $6 million, spread out over 29 contracts that are rather disparate in nature (see Table 6.7).

This set of contracts is skewed by a $3.5 million contract that KPGM held for various years with Industry Canada. In terms of contract value, units within Industry Canada (60.2 per cent) and Transport Canada (33.5 per cent) dominate the field. It is difficult to interpret the content of these contracts on the basis of the published information, but some of the GSIN codes are linked to more substantial policy advice than others. For example, contracting for Computer Systems Security, Military, and Transportation R&D involve substantive policy advice, or data upon which policy advice could be developed. Other codes,

---

[5] https://buyandsell.gc.ca/procurement-data/tender-notice/PW-ZG-421-29395

Table 6.7 *Third subset contracts most relevant to policy advice and with contracting unit with a policy name*

Contract Number	Fiscal Year	Supplier	GSIN Code	GSIN Description	Individual Contract Value	End User	Contracting UNIT
A0211-163922/001/SV	2016/17–2018/19	The Conference Board of Canada	AD217740	Military Logistics (Research)	$25,000	Aboriginal Affairs & Northern Development Canada	Policy & Coordination Branch
T4045-090001/001/TOR	2009/10–2010/11	Regional Economic Models, Inc. Remi	AD917700	Military (R&D)	$24,000	Transport Canada	Regl. Dir. Policy & Coordination
U4408-118202/001/SS	2011/12	National Cyber-Forensics and Training Alliance Canada	AJ212528	Computer Systems Security (R&D)	$225,989	Industry Canada	Digital Policy Branch
W0134-10CYFL/001/EDM	2009/10–2010/11	University of Lethbridge	AD917700	Military (R&D)	$19,690	Department of National Defence	4 Wg Sup Flt/Pol Section
W0134-11CYGF/001/EDM	2010/11–2012/13	University of Lethbridge	AD917700	Military (R&D)	$50,000	Department of National Defence	4 Wg Sup Flt/Pol Section
T7000-090001/001/XSB	2010/11	Parsons Inc.	AT919500	Transportation (R&D)	$251,265	Transport Canada	Policy & Coordination TC
T7000-090002/001/XSB	2009/10–2010/11	IBI Group	AT919500	Transportation (R&D)	$99,965	Transport Canada	Policy & Coordination TC
T7000-100001/001/XSB	2010/11	Halcrow Consulting Inc.	AT919500	Transportation (R&D)	$109,603	Transport Canada	Policy & Coordination TC
T7000-101001/001/XSB	2010/11	Aecom Canada Ltd	AT919500	Transportation (R&D)	$134,400	Transport Canada	Policy & Coordination TC
T7000-120005/001/VAN	2012/13–2013/14	The Tioga Group	AT919500	Transportation (R&D)	$174,860	Transport Canada	Policy & Coordination TC

Table 6.7 (*cont.*)

Contract Number	Fiscal Year	Supplier	GSIN Code	GSIN Description	Individual Contract Value	End User	Contracting UNIT
T8129-070003/001/XSB	2007/08–2009/10	Advanced Lithium Power Inc.	AT919500	Transportation (R&D)	$265,000	Transport Canada	Strategic Policy
T8129-070004/001/XSB	2007/08–2010/11	E One Moli Energy (Canada) Ltd	AT919500	Transportation (R&D)	$317,500	Transport Canada	Strategic Policy
T8129-120006/001/SS	2013/14	Université De Montréal	AT919500	Transportation (R&D)	$253,596	Transport Canada	Strategic Policy
T8129-130001/001/MTB	2014/15–2015/16	Université De Montréal	AT919500	Transportation (R&D)	$278,155	Transport Canada	Strategic Policy
T8159-130110/001/SS	2014/15–2015/16	Novo Energy Group Inc	AT919500	Transportation (R&D)	$226,000	Transport Canada	Env. Affairs-Policy (ACS)
T8129-120001/013/MTB	2012/13–2015/16	Université Laval	B219A	Other Engineering Studies	$-	Transport Canada	Strategic Policy
EC373-150433/001/MCT	2013/14–2015/16	Eastward Sales Ltd	D311A	Data Conversion Services	$45,200	PWGSC	Contract Policy & Admin.
U5200-095743/001/ZG	2009/10–2012/13	KPMG LLP	R199 H	Consulting Services, Change Management / Organizational Development	$3,565,480	Industry Canada	Innovation Policy Branch
EN914-120486/001/CX	2011/12	Consult Ink Ltd	T000I	Communication Projects	$11,701	PWGSC	GOS/CS Policies & Practices
KM186-101348/001/CY	2010/11	EKOS Research Associates Inc.	T001A	Public Opinion Research – Quantitative	$83,857	Environment Canada	MSC DG Policy & Corp. Affairs

Reference	Fiscal Year	Vendor	Code	Service	Amount	Department	Sector
KM186-111409/001/CY	2011/12–2012/13	Acnielsen Company of Canada	T001A	Public Opinion Research – Quantitative	$76,348	Environment Canada	MSC DG Policy & Corp. Affairs
EN914-100962/001/CX	2009/10–2010/11	Consult Ink Ltd	T004 H	Writing Services	$39,323	PWGSC	GOS/CS Policies & Practices
EN914-110902/001/CX	2010/11	Consult Ink Ltd	T004 H	Writing Services	$12,885	PWGSC	GOS/CS Policies & Practices
EN914-111803/001/CX	2010/11	Consult Ink Ltd	T004 H	Writing Services	$35,087	PWGSC	GOS/CS Policies & Practices
U6280-142331/001/CY	2013/14–2014/15	Media Q Inc.	T004 K	Media Monitoring Services	$904	Industry Canada	Bankruptcy Prog, Policy & Reg. Aff
UC250-107124/001/CY	2009/10	Media Q Inc.	T004 K	Media Monitoring Services	$22,050	Industry Canada	Strategic Policy Sector
UC250-118582/001/CY	2011/12	Media Q Inc.	T004 K	Media Monitoring Services	$13,560	Industry Canada	Strategic Policy Sector
UC250-131072/001/CY	2013/14–2014/15	Media Q Inc.	T004 K	Media Monitoring Services	$5,650	Industry Canada	Strategic Policy Sector
UC250-139992/001/CY	2012/13	Media Q Inc.	T004 K	Media Monitoring Services	$5,650	Industry Canada	Strategic Policy Sector
Total					$6,372,718		

such as Data Conversion Services and Media Monitoring Services, are less indicative of the provision of direct substantive policy advice.

6.3.2 Data on the Supply of Advice

Saint-Martin (2005, 2006) noted that the size of the companies is relevant to the nature of the contract system, and size is recognized as potentially introducing bias in contracting (Macdonald 2011). We used the open data to generally assess these dimensions. The first data set (180 GSIN Codes) contains 1,874 suppliers to which funds have been disbursed as a result of contract awards. As Table 6.8 shows, there is a significant 'top-heavy' bias in the amounts awarded – that is, relative to the size of the contracting company.

This is in keeping with previous analyses of consulting practices in Canada, where a very small set of companies essentially monopolized the awards (Howlett and Migone 2014a, 2014b).

The suppliers at the very top of this list tend to be from the aerospace and defence sector, and from a technology background more generally, the two evident exceptions of this being Resolve Corporation / D+H Ltd Partnership, which administers the Canada Student Loan Program, and Accenture (see Table 6.9).

It is not surprising to see this distribution in terms of the categories selected. As a further analysis, we compared the total awards to large consulting firms across all select GSIN service categories to understand how much their business was focused on the first 'policy-related' subset.

Table 6.8 *First subset (180 GSIN codes): distribution of supplier contract income*

Supplier Income	# of Suppliers	% of Suppliers	Value	Value %
Less than $25 K	234	12.5	$3,720,732	0.06
$25 K to $100 K	374	20.0	$22,168,836	0.3
$100 K to $500 K	508	27.1	$129,265,397	1.9
$500 K to $1 M	289	15.4	$199,229,769	3.0
$1 M to $5 M	331	17.7	$778,746,567	11.7
$5 M to $10 M	70	3.7	$499,541,960	7.5
$10 M to $50 M	59	3.1	$1,159,254,518	17.4
$50 M and over	9	0.5	$3,868,948,689	58.1

Table 6.9 *Top ten suppliers by award size*

Company	Sector	Value of Contracts Awarded
Aerex Avionics Inc.	Aerospace & Defence	$47,552,222
General Dynamics Canada Ltd	Aerospace & Defence	$51,141,453
Morneau Shepell Ltd	HR Consulting & Technology	$64,269,912
Neptec Technologies Corp	Technology	$86,156,319
COM DEV Ltd	Aerospace	$225,331,378
L-3 Communications Mas (Canada) Inc.	Aerospace & Defence	$230,873,002
Accenture	Professional Services	$451,042,244
Resolve Corporation / D+H Ltd Partnership	Finance (*Canada Student Loan Program*)	$722,543,484
Macdonald, Dettwiler And Associates Ltd	Communication and Information	$925,349,699
Calian Ltd	Technology	$1,112,241,198
Total (Top 10 Suppliers)		$3,916,500,911
Total (All Suppliers)		**$6,660,876,467**

The results in Table 6.10 show that there is a broad distribution among these companies with regard to their share of this outsourcing as a percentage of their total activity.

Finally, the 1,874 suppliers who have received payment for a contract over the period were analysed and categorized according to the type of activities they undertake by reviewing what each company's website stated as services on offer. We should note that many companies cannot be neatly classified in one single category. For example, a variety of engineering companies also undertake work in the environmental field. As a result, we took into account all areas of activity utilized by these suppliers. Thus, the Canadian Council for Canadian Studies has been tracked as both Policy and Association and is counted as a potential provider of both services.

Table 6.11 illustrates a clear trend in the sample, showcasing a set of areas of focus where suppliers cluster: the technology and engineering sector. This is partially explained by the Research and Development GSIN codes that were included in the subset and by the broad scope of

Table 6.10 *Select suppliers award comparison – $ million*

Supplier	All GSIN Codes	First Subset (180 Codes) Awards	%
EY	$58.9	$0.057	0.1
Hill+Knowlton	$5.9	$0.067	1.1
Deloitte	$128.5	$6.5	5.1
KPMG	$77.1	$10.1	13.1
PwC	$205.2	$38.1	18.6
Accenture	$496.6	$451.0	90.8

Table 6.11 *Areas of activity of suppliers – aggregated categories*

Areas of Activity	Number of Instances
Human Resources	39
Legal	43
Defence/Security	58
Information Technology	69
Management Consulting	75
Marketing/ Communication/ Public Opinion	82
Business Services/Financial	88
Environmental Services	110
Health	161
Engineering/Construction	291
Technology	533
Associations	28
Governments	36
Policy	83
University	89
Research	89

codes such as Business and Professional Services and Consulting Services and Change Management.

Only 83 suppliers were found to offer policy services, or about 4.5 per cent of the whole group.[6] It is possible to develop a proxy to

---

[6] It is complicated to assess a 'policy orientation' in suppliers. We analysed the suppliers' websites and included those that offer policy services explicitly. We also included suppliers whose outputs appeared to fall in the policy category.

Table 6.12 *(180 GSIN codes): award income – policy services firms/all firms*

Fiscal Year	'Policy Services' Firms	All Firms	%
FY2008/09	$10,412,417	$143,087,558	7.3
FY2009/10	$4,351,450	$564,710,379	0.8
FY2010/11	$12,511,589	$276,870,056	4.5
FY2011/12	$10,432,728	$390,784,405	2.7
FY2012/13	$8,728,588	$1,594,465,050	0.5
FY2013/14	$5,190,720	$781,737,697	0.7
FY2014/15	$2,532,544	$376,029,550	0.7
FY2015/16	$16,580,813	$441,464,212	3.8
FY2016/17	$8,634,689	$2,091,727,560	0.4
Total	$79,375,538	$6,660,876,467	1.2

measure the fiscal impact of policy-related outsourcing in the federal administration by looking at the value of awards received by suppliers that also offer policy services. Table 6.12 compares that number with the total awards contained in the subset by the fiscal year when the contract was awarded: they represent 1.2 per cent of the subset.

These awards can be further analysed by looking at what types of GSIN codes appear most commonly for these suppliers. As can be noted from Table 6.13, there is a fair amount of diversity in the GSIN distribution, with a strong presence of public opinion research[7] and business-related services (Business Services, Project Management and Consulting), as well as analytical, planning and advisory services.

A further aspect of the analysis is to look at what type of supplier has received awards in these areas. As can be seen from Table 6.14, the suppliers that have received larger sums in this category of awards tend to be engaged in research and strategic analysis.

However, this is a proxy for our analysis, and the lack of a precise code for policy activity obviously hinders our analysis. In particular, grouping suppliers who offer policy-related services as part of their work does not ensure that all contracts awarded to these companies are policy related, but the paucity of contract descriptions severely limits our capacity to understand the nature of specific awards.

[7] The total here results from the combining of five separate Public Opinion Research GSIN codes: Qualitative, Quantitative & Qualitative, Quantitative, Syndicated Studies and Other.

Table 6.13 *Distribution by GSIN codes of suppliers with policy-related services*

GSIN Codes	Awards
Astronautics (R&D)	$524,096
Economics (R&D)	$577,500
Writing Services (including, editing, adaptation, etc.)	$619,493
Economic Studies / Modelling and Analysis	$702,635
Data Analysis – Performance of a Survey	$878,609
Transportation (R&D)	$1,046,957
Administrative Management and Planning Services	$1,146,912
Professional Services / Programme Advisory Services	$1,277,852
Medical and Health Studies	$1,823,154
Data Collection Services	$1,951,436
Military (R&D)	$2,459,705
Adjudication Services	$2,580,776
Organization Planning/Analysis	$2,625,000
Media Monitoring Services	$3,238,100
Programme Management – Analysis/Control	$3,772,639
Real Estate Advisory Services	$4,039,256
Consulting Services, Change Management / Organizational Development	$7,797,781
Project Management Services	$11,019,908
Business Services	$13,531,604
Public Opinion Research (all streams)	$13,684,150 x
Other Codes	$4,077,975

This supports the findings from previous research (Howlett and Migone 2014b; Howlett, Migone and Tan 2014), indicating that there is a group of consultants in Canada that has specialized in the area of supporting the policy advisory capacity of the federal government.

6.4 Conclusion

Ultimately, the Government of Canada's changes to the reporting of procurement over the past decade have made it simpler to assess financial patterns of contracting in detail, but details about the content of individual contracts are still limited. The complete absence of data at

Table 6.14 *Suppliers with policy-related services and contract income over $1 million*

Supplier	Area of Contracting	Award
Mayo Moran	Policy/Research	$1,000,000
Prairie Research Associates Inc.	Policy/Research	$1,073,026
Canadian Public Safety Operations Organization	Policy/Government	$1,251,475
DPRA Canada Inc.	Policy/Environment/ Research	$1,338,199
Kathleen Mell	Policy/Research	$1,580,776
Informetrica Ltd	Policy/Research	$1,591,982
Advanis	Marketing/Policy/ Research	$1,902,582
NRG Research Group	Policy/Research	$2,148,377
The Strategic Counsel	Policy/Research	$2,314,771
Strategic Relationships Solutions Inc.	Policy/Research	$2,332,667
International Council for Canadian Studies	Policy/Association	$2,485,563
SJT Solutions Inc.	Policy/Research	$2,625,000
Fotenn Consultants Inc.	Policy/Services	$3,892,961
Quallium Corporation	Policy/Research	$3,987,200
Wyle Laboratories Inc.	Policy/Technology	$4,303,007
EKOS Research Associates Inc.	Policy/Research	$6,834,785
Social Research and Demonstration Corporation	Policy/Research	$8,637,881
Bronson Consulting Group	Policy/Management Consulting	$15,254,196

the provincial level is particularly worrisome and should be corrected as soon as possible.

Nevertheless, it is now possible to arrive at a reasonable estimation of federal expenditures and to compare these with the situation in other countries. The analysis of Canada, in this sense, while relying on a different data set organization – GSIN codes as opposed to Proactive Disclosure codes – from earlier studies, mirrors the results obtained in previous analyses in this area (Howlett and Migone 2014a, 2014b, 2017). Within the subset that we have chosen, the distribution of awards is highly skewed in terms of the end user departments, with a handful of departments accounting for the majority of the awards. The same thing is true of the concentration of large sums within a very small number of companies, again confirming previous research results (Macdonald 2011; Howlett and Migone 2017).

A similar pattern exists when addressing the distribution of awards by GSIN codes: the initial sample is unfortunately skewed by the broad categories that some GSIN codes represent, such as the Consulting Services, Change Management/Organizational Development code, and by the inclusion of all research and development codes. However, given the current status of the available data, we were unable to provide a more granular response.

Our findings also support Speers' (2007) and Saint-Martin's (2006) original claims that these consultants represent a hidden or 'invisible civil service' with a more or less permanent and fixed character largely escaping traditional reporting and accountability measures. While traditional concerns with the outsourcing of policy advice often developed around the efficiency of external sources compared to internal ones in this supply, we argue that the oligopolistic nature of the supply chain (Howlett and Migone 2013) also needs to be explored. Here, we reviewed a smaller set of contracts within our initial sample, of not only what this important set of actors in the policy advice realm has been doing, and to arrive at a clearer picture both of external consultants and their work, but also of their place in the Canadian policy advisory system. As this discussion shows, they have emerged as a key player in the Canadian system over the past several decades and have taken an important place in that system. Thus, they are worthy of the same level of research and attention as is paid to older actors in the system, such as officials in the central bureaucracy and, more recently, actors such as think tanks and research institutes (Dobuzinskis and Howlett 2018; Howlett et al. 2017; Dobuzinskis et al. 1996, 2007). Improvements in reporting and data collection on the activities of consultants, however, is required before more definitive statements can be made of their significance and impact.

7 | Swedish Government Agencies' Hiring of Policy Consultants: A Phenomenon of Increased Magnitude and Importance?

7.1 Introduction

In many Western countries, the public sector has been one of the fastest growing sectors in the consulting markets (Glassman and Winograd 2005; Saint-Martin 2012). Apart from consulting services related to ICT, public organizations hire consulting services to the extent that the public sector now forms the third-largest client sector for management consulting services in Europe (FEACO 2010, 2016). Extant research has tended to explain organizations' hiring of consultants with either rational arguments related to organizations' need for expertise and resources (Armbrüster 2006; Canbäck 1998, 1999), or the individual managers' need for reducing uncertainty and gaining legitimacy (Alvesson and Johansson 2002; Berglund and Werr 2002; Clark and Salaman 1996; Fincham 2012). While this research has grown considerably over the last decades, and has provided important insights, it has tended to focus on private organizations at a particular point in time (Sturdy, Werr and Buono 2009). Thus, we know less about the hiring of consultants in the public sector and how it might vary over time. This is somewhat surprising, given the repeated calls for more research on the use of consultants in the public sector, and the recurrent descriptions of consultants forming 'an invisible public service' (Howlett and Migone 2014), a 'shadow government' (Guttman and Willner 1976; Lapsley and Oldfield 2001), or even a 'consultocracy' (Hodge and Bowman 2006), thereby removing governing power from policy-makers (Craig with Brooks 2006).

The research that does exist has suggested that consultants can take on different roles in public sector organizations, ranging from providing extra resources, an outsider perspective and expertise, to sense-making, strategic direction, advice and legitimacy (Kipping and Armbrüster 2002; Kubr 2002; Lapsley and Oldfield 2001). It has also been argued that for both organizations and consultants, the context in the public sector is more complex than in the private sector, as it is highly political with a multiplicity of stakeholders involved and under strict scrutiny from media (Glassman and Winograd 2005; Jacobsson and Sundström 2016). The hiring of consultants in the public sector thus forms a highly relevant setting for exploration, from both a practical and a theoretical point of view (Murdoch 2015). This chapter seeks to contribute to the knowledge development in this field by exploring empirically how government agencies in Sweden hire consultants related to policy work, and how their spending develops over time. In doing so, we will first provide a short introduction to the Swedish public sector. We then discuss the data and methods used, before presenting the analyses and results. The chapter ends with a short conclusion summarizing the main findings and proposing avenues for future research.

7.2   A Brief Introduction to the Swedish Public Sector

In the literature, Sweden is recurrently depicted as a welfare state with generous benefits, high taxes and a strong legacy of a state-centric political culture (Elinder and Jordahl 2013). In accordance with this culture, the citizens expect the state to solve societal problems, and hence have a strong trust in Swedish domestic institutions (Pierre, Jacobsson and Sundström 2015). This culture is also reflected in the political system, within which there is a strong belief in social engineering and rational and pragmatic solutions, as well as in the problem-solving capacity of the state (Pierre 2016). The Swedish public sector includes more than 5,000 public contracting agencies and spends approximately SEK[1] 900 billion annually on goods and services, equalling approximately 15–20 per cent of Sweden's GDP. The Swedish government presents proposals for new laws and implements decisions taken by the Swedish *Riksdag* (the parliament). In doing so, it is assisted by roughly 400 central government agencies and public administrations. In contrast to many other countries, only a small number of civil servants work in the government's offices and ministries; instead, the majority work in government agencies (Dahlström 2016; Ehn 2016).

Each year, the government decides which goals the government agencies should pursue and what the appropriate budgets should be.

---

[1]   As of November 2017, SEK 1 equals approximately € 0.1, £ 0.09 and US$ 0.11.

However, a central feature of the Swedish politico-administrative system is 'dualism', which prohibits and protects government agencies from ministerial rule and gives them relatively high levels of autonomy (Pierre et al. 2015). This means that the government has no powers to intervene in an agency's exercise of its authority, its decisions in specific matters or its day-to-day activities (Dahlström 2016). The Riksdag ensures that ministerial rule does not occur (Pollitt and Talbot 2004); this structural arrangement implies that there is a strong need for policy coordination between the government offices and the relatively autonomous government agencies (Dahlström 2016).

7.2.1 Powerful Director Generals in Sweden

An effect of the principle of dualism is that the power to decide how to structure and run the work in the government agencies is transferred from the ministers to the Director Generals (DGs). Swedish DGs are typically described as holding extensive power in their organizations, as they have the mandate to initiate large change initiatives, appoint members of the top management teams and influence organizational structures, performance measurement and reward systems, as well as the working climate in their agencies (Asplind 2013). This was illustrated by one of the interviewed DGs: 'I think that in Sweden, if we compare to Germany or France, for instance, the DG is quite free to decide for himself what is best' (DG 5). Another DG said: 'There are not many jobs in the public sector that give you as much power as Director General' (DG 4). This large amount of freedom is, however, perceived as both a blessing and a curse by the DGs, as it also makes them ultimately responsible for the initiatives taken in their government agencies:

We [Swedish DGs] have much more freedom [than DGs in other countries]. Much more. And it makes it much more difficult because … if you are experienced enough you can just say to the minister 'I want to have a decision on this, otherwise I won't do anything'. In Germany, if the minister calls you, you say 'OK, I'll do it'. So, I think it's a big difference. (DG 2)

Included in the DGs' responsibilities is the hiring of consultants, which tends to be initiated or at least approved by the DGs. As explained by a DG: 'The government and the parliament just decide the total [budget], and then you can use it as you like' (DG 1). Although middle managers in larger government agencies may hire consultants for smaller assignments, the DG must approve larger initiatives: 'I would say for limited projects, the middle managers are free to hire consultants. Of course, if they want to do a larger project they must discuss it with me first' (DG 6). In smaller government agencies, the DG is more directly involved in the consulting projects and signs all the agreements. As described by a DG: 'Every agreement that needs to be signed must be signed by me' (DG 3). This means they are also the person media would focus on, should the agency's use of consultants be scrutinized:

So one has to be very careful when selecting a specific consultancy or asking for a specific consultant. Then the tabloids might call you and ask: 'Why did you hire them? Are they your friends? Is that your mistress?' They ask you anything! They even make stories up sometimes! So one has to be aware of that. (DG 1)

7.2.2 Reforms in the Swedish Public Sector

In recent decades, the Swedish public sector has gone through several reforms inspired by NPM ideals. These reforms have led to a stronger emphasis on management ideas and practices associated with market-ization, efficiency, transparency, performance measurements and quan-titative measures and evaluations (Pierre et al. 2015). The adoption of NPM launched in the 1980s, and included the closing, merging and forming of new government agencies and a new approach of results-oriented budgeting (Pollitt and Bouckaert 2004). In the 1990s, the Social Democratic government made it possible for private companies to enter the until then state-controlled and monopolist markets of healthcare, education and pensions (Teelken 2015). This was soon followed by similar initiatives in the municipalities and the social welfare sector. In 2006, the newly formed centre-right government continued the NPM-reforms, but at a higher speed, resulting in more complexity for Swedish public organizations (Bolton et al. 2009; Jacobsson 1994; Jarl, Fredriksson and Persson 2012; Lantto 2001; Rombach 1997; Svanborg-Sjövall 2014). The reforms have led to a reduction in the number of government agencies, as smaller local agencies have merged into larger ones and others have been corporatized.[2] Thus, although Sweden has

---

[2] See the report 'Svenska myndigheter – färre men större [Swedish government agencies – fewer but larger]', The Swedish Agency for Public Management 2010: www.statskontoret.se/globalassets/publikationer/om-offentlig-sektor-1–11/om-offentlig-sektor-6.pdf.

a long tradition of having a large public sector providing an extensive, tax-financed welfare system, including free education, pensions, tax-subventioned low costs for healthcare and day-care for young children, it has in recent decades moved towards more autonomous agencies with 'business-like' structures, procedures and languages (Denis, Ferlie and Van Gestel 2015).

In response to these developments, government agencies have increasingly sought access to new expertise on how to tackle issues related to decentralization, internationalization, ICT and wicked social problems (Pierre and Peters 2000; Pollitt 2003). Following the reduction of the number of government agencies from 643 to 377 from 2000 to 2011 due to mergers and transformations of smaller agencies into larger ones, they have also sought assistance in how to perform organizational changes. The changes have been related to various areas, such as social security administration, national defence, the tax authority and the employment office.[3] To meet these demands, consultants are frequently hired (Pemer, Börjeson and Werr 2014).

7.2.3 Policy-Making in Sweden

Policy-making in Sweden has often been characterized as a rational, matter-of-fact process built on consensus and a low degree of conflict (Dahlström 2016; Mattson 2016). As noted by Petersson (1994: 3), the 'emphasis on compromise and pragmatic solutions has led to the development of a political culture built on consensus'. This image builds on three specific features of Swedish policy-making. First, Sweden has a history of minority governments, which has given the Riksdag a stronger position in the policy-making process than in typical Westminster-type democracies, and also fostered a culture of compromise-seeking (Mattson 2016). Second, the corporatist policy-making style has traditionally enabled labour market organizations and interest organizations to influence policies. Lastly, all policy proposals are analysed by a commission of inquiry before being sent to private and public organizations for referral (Dahlström 2016). These commissions have traditionally been large and included representatives from different

---

[3] See The Swedish Agency for Public Management: www.statskontoret.se/var-verksamhet/forvaltningspolitikens-utveckling/offentliga-sektorns-utveckling/arl iga-uppfoljningar/.

societal spheres, such as NGOs, political parties, researchers and private organizations. The representatives have taken on the roles of members and experts, and have participated in the commissions' analyses and discussions. Although the commissions are temporary, they have held a strong position and almost the same degree of autonomy as the (permanent) government agencies (Pierre et al. 2015).

In Sweden, the government offices have an estimated 4,600 employees, comprising the Prime Minister's Office, the Office for Administrative Affairs and ten line ministries, which in turn are divided into approximately 100 units. The number of ministries is not regulated; rather, it is up to the government to decide how to distribute and divide the duties and tasks (Jacobsson and Sundström 2016). When compared to many other countries, Swedish ministers tend to make decisions collectively, apart from those that concern the administration and organization of their own ministries. This collective decision-making is based on a joint preparation and drafting procedure involving all relevant ministries. Formal government decisions are made at the weekly Cabinet meetings given that there is ministerial unanimity (Dahlström 2016).

Historically, the institutionalized involvement of interest representation in all stages of the policy-making process has been very strong. In recent decades, however, this involvement has weakened, and the organized interests increasingly use other channels, such as lobbying and the media (Öberg 2016). There are also signs that due to the increasingly divided political discourse following the development of two blocs (i.e. one non-socialist and one socialist/green), with different ideas on the balance between the 'market' and the 'state', this consensus-seeking behaviour might be declining (Pierre 2016).

7.2.4 Public Procurement in Sweden

Public procurement in Sweden is regulated by the Swedish Public Procurement Act (PPA), which builds on EU directives on public procurement.[4] The PPA regulates principles, processes and documentation in public procurement, and is enforced by the Riksdag, courts of law, the Swedish Competition Agency (*Konkurrensverket*) and the National Agency for Public Procurement (*Upphandlingsmyndigheten*).

---

[4] Swedish Public Procurement Act (2007: 1091), EU Directive no. 199/1994; EU Directive no. 24/2014.

It aims to increase transparency, procedural correctness and competition (e.g. by enabling smaller suppliers to bid on contracts), and to reduce corruption and nepotism in the supplier selection process. When the PPA was first implemented in 1994, the purchasing maturity among public organizations was relatively low, and little collaboration or knowledge-sharing existed at the time. Consulting services were mainly purchased by managers in public organizations, with little or no assistance from procurement professionals (Pemer and Skjølsvik 2017). To help introduce more standardized purchasing practices, the Swedish National Board for Public Procurement (*Nämnden för Offentlig Upphandling*)[5] and a newspaper[6] for publishing public procurement notices were established. In 2002, a new rule was introduced by the PPA. The rule gave suppliers the right to take the buyer organization to court if they found that the procurement process or contract award decisions had been incorrectly performed. If found guilty, the buyer organizations would have to perform the purchasing process again and/or pay penalties. To avoid court cases, many public organizations responded by focusing on 'safe' and tangible supplier selection criteria when hiring consultants, such as lowest price, number of certifications or years of experience (Pemer and Skjølsvik 2017). The public organizations also strove to increase their purchasing maturity by forming new procurement offices, and improving the skills of the procurement professionals by either offering training or hiring experienced professionals from regulating agencies and the private sector. Government agencies such as the Legal, Financial and Administrative Services Agency (*Kammarkollegiet*) increased their support by providing information and developing framework agreements with preferred suppliers that the public organizations could use.

A few years later, following intense discussions in the media on the problems associated with the PPA when buying complex services, the Riksdag invited procurement professionals, managers from public organizations, researchers and legal experts to roundtable discussions on how

---

[5] Report: Effects of the PPA, Swedish National Board for Public Procurement (1998: 14).

[6] The newspaper was called *Anbudsjournalen* [*Journal of Bids*] and existed between 1994 and 2012, when it was bought by Upphandling24, a digital platform publishing public procurement notices and bids (see www .upphandling24.se).

to improve the legislation (Pemer and Skjølsvik 2017). Following these discussions, and after several investigations,[7] the Swedish government offered a proposal on how to change the PPA regulation in the Riksdag in 2014. The changes are currently being crafted by legal experts and regulators, and will be implemented in the coming years. A central feature of the proposed changes is to make it easier for public organizations to include more qualitative and subjective evaluation criteria in the supplier evaluation, and thus enable the buyer to move from tangible aspects (e.g. the price per hour) towards focusing more on the supplier's quality and value for money (Pemer and Skjølsvik 2017). This development is illustrated in the following quote from a procurement professional:

> We used to look just at the [consultant's] CV: 'It looks good, let's hire this person'. Now the trend is that we actually meet the consultant, we look at cases, and at what the consultant actually has done. So, the focus today is more on the specific person than on the consultancy. (PP2)

Thus, in parallel with the development of the Swedish public sector towards increased reforms, contracting out and implementation of NPM practices and ideals, the purchasing maturity among public organizations has increased. The role of public procurement professionals has also changed from having a relatively low status to forming a well-respected profession with high status, its own professional association, specific training, and an institutionalized knowledge-sharing of innovative purchasing practices (Pemer and Skjølsvik 2017). Given these developments, one would have suspected that there would be an easily available overview of the spending on various types of consultants in the public sector. However, this is not the case.

7.3 Methods

Following the 'principle of openness' in the Swedish public sector, government agencies are required by law to make their documentation publicly available. On the one hand, this makes Sweden a setting with wide research access (Yin 2009), and enables the extraction of documentation regarding, for instance, public procurement and government agencies' spending. On the other hand, similar to the

---

[7] See SOU 2013: 12 and SOU 2014: 51.

situation in many other countries, there exists no available overview of data on the use of consulting services in the public sector (Howlett and Migone 2013a, 2013b). Possible explanations for this are: i) that several government agencies are involved in regulating, overseeing and informing about public procurement, and that no single office has the main responsibility for collecting and publishing the data; ii) the existing codes in the accounting systems do not fully capture the variety of consulting services that exist in practice; and iii) coding practices vary across the agencies. As a consequence, overarching information about what kind of consulting projects have been performed in the agencies, for what purposes and why, is largely lacking.

7.3.1 Types of Policy Work and Types of Consultants

As discussed in Chapters 3 and 6, separating policy consulting from other types of consulting related to management, PR/communication or ICT is difficult. This is especially so when – as in the reporting in the Swedish public sector – there are no clear classifications or codes in the data. In a recent article, Van den Berg (2017) offers a classification of what types of work policy consulting might include. *Policy advice* denotes work related to gathering policy-related information, performing policy-related research and analyses, identifying policy options, formulating policies and drafting reports, preparing and giving ministerial briefings and consulting decision-makers. *Policy implementation* denotes the implementation of policy programmes and policies. *Policy evaluation* denotes the evaluation of policy processes, outcomes and results. *Process support*, lastly, denotes preparing departmental planning and budget proposals; informing policy advisers, external stakeholders and departmental management; negotiating with the client's stakeholders; and consulting citizens. Building on this classification, in this study we have chosen to focus on two types of consulting: management consulting services and PR/communication consulting services. The reasons for this are, first, that the term 'policy consulting' is not commonly used in Sweden to denote either typical tasks or consultancies, Second, the work tasks included in Van den Berg's (2017) four types are likely to be performed by either management or PR/communication consultants in Sweden.

7.3.2 Database Information on Government Agencies' Spending on Consulting Services

In order to provide a first picture of spending on consulting services in the Swedish public sector, this chapter draws on data derived from Solidinfo (www.solidinfo.se),[8] a publicly available database. The database covers approximately 90 per cent of the transactions between Swedish government agencies and their suppliers. It includes information about the individual transactions, as well as the buyer, supplier and amount of money of each transaction for the years 2003 to 2011. Therefore, this time period is used in this study. While the database gives an overview of the spending per buying organization and supplier, both over time and per year, it does not include information about the exact nature of the consulting assignments. Nor does the coding provide much information, as only three main codes are used: Other services, Non-state educational services and Research projects. Of these, the code 'Other services' is largest, adding up to a total of SEK 3,165,461,464 between 2003 and 2011. This is followed by 'Non-state educational services', with a total of SEK 114,870,473 between 2003 and 2011. Lastly, we find 'Research projects', amounting to SEK 1,737,207 between 2003 and 2011. To understand what kind of projects the consultancies might have provided, we have instead reviewed documents, government agencies' annual reports and the identified consultancies' websites, as well as their descriptions of typical projects performed in the public sector.

Being aware of these limitations, we collected data for 76 government agencies in 2003 to 2011 (see Appendix B for an overview). Of these, 76 used management consulting services and 70 of the 76 agencies used PR/communication consulting services. The reason these government agencies were studied was that they had had transactions with a supplier of management or PR/communication consulting services.[9] To provide a quick indication of the government agencies'

---

[8] The data in Solidinfo was cross-checked with information from the database Govdata (www.govdata.se; website no longer available), which built on information from The Swedish National Financial Management Authority (*Ekonomistyrningsverket*). However, while Solidinfo covered transactions of all sizes, Govdata only showed the 50 largest suppliers within each code.

[9] Based on a classification of services in the data, we could exclude transactions related to 'IT services' in the cases where consultancies delivered both management consulting and IT services.

different fields of expertise and services, we have classified them according to the COFOG system (see Appendix A). We identified the suppliers based on Konsultguiden's[10] listing of the largest management and PR/communication consultancies in Sweden between 2003 and 2011. In the listings, 100 management consultancies and 20 PR/communication consultants were included (see Appendices C and D).

To analyse the data, we searched the Solidinfo database for each of the listed consultancies, to see which government agencies they had had as clients in the 2003–2011 period. Each search provided us with information about the size (in terms of SEK) of each project the consultancy had carried out, per year, for a particular government agency. The information was compiled in Excel sheets, which made it possible for us to identify both the total spending for all government agencies or consultancies included in the study per year, as well as for the time period 2003–2011. It also made it possible for us to break down the data in order to explore which government agencies were the largest buyers of different types of consulting services, which suppliers they hired, the amounts of money they spent on their services and how that changed over time. The results from these analyses will be presented below.

7.3.3 *Interviews and Documents*

As a complement to the quantitative analysis, we performed qualitative interviews with six DGs of Swedish government agencies, two public procurement professionals, an independent expert and an expert working at The Swedish Agency for Public Management (*Statskontoret*), which is the government's organization for analyses and evaluations of state and state-funded activities. The interviews were performed between 2015 and 2017, lasted between 30 and 120 minutes and were recorded and transcribed (see Appendix E for an overview). The interviews were aimed at providing a contextual understanding for why consultants were hired and for what type of assignments. Also collected were documents and information from the government agencies' annual reports and websites, published investigations and reports, media articles and information from the studied consultancies' websites. This material has been used to provide additional context to the data on transactions from the Solidinfo database.

[10] See www.konsultguiden.se.

7.4 Swedish Government Agencies' Spending on Management Consulting Services

A first finding from the analyses is that the studied government agencies' spending on management consulting services has increased rather steadily from 2003 to 2011, with a reduced pace between 2008 and 2009 – possibly due to the financial crisis – only to pick up speed again in from 2010 to 2011 (see Figure 7.1).[11] The total spending in 2011 was 3.5 times higher than in 2003. This finding supports claims in research from other countries that the costs and the assumed importance of management consulting in the public sector has indeed grown considerably (ACCA 2010; Howard 2006; Howlett and Migone 2013a; NAO 2016; Raudla 2013; Saint-Martin 2012). However, previous research has indicated that under-reporting and non-compliance related to the hiring of consultants decreased in Sweden in the studied period (Pemer and Skjølsvik 2017). It might therefore be likely that at

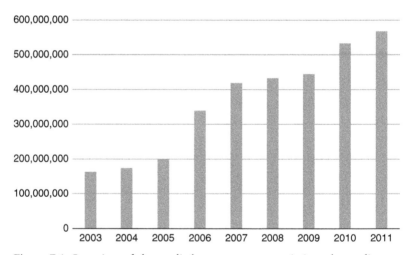

Figure 7.1 Overview of the studied government agencies' total spending on management consulting services between 2003 and 2011

---

[11] Adding to this number is the spending on management consulting services categorized in Solidinfo as made by an 'unknown' government agency. This category emanates from invoices that are difficult for SolidInfo to trace to a certain government agency. The total spending from 2003 to 2011 in this category amounts to SEK 13,501,022.

least a smaller part of the identified growth can be explained by increased reporting compliance; future research is encouraged to explore this further.

The analysis further shows that spending on management consulting services varies across the studied government agencies, so that a small fraction represents a large part of the total spending, while the majority of the agencies spend smaller amounts on consulting services. In fact, of the studied government agencies, only nine (equalling 7 per cent) spent more than SEK 100,000,000 in total on management consultants between 2003 and 2011. The largest group of agencies, amounting to 47 per cent of the studied agencies, spent between SEK 1,000,000 and SEK 10,000,000 on management consultants, followed by a group of agencies spending SEK 10,000,000 to SEK 50,000,000 on consultants from 2003 to 2011. This finding highlights that although a small number of government agencies stand for a large amount of the total spending on management consulting services, the majority of agencies hire management consultants for smaller and shorter assignments (see Figure 7.2).

The nine government agencies with a total spending on management consultants above SEK 100,000,000 from 2003 to 2011 were all large,

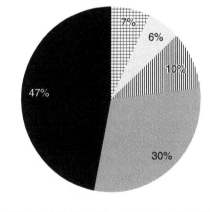

⊞ 200,000,000–500,000,000   ☐ 100,000,000–200,000,000

Ⅲ 50,000,000–100,000,000   ▨ 10,000,000–50,000,000

■ 1,000,000–10,000,000

Figure 7.2 Overview of the percentage of the studied government agencies' total spending on management consulting services in the time period 2003–2011

Table 7.1 *Overview of the nine government agencies that spent in total more than SEK 100,000,000 from 2003 to 2011*

Government Agency	Total Spending 2003–2011 in SEK	COFOG
Swedish Defence Material Administration	528,368,187	2
Swedish Armed Forces	364,336,870	2
Government Offices	359,967,246	1
Swedish Social Insurance Agency	269,111,676	10
Swedish Transport Administration	223,054,301	4
Swedish Railways	135,417,366	4
Civil Aviation Authority	107,994,469	4
Swedish Police	105,363,232	3
The National Government Employee Pensions Board	103,441,974	1

with the exception of the National Government Employee Pensions Board (*Statens Pensionsverk*). At the top of the list are two agencies related to Swedish defence: the Swedish Defence Material Administration (*Försvarets Materielverk*) and the Swedish Armed Forces (*Försvarsmakten*), followed by the Government Offices of Sweden (*Regeringskansliet*) (see Table 7.1).

Although the nine agencies showed different spending patterns, the overall trend was an increase in their spending over time, although with a small reduction (0.9 per cent) in the growth rate in 2009 (see Figure 7.3).

Different explanations for the spending patterns can be given. A first is the need for *organizational change related to the closing down and starting up of new agencies*. The Swedish Railways (*Banverket*) were closed in 2010 and replaced by a new agency: the Swedish Transport Administration (*Trafikverket*). This is mirrored in their spending. Swedish Railways shows a strong peak in 2008–2009 (i.e. the two years before the termination of the agency), while the Swedish Transport Administration launched at a high level in 2010 and 2011. As management consultants are often hired to assist in organizational changes, mergers and the closing down and starting up of new organizations (Kubr 2002), this might well be the reason they were hired extensively by the two agencies.

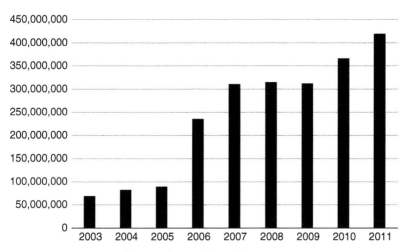

Figure 7.3 Overview of the trend in total spending on management consultants from 2003 to 2011 in the nine government agencies spending more than SEK 100,000,000

A second explanation is found in the *need for cost savings and increased efficiency*. This is closely linked to the transformation of the Swedish public sector towards ideals related to the use of more business-like practices and structurers (Denis, Ferlie and Van Gestel 2015). For example, in 2006 the Swedish government decided on large cost savings in the Swedish Defence Material Administration (*Försvarets materiel-verk*, FMV). To reach the target of reducing costs by SEK 900,000,000 in 2009, FMV needed to reorganize, and shift its focus towards increased contracting out of the production of defence materials.[12] In 2007, a large organizational change process was initiated aiming to increase customer focus and efficiency.[13] The change initiatives are reflected in the spending on management consultants, which more than tripled from 2005 (SEK 25,864,887) to 2006 (SEK 85,393,717), peaking in 2007 (SEK 111,555,057). The supplier with the largest contract by far in 2006 and 2007 was CGI Sverige (SEK 72,585,850

---

[12] See FMVs annual report, 2006: https://fmv.se/Global/Dokument/Om%20FM V/Informationsmaterial/%C3%85rsredovisningar/2006/FMV_AR2006%20tr yckt_SE.pdf
[13] See FMVs annual report, 2007: https://fmv.se/Global/Dokument/Om%20FM V/Informationsmaterial/%C3%85rsredovisningar/2007/FMV_AR2007_SE .pdf

and SEK 92,749,227). In the Swedish Police force (*Polisorganisationen*), a large reorganization was initiated in 2010, gaining momentum in 2011. The new organization aimed to increase quality, cost efficiency and flexibility and lead to better results.[14] This is reflected in the spending on management consultants, which almost tripled from roughly SEK 15,148,545 in 2010 to SEK 44,225,173 in 2011. The three suppliers with the largest contracts in 2011 were McKinsey (SEK 1, 438,800), Deloitte (SEK 5,585,438) and CGI Sverige (SEK 5,133,477), all of which provide services related to organizational change.

A third explanation is found in the *implementation of new work processes and practices* related to accounting and administration, and improving work processes and management systems. For instance, the government's decision to change the recruitment system in Swedish defence led to large changes in the Swedish Armed Forces' organization. Simultaneously, the Swedish Armed Forces changed its administrative system, used for internal accounting as well as procurement.[15] The supplier with undoubtedly the largest contract in 2009 and 2010 was CGI Sweden (SEK 51,632,414 and SEK 52,988,706, respectively). In the Swedish Social Insurance Agency (*Försäkringskassan*), the initiative to implement a new SAP-based business system led to an increase in consulting costs (Accenture having the largest contract, amounting to SEK 52,298,837 in 2008). After strong criticism of the delays and high costs, the project was closed down, the Director General was asked to leave and 80 consultants were replaced by staff from the Swedish Social Insurance Agency.

A fourth and final explanation is that the management consultants are used as *extra resources*. In this role, which can be part of an outsourcing strategy by the agency, the consultants take on everyday tasks, such as performing analyses, research and investigations. For example, the government offices and the National Government Employee Pensions Board (Statens Pensionsverk) did not have any large individual peaks in their spending on management consulting services, which might indicate that their spending was not related to externally or internally driven change or cost-reduction initiatives, as in the other government agencies.

---

[14] Justitiedepartementet (2010): 75.
[15] See the annual report of the Swedish Armed Forces 2010: www
     .forsvarsmakten.se/siteassets/4-om-myndigheten/dokumentfiler/arsredovisnin
     gar/arsredovisning-2010/huvuddokument-ar-10.pdf

7.4.1 Stable Supplier Relations with Management Consultancies

Among the nine government agencies spending the largest total sums on management consulting services, different supplier relations could be discerned. Two of the nine agencies used several suppliers throughout the studied time period: the Swedish Armed Forces hired CGI Sverige, Decision Dynamics and Gartner every year between 2003 and 2011, while the Swedish Social Insurance Agency hired CGI Sverige, Accenture and Gartner.[16] In contrast, four government agencies relied heavily on one supplier in the period 2003 to 2011: the Swedish Defence Materiel Administration (*Försvarets Materielverk*) and the National Government Employee Pensions Board (*Statens Pensionsverk*) hired CGI Sverige, using 56 per cent and 94 per cent, respectively, of their total spending on management consultants from 2003 to 2011 on them. Furthermore, the Civil Aviation Authority (*Luftfartsverket*) hired KPMG and the Swedish Police force hired Capgemini, spending 2 per cent and 18 per cent, respectively, on their services. The three remaining agencies did not provide data for all years, due to reporting (government offices) and the transformation of agencies into new ones (Swedish Railways and Swedish Transport Administration). However, in these three agencies, several suppliers were used. In the government offices, five suppliers were used throughout the 2006–2011 period: CGI Sverige, Capgemini, KPMG, Ramböll Management Consulting and Gartner. Swedish Railways used five suppliers between 2003 and 2010: Andersson och Bydler AB, CGI Sverige AB, Det Norske Veritas Certification AB, EC Effectiveness Consultants Sverige AB and Sandholm Associates AB.[17]

[16] Interestingly, 46 per cent of the Swedish Armed Forces total spending on management consulting services between 2003 and 2011 was on CGI Sverige, 1 per cent on Decision Dynamics and only 4 per cent on Gartner. The remaining 49 per cent was distributed across 30 other management consultancies. The Social Insurance Agency used 54 per cent of their total spending on Accenture, 19 per cent on CGI Sverige and 3 per cent on Gartner. The remaining 24 per cent was distributed across 32 other management consultancies.

[17] Three per cent of the government offices' total spending on management consulting services from 2006 to 2011 was on CGI Sverige, 7 per cent on Cap Gemini, 7 per cent on Ramböll Management Consulting and 3 per cent on Gartner; the remaining 80 per cent was distributed across 48 other management consultancies. The Swedish Railways used 2 per cent of their total spending on Anderson and Bydler, 15 per cent on CGI Sverige, 0.5 per cent on Det Norske Veritas, 0.9 per cent on EC Effectiveness Consultants Sverige AB, 0.7 per cent on Sandholm Associates and the remaining 80.1 per cent was distributed across 28 other management consultancies.

The Swedish Transport Administration, lastly, came into existence in 2010, and used 33 different suppliers of management consulting services in 2010 and 2011. Of these, the three largest suppliers in 2010 and 2011 were McKinsey & Co, CGI Sverige AB and Xmentor.[18] The existence of long-standing supplier relations is illustrated in Table 7.2.

In the second group, spending in total between SEK 10,000,000 and SEK 50,000,000 in the 2003–2011 period (see Table 7.4), we find large government agencies with very different preferences regarding which supplier(s) to hire. The Swedish Labour Office (*Arbetsmarknadsverket*) used Arbetslivsresurs, CGI Sverige and Ramböll Management Consulting in all years between 2003 and 2011.[19] The Swedish National Financial Management Authority (*Ekonomistyrningsverket*) used BDO Consulting Group, corresponding to 23 per cent of its total spending on management consulting services. The Swedish Mapping, Cadastral and Land Registration Authority (*Lantmäteriverket*) used CGI Sverige, corresponding to 3 per cent of its total spending on management consulting services. The Swedish Environmental Protection Agency (*Naturvårdsverket*) used Frontit, amounting to 7 per cent of its total spending on management consulting services. The Swedish Tax Authority (*Skatteverket*) used Capgemini and Gartner, corresponding to 35 per cent and 7 per cent each. Interestingly, the Swedish Migration Agency (*Migrationsverket*) used several suppliers, but none for more than six of the nine years studied (Ramböll Management Consulting)[20]. The Swedish Road Administration (*Vägverket*) used more than 15 suppliers each year from 2003 to 2005, before transforming into the new Swedish Transport Administration (see Table 7.3).

In the third group, spending in total between SEK 1,000,000 and SEK 10,000,000 in the 2003–2011 period, we find a different pattern. The most frequently used consultancy among the agencies in this group was CGI Sverige, which was hired by Lund University, the Swedish National

---

[18] McKinsey & Co represented 58 per cent of the Swedish Transport Administration's total spending on management consulting services in 2010 and 2011; CGI Sverige AB represented 11 per cent and 16 per cent each. The remaining 15 per cent was distributed across 30 other management consultancies.

[19] Arbetslivsresurs represented 13 per cent of the Swedish Labour Office's total spending on management consulting services in 2010–2011; CGI Sverige AB represented 8 per cent, and Ramböll Management Consulting 6 per cent.

[20] Corresponding to 9 per cent of the total spending on management consulting services from 2003 to 2011.

Table 7.2 Overview of the most consistently used suppliers (including only those suppliers used in at least six out of the nine studied years), in the nine government agencies with largest spending on management consulting services

Agency	2003	2004	2005	2006	2007	2008	2009	2010	2011
Swedish Defence Material Administration	CGI Sverige AB								
Swedish Armed Forces	CGI Sverige AB Decision Dynamics AB Gartner Sverige AB								
Government Offices	n/a			CGI Sverige AB Capgemini Gartner Sverige AB KPMG Ramböll					
Swedish Social Insurance Agency	Accenture CGI Sverige AB Gartner Sverige AB								
Swedish Transport Administration	n/a						CGI Sverige AB McKinsey & Co. AB Xmentor		
Swedish Railways	Andersson och Bydler AB CGI Sverige AB Det Norske Veritas Certification AB EC Effectiveness Consultants AB Sandholm Associates							n/a	
Civil Aviation Authority	KPMG								
Swedish Police	Capgemini AB								
Statens pensionsverk	CGI Sverige AB								

Table 7.3 *Overview of the government agencies that spent between SEK 50,000,000 and SEK 100,000,000 on management consulting services from 2003 to 2011*

Government Agency	Total Spending 2003–2011 in SEK	COFOG	Supplier with Largest Share of Spending	%
Swedish Tax Authority	99,770,225	1	Capgemini	35
Swedish National Financial Management Authority	92,869,780	1	KPMG	66
Swedish Labour Office	92,188,636	10	InterPares	26
The Swedish Mapping, Cadastral and Land Registration Authority	65,978,502	4	Karlöf Consulting	71
Swedish Migration Agency	63,383,758	4	Kairos Future	70
Swedish Road Administration	58,446,671	4	Capgemini	20
Swedish Environmental Protection Agency	57,742,361	5	Rewir	41

Agency for Education (*Statens skolverk*), Umeå University and Uppsala University each year from 2003 to 2011, as well as in the Swedish Prison and Probation Service (*Kriminalvården*), the National Board of Health and Welfare (*Socialstyrelsen*), and the Swedish Board of Agriculture (*Statens jordbruksverk*) in eight of the nine years studied. The second most frequently used consultancy was Ernst & Young Advisory, which was hired by the University of Gothenburg, Karolinska Institutet, the Royal Academy of Technology, Lund University and Uppsala University each year from 2003 to 2011. Additional commissioning of Ernst & Young Advisory was executed by the Swedish International Development Cooperation Agency (*Styrelsen för internationellt utvecklingssamarbete*) in eight of the nine years reviewed. In third place is Wenell Management AB, which was used by Lund University, Karolinska Institutet and Uppsala University. Interestingly, four agencies – the Swedish Work Environment Authority (*Arbetsmiljöverket*), the Swedish Forest Agency (*Skogsstyrelsen*), the Swedish Energy Agency (*Statens energimyndighet*) and the National Property Board of Sweden (*Statens fastighetsverk*) – did not have a long-standing supplier, but used different firms throughout the studied period. In addition, three agencies – the Swedish

Table 7.4 *Overview of the government agencies that spent between SEK 10,000,000 and SEK 50,000,000 on management consulting services from 2003 to 2011*

Government Agency	Total Spending in SEK	COFOG	Supplier with Largest Share of Spending	%
Swedish National Debt Office	30,138,512	1	KPMG	86
Karolinska Institutet	28,493,077	9.4	Capgemini	59
University of Gothenburg	26,252,017	9.4	Capgemini	39
Lund University	21,067,138	9.4	Capgemini	30
Swedish Insurance Administration	20,324,366	10	Accenture	54
Swedish Defence Education	19,970,954	9.4	Capgemini	57
Swedish Pensions Agency	19,432,763	1	CGI Sverige	94
Uppsala University	19,210,376	9.4	CGI Sverige	17
Swedish National Agency for Education	18,574,150	9	CGI Sverige	64
Umeå University	18,289,151	9.4	CGI Sverige	65
National Board of Health and Welfare	18,093,151	4	CGI Sverige	26
Swedish Forest Agency	17,933,880	4	Arbetslivsresurs	32
Swedish Prison and Probation Service	15,440,123	3	CGI Sverige	19
Swedish Civil Contingencies Agency	14,979,183	4	Valtech	37
Swedish Board of Agriculture	12,626,577	4	Capgemini	42
Swedish International Development Cooperation Agency	12,589,853	1	EY	44
Swedish Work Environment Authority	12,430,803	10	Karlöf Consulting	50
Stockholm University	11,625,081	9.4	EY	59
Statistics Sweden	11,351,586	1	PA Consulting Group	22
Swedish Post and Telecom Authority	11,153,511	4	Digiscope Sverige	23
National Property Board of Sweden	11,047,119	1	Sevenco	67
Swedish Energy Agency	10,881,436	5	InterPares	36
Royal Academy of Technology	10,451,769	9.4	Rewir	49

Civil Contingencies Agency (*Myndigheten för samhällsskydd och bereds-kap*), the Swedish Pensions Agency (*Premiepensionsmyndigheten*) and the Swedish Insurance Administration (*Riksförsäkringsverket*) – were trans-formed into new agencies in the period. Lastly, the Swedish National Debt Office (*Riksgäldskontoret*) is the only agency in this group that had KPMG as a long-standing supplier in eight of the nine years. The analysis suggests that although CGI Sverige was the most commonly used supplier across the agencies in this group, the universities seemed to share similar prefer-ences regarding which suppliers to hire (i.e. CGI Sverige, Ernst & Young and Wenell Management).

In the last group, spending in total up to SEK 10,000,000 in the 2003–2011 time frame, we find local universities, county boards and a variety of other agencies (see Table 7.5). Of these, 24 had no long-standing supplier, but used different consultancies from 2003 to 2011. Of the remaining agencies, Ernst & Young was hired by Mälardalen University, the Swedish University of Agricultural Sciences, Karlstad University and Luleå University of Technology each year from 2003 to 2011. This was followed by CGI Sverige, which was hired by Malmö University, SMHI and Karlstad University from 2003 to 2011. Luleå University of Technology also hired KPMG each year in the period studied. Three agencies – the Swedish Work Life Institute (*Arbetslivsinstitutet*), Linné University and the Stockholm Institute of Education – were closed down or transformed into new organizations. Thus, we find CGI Sverige and Ernst & Young in a leading position within this group too, albeit at a much lower level.

7.4.2 Dominance of Large Suppliers of Management Consulting Services

The above analyses show that one of the most frequently and repeat-edly hired consultancies among the studied government agencies was CGI Sverige AB. It was also often one of the largest suppliers in terms of spending. CGI Sverige AB is an international consultancy focusing on IT-systems and organizational change, particularly within the public sector, including government agencies related to defence, administra-tion, healthcare, public safety and municipalities. Its Swedish public sector branch has approximately 1,000 employees, many of whom have previously worked in the public sector. CGI Sverige has

Table 7.5 *Overview of the government agencies that spent up to SEK 10,000,000 on management consulting services from 2003 to 2011*

Government Agency	Total Spending 2003–2011 in SEK	COFOG	Supplier with Largest Share of Spending	%
The Riksdag Administration	9,958,791	1	Gartner	55
Luleå University of Technology	8,663,248	9.4	EY	30
Linköping University	8,143,238	9.4	CGI Sverige	61
Swedish Prosecution Authority	7,783,451	3	CGI Sverige	26
Swedish Defence Research Agency	7,661,407	2	Frontit	29
Swedish Fortifications Agency	7,365,843	1	CGI Sverige	38
Karlstad University	6,605,735	9.4	Right Sinova	14
Swedish Meteorological and Hydrological Institute	6,542,865	5	CGI Sverige	52
Swedish National Grid for Electricity	5,512,368	5	Capgemini	32
County Administrative Board of Västra Götaland	5,333,961	1	Gartner	58
Malmö University	5,250,023	9.4	CGI Sverige	30
Mälardalen University	5,234,508	9.4	CGI Sverige	47
The Swedish Courts	5,000,573	3	Capgemini	27
Patent- och registreringsverket	4,974,195	4	Implement	57
Swedish Rescue Services Agency	4,971,389	2	Alfakonsult	28
Swedish Customs	4,478,780	1	Gartner	94
Stockholm Institute of Education	4,282,194	9.4	Kvadrat	94
Linné University	4,041,277	9.4	Valtech	64
County Administrative Board of Stockholm	3,753,116	1	Ramböll Management Consulting	36
Swedish University of Agricultural Sciences	3,427,584	9.4	EY	34
Mid Sweden University	3,369,294	9.4	CGI Sverige	36
University College of Kalmar	3,336,482	9.4	Valtech	58

Table 7.5 (*cont.*)

Government Agency	Total Spending 2003–2011 in SEK	COFOG	Supplier with Largest Share of Spending	%
Swedish Research Council	3,240,073	9	Balanced Scorecard Collaborative	51
Swedish Board of Student Finance	3,003,501	9	Accenture	20
Växjö University	2,738,106	9.4	EY	28
Örebro University	2,283,195	9.4	Valtech	47
Swedish National Board of Institutional Care	2,162,142	10	Karlöf Consulting	48
County Administrative Board of Skåne län	1,914,918	1	Ramböll Management Consulting	63
University of Gävle	1,449,099	9.4	CGI Sverige	93
Swedish Work Life Institute	1,213,035	4	Kairos Future	41
Swedish Coast Guard	1,196,718	3	CGI Sverige	72
Swedish Economic Crime Authority	1,136,827	1	Valtech	37
Swedish Maritime Administration	1,115,643	4	CGI Sverige	88
Södertörn University	355,115	9.4	Capgemini	57
Dalarna University	142,025	9.4	Frontwalker	78

framework agreements with government agencies and municipalities regarding IT outsourcing, IT services, programme and system development, resource consulting, business intelligence and e-commerce. Given CGI Sweden's field of expertise, a possible explanation for its strong position as supplier to the studied government agencies is that many of these needed to implement new IT-systems in the studied time period, or decided to outsource parts of their IT to CGI Sverige. As stated on CGI Sverige's website:

Every third government agency lacks an IT-strategy that meets the organization's future needs of scalability, flexibility and management. They are also under pressure to reduce costs and many of them still use old IT-solutions and systems that need to be manually operated. There exist many possibilities to increase efficiency and save costs. We can help you to move forward.[21]

In the government agencies with lower total spending, CGI Sverige was still one of the most frequently hired consultancies, alongside Ernst & Young Advisory and Wenell Management AB. The analysis shows that Ernst & Young was preferred particularly by universities. A possible explanation for this finding is that several universities had framework agreements with Ernst & Young regarding the auditing of research projects, performing investigations and collecting statistical data.[22] Another is that it indicates a learning effect or culture of mimicking behaviour among the universities. It is also worth noting that Ernst & Young was one of the preferred suppliers in the framework agreement for management consulting services related to analysis, issued by the Legal, Financial and Administrative Services Agency in 2010 (see Appendix F).

7.5 Swedish Government Agencies' Spending on PR/Communication Consulting Services

A first finding from the analysis is that the studied government agencies' spending on PR/communication consulting services increased between 2003 and 2011, with a large increase in 2009, followed by a decrease in 2010, then an increase in 2011. The total spending in 2011 was 2.75 times higher than in 2003. This finding indicates that government agencies' perceived need for support in issues related to communication, information, analyses, opinion-building and media has indeed increased strongly throughout the studied time period (see Figure 7.4).

A closer analysis revealed that between 2003 and 2011 the government agencies' total spending amounted to SEK 330,846,192.[23] Of these, 7 agencies spent more than SEK 10,000,000 in total on PR/communication consultants, while 25 spent between SEK 1,000,000 and SEK 10,000,000, and 22 spent between SEK 100,000 and SEK 1,000,000.

---

[21] See www.cgi.se/offentlig-sektor/statlig-verksamhet-och-myndigheter.
[22] See www.imh.liu.se/imhs-veckobrev/filer-v-11/vecka-1/1.279864/Inkpsnyttn r2-3december2010.pdf.
[23] Adding to this number is the spending on communication consulting services categorized in Solidinfo as having been made by an 'unknown' government agency. This category emanates from invoices that are difficult for SolidInfo to trace to a certain government agency. However, the total spending from 2003 to 2011 in this category is rather large at SEK 8,574,854.

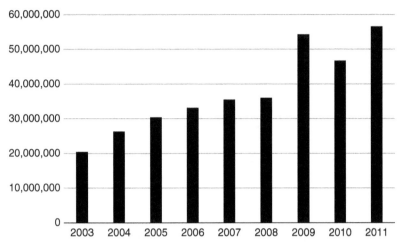

Figure 7.4 Overview of the studied government agencies' total spending on PR/communication consulting services from 2003 to 2011

A smaller group of 15 agencies spent less than SEK 100,000 from 2003 to 2011. This finding indicates that although a small number of the studied government agencies stood for a large part of the total spending on PR/communication consulting services, the majority of the agencies spent less than SEK 10,000,000 in total between 2003 and 2011 (or less than roughly SEK 1,100,000 per year) on such services (see Figure 7.5).

The seven government agencies shown in Table 7.6 spent more than SEK 10,000,000 in total on PR/communication consultants in the 2003–2011 time frame. The seven government agencies in this group are large, with number of employees ranging between 500 and 9,000, and hire PR/communication consultants frequently.

Although the seven agencies showed different spending patterns, the overall trend was an increase in their spending over time, although with two declines in 2008 and 2010, and two peaks in 2009 and 2011 (see Figure 7.6).

7.5.1 Explanations for the Spending on PR/Communication Consultants

Different explanations for the spending patterns can be offered. In the studied time period, two of the government agencies were being transformed into new agencies. This required far-reaching *organizational*

Table 7.6 *Overview of the seven government agencies that spent more than SEK 10,000,000 on PR/communication consulting services in the 2003–2011 period*

Government Agency	Total Spending 2003–2011 in SEK	COFOG
Government Offices	52,363,538 kr	1
Swedish Railways	44,940,113 kr	4
Swedish Environmental Protection Agency	33,084,775 kr	5
Swedish Energy Agency	30,085,404 kr	5
Swedish Labour Office	27,641,665 kr	10
The Riksdag Administration	19,240,108 kr	1
Swedish International Development Cooperation Agency	17,976,936 kr	1

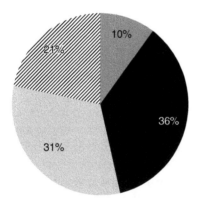

■ 10,000,000–100,000,000   ■ 1,000,000–10,000,000

▨ 100,000–1,000,000   ▨ 0–100,000

Figure 7.5 Overview of the percentage of the studied government agencies' total spending on PR/communication consulting services in different ranges, between 2003 and 2011

changes related to the closing down and starting up of the agencies. Swedish Railways, which was responsible for train traffic in Sweden, was replaced by the new agency Swedish Transport Administration, which took on a greater responsibility for both train and road traffic.

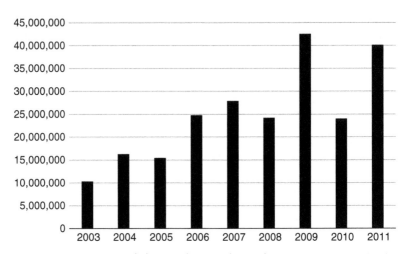

Figure 7.6 Overview of the trend in total spending on PR/communication consultants 2003–2011 in the seven government agencies spending more than SEK 10,000,000

The Swedish Labour Office (*Arbetsmarknadsverket*), in turn, was transformed into a new government agency: The Swedish Employment Office (*Arbetsförmedlingen*).

A second explanation is that PR/communication consultants are hired to *support the internal work* at the agencies. Interestingly, among the largest buyers we find the two central government agencies that are oriented towards supporting the Swedish government and the Riksdag in their work, e.g. by performing analyses and investigations, writing reports, preparing decision materials and enabling communication, as well as collaboration between ministries and administration, namely the government offices and the Riksdag Administration. While the spending on PR/communication consultants increased in the government offices, it has decreased in the Riksdag Administration since 2007.

The use of PR/communication consultants can also be *related to externally or internally initiated events, resulting in a temporary peak*. For instance, in the Swedish Environmental Protection Agency, the peak in the spending in 2008 might be explained by the fact that the agency was preparing information material, analyses and reports for the United Nations' climate meeting in 2009, in addition to Sweden's presidency in the European Union in 2009. Although not explicitly stated in the data, it is possible that PR/communication consultants were hired to assist in this work. Another example is the Swedish Labour Office, which went from spending less than SEK 100,000 per year during 2003–2009 (except in 2006 when it spent SEK 850,000) to spending SEK 26,273,354 in 2011. An explanation for this peak is that in 2008, apart from being transformed into the new agency, the Swedish Employment Office also launched a new information campaign aiming to increase awareness among employers of how individuals with disabilities can contribute to work places. The campaign was created and delivered with the help of the PR consultancy Gullers Group, and included radio, TV, workshops, surveys, interviews, information material and follow-ups.[24] Another example is the Ministry of Foreign Affairs' hiring of Springtime to help arrange Sweden's participation in the World Exhibition in Shanghai 2010.[25]

A fourth explanation is the need for government agencies to make their voice heard, and to *communicate with citizens and other stakeholders*. To do so, they hire PR/communication consultants, to provide information and advice and to prepare materials and campaigns for the agencies. Examples of such agencies are the Swedish Energy Agency (*Statens energimyndighet*) and the Swedish International Development Cooperation Agency (*Styrelsen för internationellt utvecklingsarbete*), which have spent large sums on services from the consultancy Gullers. As described in an interview in Resumé, a Swedish advertising, PR and communication magazine:

I don't find the large numbers [of government agencies' spending on PR/ communication consulting services] strange, I fully understand that the agencies need help to communicate [to the citizens] what they are doing. The agencies' PR spending can be explained by the fact that they have a mission to reach out to the citizens, and the internal resources are not always sufficient. Most of the work is done in-house, and the main part of the external budget is spent on societal information, often related to large infrastructure issues.[26]

---

[24] See www.arbetsformedlingen.se/download/18.4c507a4c135613b5bc1800065 01/1401114892417/sekraften-rapport.pdf.

[25] See www.resume.se/nyheter/artiklar/2013/01/22/nya-ministerns-nota-till-regeringskansliet–19-miljoner/.

[26] Director of the professional association PRECIS, interviewed in *Resumé*, 21 April 2010. See www.resume.se/nyheter/artiklar/2010/04/21/sa-delar-pr-byraerna-pa-statens-kaka/.

However, the media criticized the government agencies' increased use of PR/communication consultants. The main arguments have been that although government agencies should provide neutral and objective information, they are increasingly using PR/communication consultants to form an opinion and engage in public debates:

As the information flow increases, the agencies need to raise their voices to be heard. They use a tone that resembles advertising, but the role of advertising is not to be factual or neutral, the role is to sell. That does not fit well with the mission of the agencies … It is quite problematic when an agency like [The] Swedish Environmental Protection Agency becomes one of the key opinion leaders in the environmental debate. That the state takes over the debate is not exactly what is meant by a democratic debate climate.[27]

7.5.2 *Stable Supplier Relations with PR/Communication Consultancies*

The seven agencies with the largest spending on PR/communication consultants used Gullers in all or almost all of the years from 2003 to 2011, and it was the largest supplier in terms of total spending by the Swedish Labour Office, the Swedish Energy Agency and the Swedish International Development Cooperation Agency.[28] Intellecta Corporate AB was also frequently used, and was the largest supplier in terms of spending for Swedish Railways and the Riksdag Administration.[29] In the Swedish Environmental Protection Agency, Westander Publicitet & Påverkan was the largest supplier (representing 83 per cent of its total spending on PR/communication consultancies), which can be explained by the fact that it was awarded a framework agreement contract in 2005, after having 'strengthened its positioning

---

[27] Researcher in political science, interviewed in *Resumé*, 21 April 2010. See www .resume.se/nyheter/artiklar/2010/04/21/sa-delar-pr-byraerna-pa-statens-kaka/.

[28] Gullers represented 98 per cent of the Swedish Labour Office's total spending on PR/communication consultancies, 46 per cent of the Swedish Energy Agency's total spending on PR/communication consultancies and 95 per cent of the Swedish International Development Cooperation Agency's total spending on PR/communication consultancies.

[29] Intellecta Corporate AB represented 65 per cent of the Swedish Railways' total spending on PR/communication consultancies, and 84 per cent of the Riksdag Administration's total spending on PR/communication consultancies.

in lobbying related to climate and energy issues'.[30] Lastly, in the government offices, Springtime was the largest supplier (representing 35 per cent of its total spending on PR/communication consultancies in the 2003–2011 period), although it was used sporadically (see Table 7.7).

A similar pattern can be found in the group of agencies with total spending ranging from SEK 1,000,000 to SEK 10,000,000 (see Table 7.8). In this group, we find a mix of medium- to large-sized government agencies, as well as Sweden's largest universities. Among them, all but four used Gullers, and Gullers was also the consultancy with the largest total spending from 2003 to 2011 in nine of the agencies, followed by Kreab, Prime and Westander (in four agencies each).

This is also the case in the third group, which includes agencies with a total spending of between SEK 100,000 and SEK 1,000,000 from 2003 to 2011. In this group, we find a mix of smaller and local government agencies, such as the Swedish Consumer Agency (*Konsumentverket*) and the National Property Board of Sweden, as well as very large and highly specialized agencies, such as the Swedish Prison and Probation Service and the Swedish Armed Forces, both having more than 10,000 employees. Gullers is used in all but six agencies and is the most frequent, and the largest, supplier among the hired consultancies (in 10 out of 22 agencies) (see Table 7.9).

Finally, in the fourth group, which includes agencies with a total spending of between SEK 0 and SEK 1,000,000, we find smaller and very local universities, as well as highly specialized government agencies. Among these 15 agencies, nine used Gullers as their only or as one of two suppliers, and no agency used more than three suppliers in total over the studied time period (see Table 7.10).

7.5.3 Dominance of Large Suppliers

As illustrated above, a large proportion of the government agencies has tended to rely on one or two larger suppliers of PR/communication consulting services over time. Of them, Gullers stand out as the most commonly hired PR/communication consultancy. Interestingly, Gullers does not provide detailed information about its history or

---

[30] See www.westander.se/press/pressmeddelanden/naturvardsverket-skriver-ramavtal-med-westander/.

Table 7.7 Overview of the most consistently used suppliers (including only those suppliers used in at least six out of the nine studied years), in the seven government agencies with largest spending on PR/communication consulting services

Agency	2003	2004	2005	2006	2007	2008	2009	2010	2011
Swedish Labour Office	Gullers							Gullers	
Swedish Railways	Gullers								n/a
Swedish Environmental Protection Agency	Intellecta Corporate AB				–	Gullers			
Government Offices		n/a	Westander Publicitet & Påverkan AB	Gullers		Intellecta Corporate AB			
The Riksdag Administration	Gullers	Intellecta Corporate AB		–	Gullers				
Swedish Energy Agency	Gullers		–	Kreab					
Swedish International Development Cooperation Agency	Gullers							–	

Table 7.8 *Overview of the government agencies' spending between SEK 1,000,000 and SEK 10,000,000 in total on PR/communication consulting services in the 2003–2011 time frame*

Government Agency	Total Spending 2003–2011, in SEK	COFOG	Supplier with Largest Share of Spending	%
Swedish Transport Administration	7,831,705	4	Intellecta Corporate	40
National Board of Health and Welfare	7,746,819	4	Gullers	94
Swedish Road Administration	7,154,232	4	Prime	43
The Swedish Fortifications Agency	6,603,576	1	Gullers	95
The Swedish Mapping, Cadastral and Land Registration Authority	6,600,089	4	Gullers	58
The Swedish National Grid for Electricity	6,095,562	5	Kreab	93
Swedish Civil Contingencies Agency	5,856,396	4	Gullers	50
The Civil Aviation Authority	4,572,219	4	Burson-Marsteller AB	38
Royal Institute of Technology	4,202,871	9.4	Intellecta Corporate	75
Swedish Rescue Services Agency	3,785,619	2	Westander	98
Swedish National Agency for Education	2,775,358	9	Gullers	51
Stockholm University	2,763,698	9.4	Gullers	84
Karolinska Institutet	2,582,187	9.4	Cohn & Wolfe Stockholm AB	18
Swedish Board of Student Finance	2,321,589	9	Gullers	100
Swedish Board of Agriculture	2,266,062	4	Gullers	91

Table 7.8 (*cont.*)

Government Agency	Total Spending 2003–2011, in SEK	COFOG	Supplier with Largest Share of Spending	%
Uppsala University	2,238,555	9.4	JKL	47
Swedish Tax Authority	1,986,575	1	Publik Kommunikation	42
Swedish Defence Material Administration	1,763,653	2	Halvarson & Hallvarson	78
Lund University	1,602,609	9.4	Kreab	80
Swedish Work Environment Authority	1,595,663	10	Intellecta Corporate	62
Swedish Social Insurance Agency	1,581,610	10	Prime	90
Swedish Defence Research Agency	1,407,625	2	Gullers	89
Örebro University	1,392,856	9.4	Westander	97
Göteborgs University	1,236,646	9.4	JKL	91
Swedish Prosecution Authority	1,218,730	3	Gullers	84

Table 7.9 *Overview of the government agencies' spending between SEK 100,000 and 1,000,000 in total on PR/communication consulting services in the 2003–2011 period*

Government Agency	Total Spending 2003–2011, in SEK	COFOG	Supplier with Largest Share of Spending	%
County Administrative Board of Stockholm	926,539	1	Prime	51
Swedish Prison and Probation Service	593,911	3	Publik Kommunikation	79
Swedish Consumer Agency	534,110	1	Gullers	42
Swedish University of Agricultural Sciences	532,602	9.4	Gullers	50
National Property Board of Sweden	527,635	1	Gullers	54
Swedish Work Life Institute	482,555	4	Gullers	100
Swedish Research Council	478,150	9	Gullers	67
Swedish Armed Forces	467,235	2	Geelmuyden.Kiese	85
Swedish Pensions Agency	430,662	1	Publik Kommunikation	100
Swedish Defence Education	408,665	9.4	Gullers	89
Swedish Courts	403,800	3	JKL	87
Linköping University	380,225	9.4	Narva Communications	54
Luleå University of Technology	289,128	9.4	Kreab	52
Swedish Post and Telecom Authority	263,856	4	Gullers	66
Swedish Insurance Administration	206,600	10	Prime	90
Swedish National Financial Management Authority	150,590	1	Gullers	100
Swedish Economic Crime Authority	138,320	1	Cohn & Wolfe	68
University of Gävle	125,264	9.4	Gullers	100
Swedish National Board of Institutional Care	117,150	10	Narva Communications	95
Swedish Migration Agency	113,986	4	Gullers	100
Södertörn University	113,565	9.4	Westander	63
Malmö University	109,780	9.4	Gullers	100

Table 7.10 *Overview of the government agencies spending between SEK 0 and SEK 100,000 in total on PR/communication consulting services in the 2003–2011 time frame*

Government Agency	Total Spending 2003–2011, in SEK	COFOG	Supplier with Largest Share of Spending	%
Karlstad University	75,500	9.4	Cohn & Wolfe	62
Swedish National Debt Office	69,000	1	Kreab	78
Patent- och registreringsverket	62,535	4	Narva Communications	60
Swedish Forest Agency	56,930	4	Gullers	100
County Administrative Board of Skåne län	52,010	1	Gullers	100
County Administrative Board of Västra Götaland	46,920	1	Gullers	74
Mid Sweden University	46,100	9.4	Prime	56
Linné University	20,100	9.4	Gullers	100
Swedish Customs	19,203	1	Prime	100
Swedish Meteorological and Hydrological Institute	18,200	5	Gullers	100
Mälardalen University	18,000	9.4	Cohn & Wolfe	94
Stockholm Institute of Education	12,000	9.4	Gullers	100
University College of Kalmar	7,800	9.4	Westander	100
Växjö University	4,169	9.4	Gullers	100
Statistics Sweden	3,350	1	Gullers	100

organization via their website. The description of its activities given here is instead retrieved from its LinkedIn page.[31] The text illustrates well that Gullers is specialized in working with organizations within the public sector; only at the end of the text are two examples offered, from what could possibly be a mention of the private sector:

[Gullers is] Sweden's leading communication consultancy for societal actors. [We have] offices in Stockholm, Gothenburg, Malmö and Sundsvall. Common for many of our clients is that they are of high societal interest and have complex organizations. The organizations are expected to be neutral, balanced and trustworthy. The organizations form the very core of Swedish democracy and the development of democracy, and often are required to both administer and renew [their work and services]. The societal actors are often part of the top level of the political system. We work with municipalities, regions and organizations, with universities and university colleges, with government agencies and unions, and with leading companies within medical drugs and infrastructure. In order to create creative, clear, relevant and well-functioning communication for societal actors, a specific type of expertise and experience is needed. We have that.

Possible explanations for the government agencies' reliance on large, specialized consultancies such as Gullers are, first, the increased use of framework agreements and, second, that they prefer consultancies that are specialized in opinion-building or issues related to the public sector, and thus have experience and expertise in such areas. The fact that government agencies often work with several PR/communication consultancies, apart from those they have long-standing business relations with, can be explained by a decentralized purchasing behaviour in the larger agencies, so that each region or division can make its own purchases.[32]

A last observation is that the large PR/communication consultants are populated with former prime ministers, members of government and highly experienced politicians. For instance, after having lost the elections, the former Social Democratic prime minister Göran Persson left his position as party leader, and took up a position in JKL.[33] While this has been frequently reported on and criticized in the media, it also indicates that there is a perception among the consultancies that

---

[31] See www.gullers.se and www.linkedin.com/company/82142/.
[32] See www.resume.se/nyheter/artiklar/2010/04/21/sa-delar-pr-byraerna-pa-statens-kaka/.
[33] See www.dn.se/arkiv/nyheter/politiker-da-pr-konsulter-nu/?forceScript=1&variantType=large.

organizations in both the public and private sectors will continue to demand expertise and experience in how to operate and communicate in government agencies.

7.6 Framework Agreements

In the studied time period, government agencies such as the Swedish National Financial Management Authority and the Legal, Financial and Administrative Services Agency started to develop framework agreements with suppliers within management consulting and PR/communication consultants. Although this development took time, not least regarding the learning process in how to formulate the demands and what aspects of the services the agreements should focus on, the use of framework agreements slowly became institutionalized between 2003 and 2011 (see Pemer and Skjolsvik 2017). In the framework agreements, a short description of the type of services was included, as well as a list of the selected suppliers, their price lists and any sub-consultants. The government agencies were supposed to follow and use these agreements, unless they applied for an exception to the Legal, Financial and Administrative Services Agency, for instance.[34]

7.6.1 Framework Agreements for Management Consulting Services

Following a period of preparations, pre-studies and consultations with legal experts, government agency representatives and suppliers, the Legal, Financial and Administrative Services Agency developed three framework agreements for management consulting services. The agreements indicate that management consultants could be hired for three main types of work (see Appendix F for details of the framework agreements):

– Analyses, investigations and pre-studies
– Management and leadership development
– Business and organizational development

---

[34] See www.precis.se/wp-content/uploads/2012/09/DI120912.pdf.

Interestingly, several of the selected preferred suppliers were not among the 100 largest management consultancies (compared with Chapter 2, in which it is found that the UK government's top suppliers of consulting services are large, international consultancies)[35]. While this was criticized by representatives from large consultancies, as well as managers in public organizations, who argued that it was difficult to foresee how the bids would be evaluated and that the 'wrong' suppliers won the contracts, it has also been described as a success, for the ambition within Swedish public procurement was to enable smaller suppliers to also compete for large contracts.

In 2016, the old framework agreements were replaced by new ones, which are currently in use. In these, the descriptions of what the different types of work entail are longer and more elaborate and specific. All selected suppliers but three (IPF AB, Riddarfjärdens Implement AB and Sandahl Partners AB) are on the list of the largest management consultancies in Sweden. This development indicates, first, that the Legal, Financial and Administrative Services Agency has developed new knowledge in how to define the services needed and, second, that the larger consultancies have learned how to bid on the framework agreements. The descriptions of what is included in the different areas of management consulting services also give an illustration of what tasks government agencies might seek external assistance from consultants to perform, which in turn reflects both what kind of challenges they might encounter, and what kind of internal capabilities they have available. In short, the tasks range from assisting the government agencies in managing internally and externally induced change, improving internal management and control, performing follow-ups and evaluations and improving the recruitment, development and retaining of staff, to performing analyses and investigations and preparing decision materials. Interestingly, the new framework agreements tend to be more closely related to fundamental policy matters than the previous ones. While most of their content is still oriented to management policy, the final one (in Appendix F) especially provides examples that relate to fundamental questions of agency purpose and policy. This could indicate a trend towards using framework agreements for hiring consultants to provide input in policy matters. More longitudinal research in the future is warranted to verify this.

[35] See Konsultguiden's ranking lists: www.konsultguiden.se.

7.6.2 Framework Agreements for PR/Communication Consultants

It is also notable that despite the existence of central framework agreements for media and PR/Communication consultants in the studied time period, of which Gullers was one of the selected suppliers, the government agencies did not always adhere to them.[36] There was also a perceived need among the agencies for a framework agreement that did not only focus on media distribution, but also included more strategic advice regarding PR and communication. This is illustrated in the two quotes given below, collected from the Legal, Financial and Administrative Services Agency's pre-study report on media consulting (2017):[37]

I would prefer a framework agreement including for example services like media counseling, crisis management in media and trust crises, media training and communication support in general. (p. 26)

I miss a framework agreement for strategic communication counseling, which includes both counseling in communication and PR, and counseling and production of information and advertising campaigns. (p. 31)

In response, a new framework agreement is being developed by the Legal, Financial and Administrative Services Agency, with the intention of covering both media houses and PR/communication consultants.[38] A number of government agencies are also forming their own framework agreements with consultancies in PR/communication. This can be interpreted as a sign of the increased purchasing maturity in many government agencies, making them less eager to rely on centrally developed agreements. An example of this development is that the government offices recently decided to set up framework agreements with five preferred suppliers. The suppliers will provide analyses and investigations and prepare decision materials used in further investigative and legislative processes, as well as provide strategic advice. One of them is Ramböll Management Consulting, which specializes in assisting government agencies, regions, county councils and municipalities with investigations, evaluations and analyses. In a recent article about

---

[36] See www.precis.se/wp-content/uploads/2012/09/DI120912.pdf.
[37] In Swedish: Kammarkollegiet. Förstudierapport inom medieförmedling. Dnr 23.2–67-2017.
[38] Ibid.

the framework agreement, a manager at the firm explains what services they will deliver to the government offices: 'We are incredibly proud and happy that we, together with our partners, are trusted by the government offices to assist the ministries and state-led investigations with our competences within policy analysis, implementation and management in questions that are highly relevant to society.'[39]

The selected suppliers will work on policy matters related to integration, environment, the job market, business development, digitalization, research and education, societal development, energy and environment, healthcare and social insurance.

7.7 Comparison: Management and PR/Communication Consulting

The analysis herein shows that the spending on both management consulting services and PR/communication consulting services has increased in the studied time period. Although the spending on management consulting services lies on a much higher level than PR/communication consulting services, it is interesting to see how the perceived need to communicate, and also the communication patterns of the studied government agencies, has changed over time. This development might be a reflection of both the need for cost reductions and the need to become more 'business-like' and communicate with 'customers' as well as 'suppliers' in the public sector ecosystem (Denis, Ferlie and Van Gestel 2015; Perl and White 2002).

The reasons consultants are hired vary quite naturally between the two types of services. While management consultants are hired to improve organizational effectiveness and cost reductions, or as extra resources carrying out everyday work practices, PR/communication consultants are hired to communicate with citizens and other stakeholders and for forming opinions. However, other reasons are similar between them. It seems as if organizational changes such as the closing down, merging or starting up of a new agency sparks a need for both management and PR/communication consulting services. It also seems

---

[39] Anna Halvarsson, Business Area Manager Policy and Planning: www .mynewsdesk.com/se/ramboll/pressreleases/regeringskansliet-vaeljer-ramboell-som-leverantoer-2244132

as if both types of consultants are used by the agencies to support their internal work and help in temporary peaks.

The analysis shows that the government agencies tend to use the same purchasing behaviour when it comes to management and PR/communication consulting services. In both cases, the government agencies rely on one or very few suppliers over a long period, such as CGI Sverige and Gullers. These suppliers have a strong focus on the public sector in their businesses and generally stand for one of or even the largest share of the agencies' total spending. The reliance on few, large and well-established firms might be due to risk aversion in the government agencies, as failed projects often attract media attention (Pemer and Skjolsvik 2017), as well as the increased existence of framework agreements. This finding correlates well with the results from Canada, as presented in Chapter 6, showing that a large part of the overall spending is concentrated on a small number of suppliers (see also Howlett and Migone 2014). It is also interesting to see that in contrast to the Netherlands (see Chapter 5), the Swedish government's defence-related agencies were among the top users of management consulting services. Thus, it is possible that the reason consultants are hired is more related to externally driven initiatives, such as reorganizations, cost-saving targets or new technologies, than to the domain of the government agency. More research is needed to shed further light on this issue.

A final observation is that only two agencies are on both lists for the largest buyers of management and PR/communication consulting services: Swedish Railways and the government offices. The analysis also shows that some of the agencies hiring management consultants – such as Dalarna University, the Swedish Board of Agriculture, the Swedish National Board of Institutional Care and the Swedish Maritime Administration – did not use PR/communication consultants in the studied period. Thus, it does not seem to be that a buyer of one type of consulting services is necessarily a buyer of other types of consulting services, too.

7.8 Conclusion

The development in Sweden points in the direction of fewer but larger and relatively independent government agencies. The agencies, in turn, have developed higher levels of purchasing maturity and are now establishing frame agreements with preferred suppliers of consulting services. It is also suggested, based on the analysis presented herein, that the use of consultants may take many different forms, from providing strategic advice, performing analyses, investigations, campaigns and preparing decision materials, to induce and implement organizational changes, new work practices, systems and routines, in order to improve efficiency and reduce costs. Thus, their activities seem to cover all four types of tasks as described by Van den Berg (2017).

It is possible that the identified patterns are linked to the movement in Sweden towards a 'service state' (Butcher, Freyers and Wanna 2009). As discussed in Chapters 1 and 6, characteristic for the 'service state' is the adoption of 'business-like' work practices, ideals of marketization, the corporatization of government agencies and increased contracting-out (Denis, Ferlie and Van Gestel 2015; Perl and White 2002). To meet the demand for new competencies related to the transition towards more 'business-like' government agencies, the managers also need to develop their skills – often with the help of consultants. This would explain the need for government agencies to contract out larger campaigns and investigations, as well as for organizational change and new communication strategies – not least to keep up with the technological developments towards increased digitalization. As described in interview by a Director General:

We have used management consultants to educate our managers in our organization in order to make them better leaders and to be able to communicate better with the employees, and guide them. But also as part of building the whole organization. So that is the type of consultants we have mainly used. We have used communications consultants as well. We have not used any PR consultants. Not yet. But we will, because we are entering a new phase in how we communicate. We have not communicated with society before, only with companies. (DG 3)

Against this background, future research is advised to explore the following in more depth: i) what types of assignments, tasks, and roles the hired consultants are supposed to perform; ii) the effects of digitalization on government agencies and their hiring of consultants; and iii) the organizational context in government agencies. Examples of questions to pursue are: i) why do agencies perceive a need to hire consultants? ii) who are involved in the decision and the selection of suppliers?

iii) what consequences does the use of consultants have for the agency's knowledge development, employees, and supply of resources and expertise? and iv) how is the performance and results of the consulting assignments followed-up and measured in the agencies?

In Sweden, the National Audit Office recently initiated an investigation into the hiring of consulting services, particularly related to management, which will provide new information and answers to these questions. More qualitative and quantitative research is, however, still needed.

8 Conclusion: Policy Consulting in Comparative Perspective

8.1 A Cross-Disciplinary Approach to Policy Consulting

Policy consulting, as pointed out in the Introduction to this book, is an important but under-researched topic in policy studies. Policy consultancy has been a problematic blind spot for scholars, politicians and other commentators who are concerned with the substantive and procedural quality of the policies that shape our societies, and it is a far more important and sizeable component of the work that happens within government than the literature currently acknowledges. However, many questions about the roles and activities of policy consultants remain shrouded in mystery.

Many of these questions are comparative in nature but require nuanced analysis. That is, the use and role of policy consultancy needs to be understood in terms of the political-administrative culture and structures of a given national polity, but the use of policy consultants is unevenly distributed across types of policy organizations and policy sectors.

The chapters in this book provide such analysis and address, among other questions:

– What is the extent of government consulting use and how has that use changed over time?
– What role(s) do consultants play in the public sector and what is their share of expenditures and employment?
– What are the different kinds of public sector consulting and how large are different portions such as management consulting, consulting around ICT issues, and consulting over policy advice? and
– How much of policy consultants' work is procedural in nature versus making recommendations on substantive policy content?

Each chapter aims to bring more conceptual and empirical clarity to the type and extent of policy consultancy in the jurisdiction examined, the role and impact of consultants on public policy found in that country, and the similarities and particularities in the use of policy consulting in and across various countries and political-administrative systems.

This is a cross-disciplinary effort, with studies from fields such as public administration, public management, the policy sciences, comparative politics, the sociology of professions and business administration, among others, brought to bear on the subject. A key central problematic addressed by all the chapters, however, is the impact of consulting and the evaluation of whether this phenomenon has advanced to the point where modern states have become 'consultocracies', or if this is just one part of the more general evolution of the 'contractor state'. The difference is important since consultocracy equals the usurpation of traditional administrators' decision-making power and their ability to influence governments, without the traditional means of accountability of civil servants to elected representatives, while emergence in the 'contractor state' implies a more dispassionate critique of the results and impact of various forms of contracting on public service delivery, without necessarily challenging the very basis of the modern state.

In this concluding chapter we bring together a number of overarching insights and considerations and give an overview of the findings per chapter, followed by the pointers for further research emanating from this study.

8.2 The Central Problematic: Consultocracy versus the Contractor State

The explanations for the emergence of policy and management consulting practices in government and the reasons at its root are varied. Some accounts place consulting within the larger framework of increased contracting out and part-time service delivery in government and see it as part of a more general shift in the overall nature of state–societal relations – away from the 'positive' or 'regulatory' state (Majone 1997) and towards the 'service', 'franchise' or 'competition' state (Butcher et al. 2009; Perl and White 2002; Radcliffe 2010; Bilodeau, Laurin and Vining 2007). This is an approach shared by Hood and Jackson (1991) and the later, more historically inclined analysis of Saint-Martin

(1998b, 2005, 2006), both of whom suggested that rising 'consultoc-racy' led to a weakening of democratic practices and public direction of policy and administrative developments.

Notions of the rise of the so-called franchise state, for example, are centred on the idea that the contemporary 'service state' is based on many more external–internal links in the provision of services – in which con-tracting is the norm in many areas – than the pre–World War II 'autarkic state' which was based on in-house provision of all kinds of services. The primary aim of in-house provision was usually to provide 'consistency, reliability and standardization' in service provision (Butcher et al. 2009: 22) – concerns which have been replaced, it is argued, by 'a hybrid mixture of part public, part private, activities, delivery that does not remain in neat boxes or organizational settings, (with) loose combination of actors and providers who are each necessary to see something delivered' (Butcher et al. 2010: 31). Here, the state is seen as the chief contractor, and variety in the nature of goods and services provided and their provision is seen as neither surprising nor unexpected.

Some scholars have noted that the use of for-hire consultants has extended far beyond public service provision to now play an increasing role in policy-making and organizational management activities within government, and arguably an increasingly influential one (Guttman and Willner 1976; Kipping and Engwall 2003; Martin 1998). Others, however, see the use of consultants in policy-making as a less significant activity linked to the normal development of policy advice systems in modern government, as business groups and others require specialized expertise in their efforts to lobby governments. Government agencies in turn require similar expertise in order to deal with ever-more active businesses, NGOs and other participants in policy-making processes (Halligan 1995; Lahusen 2002). As Lahusen put it:

Consultancies are at the head of a growing professionalization and institu-tionalization of interest intermediation: first, these companies are able to establish themselves successfully beside trade associations; second they are able to expand in terms of staff and national branches; third they successfully provide professional skills and services above and beyond the specific inter-ests or issues to be dealt with, i.e. they possess 'neutral' professional tools to be learned and applied by new managerial staff. (2002: 697)

Czarniawska and Mazza (2003) also suggest that consultants are likely to play a limited role in policy-making, arguing that they are too poorly organized to exercise any kind of permanent policy influence and rely very much on the existence of a variety of appropriate political and institutional characteristics – such as the rise of the service state – in order to exercise any influence at all. This is a view which has been supported by the findings of van Houten and Goldman (1981) and, to a lesser extent, Saint-Martin (1998a and 1998b).

Such dichotomous views cry out for more nuanced analyses (Clark and Fincham 2002), which not only can more accurately assess basic quantitative questions such as how many consultants and contracts there are, and if their numbers have grown over recent decades, but can also carefully examine the qualitative questions around the nature of influence in governments and the role consultants play in it – for instance, from the provision of direct advice to the more indirect creation of specific kinds of knowledge and its mobilization and/or utilization in policy deliberations (Van Helden et al. 2010; Weiss 1977, 1986).

However, as the chapters in this book attest, there has been a continued problem with developing effective policy work variables with which to measure the scope and shape of policy advice within modern public administrations. Lack of thematically and historically comprehensive repositories for contracts at any level of the system have hindered this type of analysis. The default proxies have been drawn mainly from procurement data, which is not designed for this purpose, and surveys, which tend to reach a limited number of respondents and seldom have robust longitudinal dimensions.

8.3 The Role of Consultants in Policy Advisory Systems: Beyond the Two Communities Model

Public policy scholars have long studied the connection between decision-making, policy advice and evidence. One of the threads that runs through the policy literature is the relationship between external experts and public bodies as producers and consumers of knowledge. During the 1970s, scholars focused on research utilization, and the privileged metric was the amount of academic research used by the public service (Caplan 1979; Booth 1990). The image that resulted from these analyses was one of 'two communities', with policy-makers and academics standing as separate and different in their goals, focuses and approaches (Weiss 1979, 1980). The literature also argued that external policy experts had become progressively less relevant in solving social problems by working with governments (Laswell 1970; Howard 2005). At the same time, in the late twentieth century, policy advisory systems and policy-making processes became increasingly complex and multi-layered (Gregory and Lonti 2008; Veselý 2017) and some of the internal logics shifted. As a result, the 'two-communities' notion became empirically less prevalent, partly because it became increasingly common in various countries for academics to become consultants with government, or to enter government for short periods of time (Gunter 2012; Gunter and Mills 2017).

However, in the early twenty-first century this scholarship has evolved considerably in its description and analysis of the field. The 'two communities' metaphor has been abandoned as a much more complex approach to the policy system has been introduced (Howlett and Wellstead 2011; Veselý, Wellstead and Evans 2014; Cherney et al. 2015), where the 'main focus is no longer to improve the uptake of academic research for the sake of research salience; it is now to improve the use of relevant research because it is believed that policy fully informed by research evidence will produce better outcomes for citizens' (Newman and Head 2015b: 384).

Ultimately, the literature acknowledges that policy-making is a complex process, where policy success is a multi-dimensional and – at least in part – political and therefore subjective exercise (Newman 2014). Policy-makers are bounded rational actors who use both rational strategies to reduce empirical uncertainty and irrational ones to reduce political ambiguity. In this environment, multiple actors compete as sources of knowledge and engage over the long-term with policy-makers (Cairney 2016; Cairney, Oliver and Wellstead 2016), and simply supplying policy advice does not ensure that it will be used (Head 2015b). As a result, policy advice exists in a highly contextualized environment (Wesselink and Gouldson 2014), where there is no immediate linear connection between it and policy decisions (Head 2013; Wesselink, Colebatch and Pearce 2014). In reality, political and other considerations mediate between the two, multiple evidence sources add to the 'messiness' of the process and ideal decision-making conditions are about as common as perfect competition.

At least since the 1970s, that focus has shifted towards evidentiary advice, which the literature generally considers desirable and positively correlated with successful implementation. As a result, evidence-based decision-making (EBDM) and policy advice have become common concepts in the effort to analyse and explain the inputs, roles and patterns of activity that exist in the public policy ecosystem.

Notably, by the late 1990s the use of evidence-based advice, fashioned after the approach taken in health care (Boaz et al. 2008), was considered a necessary ingredient of policy-making by the UK's Cabinet Office (1999), and was taking hold there (Boaz et al. 2008), in Canada (Howlett 2009c; Young 2013), Australia (Head 2010), the USA (Hall and Jennings 2010), the European Union (Böhme 2002) and the OECD. At the same time, however, this movement has been at the centre of three major debates in the discipline. The first is a constructivist–rationalist debate on the nature of knowledge. A second involves the historical evolution of the use of knowledge and advice within policy-making environments, including the relationship between policy-makers and knowledge producers. Additionally, various questions hinge on understanding why something like EBDM seems to have had so little measurable effect on actual policy implementation. The third debate has to do with the politics of evidence – that is, who decided what is evidence and what is policy-relevant information (Newman, Cherney and Head 2017; Craft and Halligan 2017)?

With respect to these concerns, a perceptible shift by part of the scholarship and practice towards evidence-informed (as opposed to evidence-based) decision-making (Head 2015b) has occurred. This corrects some issues with the original approach by recognizing that the limited ascertained impact of EBDM on the policy field can be explained by the different information needs and practices of public organizations. Hence, while the instrumental use of knowledge (where knowledge is used to directly solve a social problem) may be theoretically desirable, it is likely that both conceptual (to generate ideas that affect an issue over longer periods) and political (to rationalize previously chosen policy) uses will be rather common within political environments (Daviter 2015). This is especially so if these political environments underwent a process of 'procedural politicization' (Eichbaum and Shaw 2008: 343). Furthermore, both the rigorous methodological and resource premises required by evidence-based policy advice (Head 2015b; Howlett and Craft 2013) and the availability of practical elements, such as the capacity of the public service to understand evidence (Newman, Cherney and Head 2017) and process it into policy (Howlett 2015), are now seen as critical components affecting the success of any evidence-based or evidence-informed approach. In practice, the careful assessment of the connections between policy advice and policy outcomes that has been at the core of a large part of the recent literature has partially shifted the focus of inquiry from 'what works' to the 'best available evidence'.

The focus on so-called evidence-based policy-making, which in most western countries became truly en vogue in the mid-1990s, required researchers to get on board with policy, where government actors commission large numbers of projects to support and evaluate policy. One of the results of this was a type of resource–exchange relationship between ministers and their civil servants on the one hand, and academics, business, philanthropy and consultancy firms on the other. Ministers and civil servants need the knowledge to legitimize policy, and the knowledge providers needed the status, acclaim and funding from contractual exchange relationships (see Gunter 2012).

The second issue existing in the literature surrounding policy advice and knowledge is how can we explain what appears to be a minimal impact of evidence on the actual process of policy-making (Head 2010, 2015b; Corbett and Bogenschneider 2011; Cartwright and Hardie 2012; John 2013; Watts 2014; Newman 2016), even as both the literature and folk wisdom underscore its relevance and there is a substantial body of literature arguing for its use (Head 2013; Howlett and Wellstead 2011)? Attempts at explaining these underwhelming results rely on four arguments. The *political use of evidence* reduces the effectiveness of the process – for example, through biased selection of information and goals (Weiss 1979; Head 2013; Knaggård 2014). The existence of *multiple potential interpretations of evidence* (Watts 2014), especially in social policy fields and with *existing cultural differences* between those who produce evidence and those who use it, both affect the process (Mead 2015). The *poorly and/or broadly defined policy objectives* often associated with complex policy areas can reduce the effectiveness of EBDM (Newman and Head 2015; Head 2015b). Finally, the possibility that *public service personnel and organizations may be unprepared to deal effectively with diverse forms of evidence* is noted as a further potential dampening effect (Howlett 2015; Newman, Cherney and Head 2017). In addition, decision-makers in government may be resistant to evidence. For ideological, political–strategic, financial or personal reasons, ministers and civil servants may decide on policy measures that run counter to available evidence (Gorard 2018; Gunter 2018).

As for the third concern, the main subject of the chapters in this book, the use of knowledge in policy-making has led to an increase in discussions about the sources of that knowledge, its connection with established power relations and its potential applications. This work begins from the recognition that multiple communities are engaged in the policy-making ecosystem and in the production, distribution and use of knowledge within it. These communities differ in terms of values, internal logics and structures (Veselý 2017), as well as across jurisdictions (Craft and Halligan 2017).

Historically, these relationships among these actors were originally studied through locational models where influence depended on whether they produced, consumed or brokered advice and knowledge (Clark and Jones 1999; Howlett 2011; Cappe 2011). These models tended to be unidimensional, focusing on government knowledge uptake (Craft and Halligan 2017). However, over time increasing attention was paid to processes of externalization, which created intense competition in the supply of advice, and to the manner in which advisory processes have evolved over time (Savoie 2015; Weller 2015), where administrators increasingly became more engaged in 'the politics of policy advice' (Halligan 1995: 160). If Wildavsky (1979) focused on 'speaking truth to power', later authors found 'weaving' (Parsons 2004) or 'sharing truth with many actors of influence' (Prince 2007: 179) closer to the reality of policy advice. In short, much more attention is now paid to 'the configuration, operation and dynamics of *policy advisory systems*' (Craft and Halligan 2017: 57) than was the case in the past, including the role of outside consultants within it. The identification of government regimes of practice (Gunter 2012) means that the label 'consultant' and the process of consultancy are no longer the sole preserve of those who are directly employed as consultants in consultancy firms. This underlines the necessity to be aware of the stretching of the terminology and the activity of non-formal consultants as consultants.

8.4 Methodological and Data Limitations in Researching Policy Consultants

Concerns about the use of consultants in government are not recent. However, current concerns are not just about the size and number of consultancies, but also about their *apparent growth* as both a percentage of government employees and expenditures and concomitantly about their *increased influence* and impact on the content and direction of government decision-making.

As the chapters in this book highlight, both policy and management consultants can be seen as either independent 'agents of change' or as weak, 'liminal' subjects, dependent for any potential influence on allowances made for this by their employers. While such dichotomous views should be easily resolvable through empirical analyses of quantitative questions, such as how many consultants there are and whether these numbers have grown over time, and of qualitative questions around the nature of their influence on governments, from the provision of direct advice to the more indirect creation of specific kinds of knowledge and its mobilization/utilization in policy deliberations, several significant methodological and data problems stand in the way of clarifying this debate.

First, in many jurisdictions (including the most developed states examined in this book) data is limited or of poor quality. In many cases, data on contracts and contract purposes and sizes does not exist or exists for only a few years, and often is not standardized. In particular, as each chapter has detailed, in many cases it has proven almost impossible to separate 'policy consulting' from other categories such as engineering or technical services consulting as well as from 'management consulting' – the category often used to capture policy consulting in official government reports and documents. Second, not only are policy 'consulting' activities difficult to distinguish, it is often difficult in official statistics to distinguish 'consultants' from 'temporary and part-time workers' within government, meaning any data that does exist on 'external' contracting may underestimate the size and extent of the central variable. Third, notwithstanding this quantitative concern, it is also difficult to determine extent of *policy* influence consultants enjoy.

Nevertheless, despite these problems, each chapter has aimed to shed as much light as possible on the study of the 'invisible public service' in the six jurisdictions examined. The authors apply a definition of policy consultancy that isolates the policy roles consultants fulfil from other categories of consulting and based on the six country cases, assess consulting growth and expenditures per country (and per policy sector). In so doing, they help explain the role of policy consultants in the marketplace for policies, ideas and information, and shed theoretical light on the circumstances under which core actors are more likely to rely on policy consultants than on within-system advisers, and under what circumstances policy consultants may influence or shape policies' content. Each chapter describes the variation in different countries' overall political-administrative systems and, related to it, their policy advisory systems and the role(s) played by consultants within them, and defines and demarcates the range of consultants to be examined in the study.

Each country-level chapter categorizes consulting activities identified by the stages of the policy cycle (such as policy analysis, preparation, evaluation) and related to the professional disciplines and fields of activity in which consultants are commonly deployed. Focusing on the central government level, the chapters address possible reasons for consultants' employment including:

- legitimizing proposed courses of action
- helping develop ideas on how to proceed
- cleaning up after scandals
- reviewing agencies/programmes
- providing external feedback on government performance and
- creating wiggle room for politicians facing difficult challenges.

8.5 Findings from Our Country Studies

8.5.1 *The United Kingdom*

Consultants in the UK were found to be major providers of costly services as a means of modernizing knowledge production for public policy. However, the concerns are that while spending on policy consultants is discretionary, the civil service itself was found to be 'like an addict hooked on consultancy' (Shah, 2016). Therefore, consulting costs soared even though civil service numbers declined.

Furthermore, evidence presented in the chapter demonstrates that consultants' problem-solving expertise may actually be a problem in itself, with concerns over conflicts of interest and the promotion of fads at the expense of professional expertise, as well as how reforms may not be in the public interest. Value for money regarding control and deployment of consultants continues to be raised alongside wider concerns about democratic accountability.

Three trends in particular stand out in the UK:

1) Concerns about the role of the government as client and contractor, or how those in government are active participants in the construction of knowledge.
2) How inefficiencies and a failure to evaluate the contribution by consultants may be generated by political turf-wars between departments in Whitehall (e.g. Brexit).
3) How central to the management processes underpinning public policy are arguments for the more active use, capacity building and development of in-house civil servants.

In summary, while the formal contracting of external consultants has been part of the modernization of 'club government' dominated by elite civil servants, it remains the case that knowledge production for and within public policy remains in the control of government, where ideology and party politics continue to dominate.

8.5.2 The United States

In the United States, the situation is much the same. In 2011, the GAO found a 44 per cent increase in professional/management support services contracts between 2005 and 2010, and found that 'more than half of the 230 statements of work for professional and management support service contracts requested services that closely support the performance of inherently governmental functions' (GAO 2011), thereby threatening to undermine at least some aspects of their provision.

Secondary data from the GAO (2011) indicates an increase from 2005 to 2010; in the years where Service Contract Inventories were available for analysis (2010–2015), all these units saw relative declines, not increases, in their purchasing of such services in the final years of the Obama administration. Most GAO reviews do not make an explicit distinction for policy consulting services, however, as most of the research has either looked at consulting services generally, or at management consulting specifically, as well as its effects on the organization and administration of government. However, defining policy consulting is not easy using available US statistics, and it is also the case that management consultancy firms often offer policy-related services, meaning it is difficult to be definitive about trends in administrative activities often performed by consultants.

It is also the case in the USA that the picture varies by different units of government. Contrary to much anecdotal evidence, policy services contracting in most main-line ministries of US government has stagnated since 2012, peaking in 2014 for most agencies and dropping in 2015. The weight of consulting for policy services varies from agency to agency, but remains below 20 per cent of the services listed in the inventories. The Department of Defence, however, is an outlier in many respects and needs to be examined separately. Even here, though, total obligated USD by the DoD on selected codes has also decreased every year from 2012 to 2015, with the drop in total USD obligated for the contracts coded driven by a decrease in programme management and support services. And this picture is very different from that found among the many other FAIR Act agencies which comprise the US government. There, the picture is highly variable and distinct trends are difficult to discern.

8.5.3 Australia

In Australia, the role of external consultants and contractors in public policy and administration was stimulated by two wider strategic developments from the early 1980s; both involved a lessening in the role of the tenured bureaucracy. The first was a successful push by the major parties to lever a shift in power from the appointed bureaucracy to the political executive; the second was a push, extending well beyond the leadership of the political parties, to open the bureaucracy to management techniques and competition practices ascribed to the private sector. From the mid-to-late 1980s the use of consultants as an alternative to in-house staff gained media attention, often anecdotal and unfavourable. This was not matched, however, by systematic academic scholarship. To help address this gap, Chapter 4 undertook a quantitative analysis of publicly listed summary information on consultancies and, for reasons explained, other contracts let by the national government during the past three decades. For the years prior to 1997, information could only be collated for 'consultancies'; for the years after 1997, however, the chapter was able to access data on all contracts, since this information had become much easier to collate since 2015. A massive contrast was confirmed for the past two to three decades: large, long-term increases in spending in real terms on consultancies and other contracts, but reduction in in-house staffing levels and related spending.

The chapter focuses on contracts that had the hallmarks of policy relevance. By manually analysing the summary description of consultancies listed by department in the first six years of mandatory reporting (1987–1993), the chapter found that just over half of total spending was taken up with consultancies oriented to research and review of substantive programme content, with the balance devoted to review of programme administration and corporate services. For contracts for the years 1997–2017, the chapter undertook computer rather than manual searching, using keywords relevant to policy activity. In this, it drew on three fields in the databases – the 'description' of the contract, its 'product and service code' and the title of the Division and Branch of the agency letting the contract. Sixteen searches were undertaken, plus two 'composite' searches: in all but one of these searches, spending in real terms was very significantly, and often multiple times, higher in the decade after 2007 compared to the decade before.

The chapter also reported on the demand and supply composition of spending on consultancies in the 'take-off' years and on those policy-related contracts identified through the keyword searches for 1997–2017. The government-wide pattern of increased spending on these projects was found to encompass all departments. Taking into account changing names and boundaries, most departments did increase their annual spending more often than not; where there was a decrease in a particular year, it was sometimes in the wake of an abnormally large, multi-year contract in the preceding year. At the same time there was variation in the amount of 'absolute' spending amongst departments, with a three-tier pattern emerging in both the 'take-off' 1987–1993 period and in the two decades before and after 2007. Whether there was a similar variation in spending relative to spending on in-house staff is a different matter; research for 1997–1993, for which years data was more readily available, indicates much less variation. A major finding was the standout spending of the Defence Department throughout the whole period. Nonetheless, the relative share of this department was significantly lower during 2007–2017 than in the decade prior; and in both decades, Defence's share of spending was significantly lower for contracts identified through some keywords, such as 'policy' and 'evaluation'.

On the supply side, a consistent pattern was a high and rising degree of concentration in the distribution of spending amongst suppliers. Supplier names were used for the 1987–1993 period, while the ABN

(Australian Business Number) was used to measure, more precisely, supplier shares for the years 1997–2017. Across almost all of the sixteen keyword searches, the share of the top 1 per cent of ABNs (ranked by income) during 1997–2007 fell within the range 30–70 per cent, while for 1997–2017 the corresponding figures were generally higher still. When all contracts identified through the searches of 1997–2017 were counted, the share of the top 1 per cent of ABNs was 76 per cent; when two searches perhaps less relevant to policy were excluded, the share was still 64 per cent. Using the same two composite searches, the top 10 ABNs, ranked by income, received 28 per cent and 24 per cent of total spending across the Commonwealth government. At the same time, for those fearful of concentration and a commercial monopoly of the contract market, a somewhat more consoling, if secondary, pattern emerged. While non-commercial and 'not-for-profit' entities received less income than commercial entities across all types of consultancies and contracts examined, their share was distinctly higher, and quite significant, for consultancies and contracts bearing the most plausible hallmarks of policy relevance. This was true for both 1987–1993 and 1997–2017.

Nonetheless, the pattern of a rising spending by all departments flowing disproportionately to a relatively small number of firms points to a structural shift in the programme development process in Australia. While the biggest earners, such as Broadspectrum Pty Ltd and Serco Pty Ltd, are known primarily as facility and services management firms, the scale of their operations within programmes give such players potential leverage over policy decisions. The same is even truer for the Big Four accountancy-consulting firms, since their prominent and rising share of contract income is based on an unambiguously broader range of functions. Moreover, the potential influence of these players is compounded by their involvement as consultants and contractors to private sector entities, their involvement in lobbying by various business peaks and their donations to the political parties. Just how far their influence has grown relative to more long-standing companies and institutions is a matter warranting priority qualitative research.

8.5.4 Canada

The study of government procurement of policy advice in Canada shows that between 1981 and 2000 there was absolute growth in government-wide expenditures on professional services matched by the growth of consulting as a share of total government expenditures. Although the study encountered long-standing data issues (described in more detail below), it showed a predominance of consulting work as part of 'firefighting' approaches to policy-making and highlighted the relevance of process expertise as opposed to subject-matter expertise.

The data issues encountered, however, were severe. First, no data at all was found on the situation in the powerful Canadian provincial governments who handle major areas of government activity such as healthcare, welfare and environmental protection. Second, although some recent developments have provided better and more standardized data on the Canadian federal government, there remain long-standing problems related to separating consultants hired for IT or management, for example, or for actual policy advice, and current data often does not cover smaller contracts while blending policy-related work with other (vague) activities. And, in most cases, reporting matters are often left up to individual units, meaning it is difficult to compare data across units.

While the continuing absence of data at the provincial level is worrisome, at the federal level it is possible to arrive at a reasonable estimation of federal expenditures. These figures show the distribution of awards highly skewed in terms of end user departments, with a handful of departments accounting for the majority of the awards – and the same goes for the concentration of large contracting sums within a small number of companies. This supports the notion of consultants representing an 'invisible civil service' with a more or less permanent and fixed character largely escaping traditional reporting and accountability measures, while the oligopolistic nature of the supply chain needs to be further explored.

8.5.5 The Netherlands

Our study of the Netherlands explored the practice of deploying temporary external staff by central government. The Netherlands is a noteworthy case in the sense that, on the one hand, it has been known for the openness of its policy system and the high usage of external staff, in ways comparable to the United States and Australia. On the other hand, however, it is markedly different from the Anglo set of countries, as it is characterized by a consensus-driven policy-making style and a neo-corporatist policy advisory system. The analysis shows that externally hired staff was long seen as the strength of the system, demonstrating leanness and adaptability and securing the capacity to take in new ideas and practices from the outside world. Only in recent years has there been a substantive parliamentary debate on the proportions and costs of external hiring.

To understand the nature of external hiring in the Netherlands it is necessary to distinguish between two types: a) outsourcing, or the external procurement of policy activities, leading up to the delivery of a given product; and b) external hiring, where external personnel capacity and expertise is deployed within the organization, under direct supervision of the commissioning public organization. For outsourcing, no systematic aggregate data are available; for external hiring, there are. Survey data indicate that consultants who deliver outsourced policy products have usually specialized in policy consultancy for the government, and that most of the outsourced tasks indeed involve policy advice and process support, where policy implementation and policy evaluation are also important but slightly less-sought activities. For external hiring, systematic data are available, which indicate that the large majority of temporary staff is deployed for operational and implementation activities, and mostly in implementation agencies such as the tax service and public works. As to the distribution of external hiring across ministerial departments, the high-using category consists of the Ministry of Justice and Security, the Ministry of Infrastructure and the Environment and the Ministry of Finance. The moderate users are the Ministry of Defense, the Ministry of the Interior and the Ministry of Economic Affairs, followed by a larger group of low-using departments: the Ministry of Health, the Ministry of Education, Foreign Affairs, Social Affairs and the Prime Minister's Office.

Over the period 2007–2016, the volume of externally hired capacity has remained stable at a high level, while organizational and policy advice, which was substantial before the crisis, dropped from 2010, and was not to recover in the remainder of the period studied. By contrast, external hiring in the field of ICT support grew steadily in the period from 2007 and was therefore not affected by the crisis. A final finding of this exploration is that the volumes of external hiring per ministerial department seem to evolve over the years relatively independently from the changes in the size of the permanent civil service apparatus. No support was found for either the 'communicat-ing vessels' or the 'co-varying volumes' hypothesis.

All in all, the findings give some valuable insights into the Dutch practice of externally hired policy work. However, the full availability of systematic data on the hiring and precise activities of external con-sultants will be necessary to gain a clearer and more fine-grained picture of the state of consultocracy in the Netherlands.

8.5.6 Sweden

Policy-making in Sweden has often been characterized as a rational, matter-of-fact process built on consensus and a low degree of conflict. This image builds on three specific features of Swedish policy-making:

- Sweden has a history of minority governments, which has given the Riksdag a stronger position in the policy-making process than in typical Westminster-type democracies, and has also fostered a culture of compromise-seeking
- the corporatist policy-making style has traditionally enabled labour market organizations and interest organizations to influence policies
- all policy proposals are analysed by a commission of inquiry before being sent to private and public organizations for referral. These commissions have traditionally been large and included representa-tives from different societal spheres, such as NGOs, political parties, researchers and private organizations. The representatives have taken on the roles of members and experts, and participated in the commissions' analyses and discussions.

Collective decision-making is based on a joint preparation and drafting procedure involving all relevant ministries.

Historically, the institutionalized involvement of interest representa-tion in all stages of the policy-making process has been very strong. In recent decades, however, this involvement has weakened, and the organized interests increasingly use other channels, such as lobbying and the media.

The development in Sweden points in the direction of fewer, but larger, quite independent government agencies. These agencies, in turn, have developed higher levels of purchasing maturity and are now establishing frame agreements with preferred suppliers of consulting services.

These patterns are linked to the development of Sweden towards a 'service state' (characteristic for the 'service state' is the adoption of 'business-like' work practices, ideals of marketization, the corporatization of government agencies and increased contracting out). To meet the demand for new competencies related to the transition towards more 'business-like' government agencies, the managers also need to develop their skills – often with the help of consultants. This explains the need for government agencies to contract out larger campaigns and investigations, as well as for organizational change and new communication strategies.

Future research is advised to explore the following in more depth:

1) what types of assignments, tasks and roles the hired consultants are supposed to perform;
2) the effects of digitalization on government agencies and their hiring of consultants;
3) the organizational context in government agencies.

8.6 Avenues for Further Research

All of these country studies demonstrate the use of policy consultants in line with the *contractor state*, in the sense that central government is using externally hired policy professionals on a considerable scale, and the extent to which this is practised has grown over recent decades. The economic crisis that started in 2008 did something to bring the volumes of externally hired policy consultancy down, but not as much as might be expected; also, the effect seems to have been temporary. In addition, increased flexibility in the labour market at the system level, and in career trajectories at the individual level, have in all countries relaxed the binary conception that strictly separates internal civil servants from external policy consultants. Hybrid types of positions and the more frequent occurrence of career switches from internal to external, and vice versa, have made this distinctive markedly less significant than a few decades ago.

On the question of *consultocracy*, the picture is less clear. On the one hand, is the role of policy consultants in the making, implementing and evaluation of policies present in the large majority of sectors in all countries? On the other hand, the available data do not enable us to assess to what extent external policy professionals are competitors of or replacements for internal policy advisers (public servants), so ascertaining the degree to which policy consultancy is diminishing the 'public' in 'public policy' generally across sectors, and across systems, is an issue that needs substantial further investigation.

What we take away from the country studies is that explanations for the use of policy consultants are multiple and interrelated, ranging from *economic* factors (the economic tide and budgetary room at a given point in time) to *political* factors (a prevalent political ideology of a small and/or flexible government, a cap or free pass that parliament gives on using temporary external staff, but also other political reasons why it is opportune in certain situations to not rely on internal staff, such as mistrust of the civil service by political leadership, or the specific value of independent outsiders advising on or monitoring policy or policy performance). The last major cluster of factors has to do with the *policy field* itself, such as the substantive nature of the policy field, the structural organization of the policy sector and whether the sector's focus of activity is more active, producing service providing on the one hand, or regulatory and enforcing on the other hand.

The next steps in this interdisciplinary line of research can be divided into within-country and across-country avenues. Within countries, we can distinguish between conceptual and empirical questions. The conceptual questions are centred on the development of dominant ideas about policy work in a given system into analytical concepts. To what extent is policy work in a specific system seen as the monopoly of government agencies and their public servants, and to what extent can policy work be contracted out and still be widely accepted as a publicly and democratically legitimized course for action? What cultural, institutional and other factors determine this normative framework for a given system? Empirically, the present frontier is, first, clearly the availability of systematic, comparable, cross-time and cross-sectoral data about the use of policy consultants. While we mostly have had to rely on procurement data, richer and more focused data are necessary to ascertain the type of policy work carried out by external consultants and its variation across time, policy sectors and government organization types. Second, the set of questions around impact come to the fore. How far does the influence of policy consultants reach, ranging from providing non-committal advice to actually taking policy decisions and writing legislative texts? Under what circumstances is this influence greater than others?

Concerning avenues for further cross-national comparative research (which includes the use of policy consultants in intergovernmental organizations and other types of international policy-making organizations), the primary frontier is the harmonization of definitions and terms surrounding policy consultancy. Our country studies show that they vary greatly from system to system, making systemic international comparisons still relatively challenging. In addition, particularly when it comes to the use of policy consultants cross-nationally, a widening of the range of studied countries is desirable. While our study includes both countries from the set of Anglo-Saxon majoritarian countries and of Continental European consensus-systems, important new insights are to be expected from the extension of this research to countries with a more statist orientation, such as the Napoleonic-inspired systems in south-western Europe, but also non-Western advanced economies such as Japan and South-Korea as well as middle- and lower-income countries. Enhanced and further conceptualized sensitivity towards differing economic circumstances and political-administrative cultures will further deepen our understanding of how the institutional framework is driving or constraining both the contractor state and consultocracy.

Appendix A

COFOG (Classification of the Functions of Government)

- <u>01</u> – General public services
  - <u>01.1</u> – Executive and legislative organs, financial and fiscal affairs, external affairs
  - <u>01.2</u> – Foreign economic aid
  - <u>01.3</u> – General services
  - <u>01.4</u> – Basic research
  - <u>01.5</u> – R&D General public services
  - <u>01.6</u> – General public services n.e.c.
  - <u>01.7</u> – Public debt transactions
  - <u>01.8</u> – Transfers of a general character between different levels of government
- <u>02</u> – Defence
  - <u>02.1</u> – Military defence
  - <u>02.2</u> – Civil defence
  - <u>02.3</u> – Foreign military aid
  - <u>02.4</u> – R&D Defence
  - <u>02.5</u> – Defence n.e.c.
- <u>03</u> – Public order and safety
  - <u>03.1</u> – Police services
  - <u>03.2</u> – Fire-protection services
  - <u>03.3</u> – Law courts
  - <u>03.4</u> – Prisons
  - <u>03.5</u> – R&D Public order and safety
  - <u>03.6</u> – Public order and safety n.e.c.
- <u>04</u> – Economic affairs
  - <u>04.1</u> – General economic, commercial and labour affairs
  - <u>04.2</u> – Agriculture, forestry, fishing and hunting
  - <u>04.3</u> – Fuel and energy
  - <u>04.4</u> – Mining, manufacturing and construction
  - <u>04.5</u> – Transport
  - <u>04.6</u> – Communication
  - <u>04.7</u> – Other industries

- 04.8 – R&D Economic affairs
- 04.9 – Economic affairs n.e.c.
- 05 – Environmental protection
  - 05.1 – Waste management
  - 05.2 – Waste water management
  - 05.3 – Pollution abatement
  - 05.4 – Protection of biodiversity and landscape
  - 05.5 – R&D Environmental protection
  - 05.6 – Environmental protection n.e.c.
- 06 – Housing and community amenities
  - 06.1 – Housing development
  - 06.2 – Community development
  - 06.3 – Water supply
  - 06.4 – Street lighting
  - 06.5 – R&D Housing and community amenities
  - 06.6 – Housing and community amenities n.e.c.
- 07 – Health
  - 07.1 – Medical products, appliances and equipment
  - 07.2 – Outpatient services
  - 07.3 – Hospital services
  - 07.4 – Public health services
  - 07.5 – R&D Health
  - 07.6 – Health n.e.c.
- 08 – Recreation, culture and religion
  - 08.1 – Recreational and sporting services
  - 08.2 – Cultural services
  - 08.3 – Broadcasting and publishing services
  - 08.4 – Religious and other community services
  - 08.5 – R&D Recreation, culture and religion
  - 08.6 – Recreation, culture and religion n.e.c.
- 09 – Education
  - 09.1 – Pre-primary and primary education
  - 09.2 – Secondary education
  - 09.3 – Post-secondary non-tertiary education
  - 09.4 – Tertiary education
  - 09.5 – Education not definable by level
  - 09.6 – Subsidiary services to education

- <u>09.7</u> – R&D Education
- <u>09.8</u> – Education n.e.c.

- <u>10</u> – Social protection
  - <u>10.1</u> – Sickness and disability
  - <u>10.2</u> – Old age
  - <u>10.3</u> – Survivors
  - <u>10.4</u> – Family and children
  - <u>10.5</u> – Unemployment
  - <u>10.6</u> – Housing
  - <u>10.7</u> – Social exclusion n.e.c.
  - <u>10.8</u> – R&D Social protection
  - <u>10.9</u> – Social protection n.e.c.

Appendix B

List of the studied government agencies, with names in English and Swedish and COFOG classifications.

Swedish	English	COFOG
Arbetslivsinstitutet	The Swedish Work Life Institute	4
Arbetsmarknadsverket	The Swedish Labour Office	10
Arbetsmiljöverket	The Swedish Work Environment Authority	10
Banverket	Swedish Railways	4
Centrala studiestödsnämnden	The Swedish Board of Student Finance	9
Ekobrottsmyndigheten	The Swedish Economic Crime Authority	1
Ekonomistyrningsverket	The Swedish National Financial Management Authority	1
Fortifikationsverket	The Swedish Fortifications Agency	1
Försvarets materielverk	The Swedish Defence Material Administration	2
Försvarshögskolan	Swedish Defence Education	9.4
Försvarsmakten	The Swedish Armed Forces	2
Försäkringskassan	The Swedish Social Insurance Agency	10
Göteborgs Universitet	University of Gothenburg	9.4
Högskolan i Dalarna	Dalarna University	9.4
Högskolan i Gävle	University of Gävle	9.4
Högskolan i Kalmar	University College of Kalmar	9.4
Karlstad Universitet	Karlstad University	9.4
Karolinska institutet	Karolinska institutet	9.4
Konsumentverket	The Swedish Consumer Agency	1
Kriminalvården	The Swedish Prison and Probation Service	3

(*cont.*)

Swedish	English	COFOG
Kungliga tekniska högskolan	Royal Academy of Technology	9.4
Kustbevakningen	The Swedish Coast Guard	3
Lantmäteriverket	The Swedish Mapping, Cadastral and Land Registration Authority	4
Linköpings universitet	Linköping University	9.4
Linnéuniversitetet	Linné University	9.4
Luftfartsverket	The Civil Aviation Authority	4
Luleå tekniska högskola	Luleå University of Technology	9.4
Lunds universitet	Lund University	9.4
Länsstyrelsen i Skåne län	The County Administrative Board of Skåne	1
Länsstyrelsen i Stockholms län	The County Administrative Board of Stockholm	1
Länsstyrelsen i västra götalands län	The County Administrative Board of Västra Götaland	1
Lärarhögskolan i Stockholm	Stockholm Institute of Education	9.4
Malmö högskola	Malmö University	9.4
Migrationsverket	The Swedish Migration Agency	4
Mittuniversitetet	Mid Sweden University	9.4
Myndigheten för samhällsskydd och beredskap	Swedish Civil Contingencies Agency	4
Mälardalens högskola	Mälardalen University	9.4
Naturvårdsverket	Swedish Environmental Protection Agency	5
Patent-och registreringsverket	The Swedish Patent and Registration Office	4
Polisorganisationen	The Swedish Police	3
Post och telestyrelsen	The Swedish Post and Telecom Authority	4
Premiepensionsmyndigheten	The Swedish Pensions Agency	1
Regeringskansliet	Government Offices	1
Riksdagsförvaltningen	The Riksdag Administration	1
Riksförsäkringsverket	The Swedish Insurance Administration	10
Riksgäldskontoret	The Swedish National Debt Office	1
Sjöfartsverket	The Swedish Maritime Administration	4

(*cont.*)

Swedish	English	COFOG
Skatteverket	The Swedish Tax Authority	1
Skogsstyrelsen	The Swedish Forest Agency	4
Socialstyrelsen	The National Board of Health and Welfare	4
Statens energimyndighet	The Swedish Energy Agency	5
Statens fastighetsverk	The National Property Board of Sweden	1
Statens institutionsstyrelse	The Swedish National Board of Institutional Care	10
Statens jordbruksverk	The Swedish Board of Agriculture	4
Statens lantbruksuniversitet	Swedish University of Agricultural Sciences	9.4
Statens pensionsverk	The National Government Employee Pensions Board	1
Statens räddningsverk	The Swedish Rescue Services Agency	2
Statens skolverk	The Swedish National Agency for Education	9
Statistiska centralbyrån	Statistics Sweden	1
Stockholms universitet	Stockholm University	9.4
Styrelsen för internationellt utvecklingssamarbete	The Swedish International Development Cooperation Agency	1
Svenska kraftnät	The Swedish National Grid for Electricity	5
Sveriges domstolar	The Swedish Courts	3
Sveriges Lantbruksuniversitet	Swedish University of Agricultural Sciences	9.4
Sveriges meteorologiska och hydrologiska institut	Swedish Meteorological and Hydrological Institute	5
Södertörns högskola	Södertörn University	9.4
Totalförsvarets forskningsinstitut	The Swedish Defence Research Agency	2
Trafikverket	Swedish Transport Administration	4
Tullverket	Swedish Customs	1
Umeå universitet	Umeå University	9.4
Uppsala universitet	Uppsala University	9.4

(*cont.*)

Swedish	English	COFOG
Vetenskapsrådet	The Swedish Research Council	9
Vägverket	The Swedish Road Administration	4
Växjö universitet	Växjö University	9.4
Åklagarmyndigheten	The Swedish Prosecution Authority	3
Örebro universitet	Örebro University	9.4

Appendix C

The Swedish Standard Industrial Classification (SNI codes) is based on the EU's recommended standard NACE Rev.2, and is an activity classification. Production units as companies and local units are classified in terms of the activity they perform. All Swedish companies need to classify their activities and report their SNI codes to Statistics Sweden's company register. One company, or a local unit, can have several activities (SNI codes).[1]

The following SNI codes are used by the studied management and PR/communication consultants to describe their activities.[2]

SNI codes	Description
46510	Wholesale of computers, computer peripheral equipment and software
47410	Retail sale of computers, peripheral units and software in specialized stores
47420	Retail sale of telecommunications equipment in specialized stores
62010	Computer programming activities
62020	Computer consultancy activities
62090	Other information technology and computer service activities
63110	Data processing, hosting and related activities
66190	Other activities auxiliary to financial services, except insurance and pension funding
66290	Other activities auxiliary to insurance and pension funding
68203	Renting and operating of own or leased other premises
68310	Real estate agencies
68320	Management of real estate on a fee or contract basis

[1] See www.sni2007.scb.se/snisokeng.asp.
[2] The official public data (e.g. the Solidinfo database) does not show which of the SNI codes best fits the work that is actually undertaken in each contract.

(*cont.*)

SNI codes	Description
69201	Accounting and book-keeping activities
69202	Auditing activities
69203	Tax consultancy
70210	Public relations and communication activities
70220	Business and other management consultancy activities
71121	Construction and civil engineering activities and related technical consultancy
71129	Other engineering activities and related technical consultancy
73111	Advertising agency activities
73119	Other advertising activities
73120	Media representation
73200	Market research and public opinion polling
74102	Graphic design
74900	Other professional, scientific and technical activities n.e.c.
78100	Activities of employment placement agencies
85594	Staff training
85599	Various other education n.e.c.
85600	Educational support activities

Appendix D

Appendix D:1

Below is a list of the 100 largest management consultancies used in the study, retrieved from Konsultguiden (www.konsultguiden.se).

Management consultancy	SNI codes	No. of employees
Capgemini Consulting	62020, 63110	1,343
Accenture AB	62020, 70220	728
Acando	62010, 62020, 62090, 70220	1,065
BCG	70220	384
Ernst & Young, Advisory	69201, 69202, 69203	760
McKinsey & Company	70220	221
Connecta	47410, 47420, 62020, 70220, 74900	805
KPMG Advisory & Tax	69202	1,594
Bain & Company	70220	168
PA Consulting Group	70220	275
PwC Advisory	69201, 69202, 69203, 70220	310
Deloitte	69201, 69202	168
Quartz+Co	70220	133
Valcon	70220	220
BearingPoint	70220	173
Avalon Innovation	71121	204
Centigo AB	70220	213
Kvadrat	62020	420
Frontwalker	46510, 62020	101
A.T. Kearney	70220	75
Meritmind	70220, 78100	124
Gartner	62010	60
Arbetslivsresurs	70220	170
Monitor ERP System	46510, 62010, 62020	101

(*cont.*)

Management consultancy	SNI codes	No. of employees
Stretch	70220	123
Mantec	70220, 74900	39
XLENT Consulting Group	70220	130
Resources Global Professionals	70220	70
Capacent	70220	91
Applied Value	70220	27
Mercer	70220	74
Arthur D. Little	70220	54
Rewir	70210	55
Actea	70220, 85594	83
Donald Davies & Partners	62010, 62020, 70220, 85599	63
Frontit	70220	75
IT Ledarna	70220	49
Canvisa Consulting	62020	49
Preera AB	63110, 70220	43
LynxEye	73111	39
Samarbetande Konsulter	70220	20
Level21	70220	30
Solving Efeso	70220	27
Ramböll Management Consulting	70220	58
Crescore	66290	38
Cordial Business Advisers AB	70220	21
Sweco Eurofutures	70220, 74900	46
Enfo Pointer	62010, 62020, 63110	44
Nextport	70220	17
Occam Associates	70220	30
Trinova	70220	29
Navet	62020, 68310, 68320, 69201, 70220	31
Triathlon	70220, 71129	37
CFI Group	70220	32
Eurostep	70220, 73200	32
Canea Partner Group	70220	39
Xmentor	85600	35
Omeo Financial Consulting AB	69201, 70220	25

(*cont.*)

Management consultancy	SNI codes	No. of employees
Procure It Right	70220	37
Ekan Management	70220	28
Visab Consulting	70220	38
Kairos Future	70220	26
Ontrax	62020	29
Wenell Management AB	70220	19
Implement Consulting Group	70220	25
Northstream	70220	18
Affärslogik Svenska	70220	5
Towers Watson	70220	43
Prosales	70220	19
Fasticon	70220	25
Karlöf Consulting AB	70220	21
Pqm	70220	21
SRC	0	23
Alfakonsult	70220	22
Indea	70220	16
Lind & Schultz	66190, 70220	2
Qeep Sverige AB	70220	10
Axholmen	70220	10
Askus Consulting AB	70220	15
Governo	70220	12
Propia	70220	13
Consultus	70220	14
Mason Management	70220, 78100	3
FranklinCovey Radical Change Sweden	85594	9
Element AB	70220	15
Greenwich Consulting Nordic	70220	15
Long & Partners	70220	4
Göran Hägglund	0	4
VEGA	74900	13
Neuman & Nydahl	70220	5
Ifa Produktionsutveckling	71122	3
InterPares	70220	11
Vadestra Strategy	70220	10
Kandidata	70220	8

(*cont.*)

Management consultancy	SNI codes	No. of employees
BDO Consulting Group	70220, 74900	5
PriceGain	70220	8
Allmentor	70220	4
Norlin & Partners	85600	4
Cecia Consulting	70220	3
Malmeken	70220	2

Appendix D:2

Below is a list of the largest PR/communication consultancies used in the study, retrieved from Konsultguiden (www.konsultguiden.se):

PR/communication consultancy	SNI codes	No. of employees
Hallvarsson & Halvarsson	70210	133
Kreab	70220, 73111, 73119, 73120, 74102	83
Prime	70210	93
JKL	70210	50
Gullers	70210	56
Intellecta Corporate AB	62010, 70210, 73111, 74102	48
Solberg	73111	47
Narva	70210, 74102	31
Jung Relations	73119	35
Patriksson	73111	44
Diplomat	70210	24
Springtime	70220	33
Westander	70210	29
Cohn & Wolfe	70210	23
Geelmuyden Kiese	70220	22
Paues Åberg	70210	12
Hill+Knowlton	70220	18
Burson-Marsteller	70210, 70220	12
Vero Kommunikation	70210, 70220	11
Aspekta	70210	13
Publik	70210	11
Nordic Public Affairs	70220	8
Grayling & Citigate	70210	17
Oxenstierna & Partners	70210	11
Fogel & Partners	70220	4
Hegeli Public Affairs	70210, 70220	6
Comma	70220	8
Angselius Rönn	68203, 70210	5

Appendix E

Overview of the interviewed Director Generals (DGs), experts and procurement professionals:

Name (anonymized)	Year	Duration	Type of interview	Size of government agency (No. of employees)
DG 1	2017	70 min.	Face-to-face	1,100
DG 2	2017	90 min.	Face-to-face	1,500
DG 3	2017	75 min.	Face-to-face	350
DG 4	2017	65 min.	Face-to-face	600
DG 5	2017	120 min.	Face-to-face	500
DG 6	2017	65 min.	Telephone	6,500
Expert	2017	45 min.	Face-to-face	n/a
Expert	2017	120 min.	Face-to-face	n/a
Procurement professional (PP1)	2016	30 min.	Telephone	n/a
Procurement professional (PP2)	2015	50 min.	Face-to-face	n/a

Appendix F

In this appendix, descriptions of framework agreements for management and consulting services, issued by the Legal, Financial and Administrative Services Agency, are given.

Appendix F:1

Examples of framework agreements for management consultants issued by the Legal, Financial and Administrative Services Agency.

Management Consulting Services: Analysis[1]

Time Period: 18 October 2010–31 October 2014

'This agreement includes the governmental administration's hiring and use of management consultants aiming to provide the needed competences to a high quality and good conditions. The field includes elaborated analyses/investigations usually performed to assess the possibilities for a later organizational development or change. The analysis or investigation is usually compiled into a written, solid basis for decision making that can be used by the top management.'

Selected suppliers:

- Ernst & Young AB
- Gartner Sverige AB
- IBM Svenska AB
- PA Consulting Group AB

---

[1] See: www.avropa.se/ramavtal/utgangna-ramavtal/Ovriga-tjanster/Management konsulttjanster/Managementkonsulttjanster-analys/.

Management Consulting Services: Management and Leadership Development[2]

Time Period: 29 April 2011–30 April 2015

'This framework agreement includes services related to managers' and key persons' development and assistance in changes of the managers'/leaders' and employees' actions and practices. The agreement shall support the governmental administration's hiring and use of management consultants aiming to provide the needed competences to a high quality and good conditions. The services should be performed independently by taking an overall responsibility or be provided as personal advisory/coaching services to persons in leading positions at different levels.'

Selected suppliers:

- ABC Karriär & Kompetens AB
- eWork Group AB
- Gaia Leadership AB
- Gällöfsta Perlan AB
- Indea AB
- Riddarfjärden Ledarskap & Utveckling AB
- Sandahl Partners Stockholm AB

Management Consulting Services: Business and Organizational Development[3]

Time Period: 21 January 2011–31 January 2015

'This agreement includes the governmental administration's hiring and use of management consultants aiming to provide the needed competences to a high quality and under good conditions. Within this agreement, the supplier should be able to take overall responsibility for the problems that might occur in different types of organizations. The government agencies may choose to buy parts of such competences,

---

[2] See www.avropa.se/ramavtal/utgangna-ramavtal/Ovriga-tjanster/Management konsulttjanster/Managementkonsulttjanster-chef–och-ledarutveckling/.
[3] See www.avropa.se/ramavtal/utgangna-ramavtal/Ovriga-tjanster/Management konsulttjanster/Managementkonsulttjanster-verksamhets–och-organisationsutveckling/.

e.g. strategy services. The supplier should be able to work with problem identification, deliver analyses of the current and desired future situations, and implement suggested solutions in the organization.'

Selected suppliers:

- Capgemini Sverige AB
- Centigo AB
- Connecta AB
- Karlöf Consulting AB
- Preera AB

Appendix F:2

Examples of framework agreements for management consultants issued by the Legal, Financial and Administrative Services Agency, from 2016 onwards.

Management Consulting Services: Analyses, Management, and Operations[1]

Time Period: 28 June 2016–31 December 2017, Option of Prolongation to 30 June 2020

The framework agreement for management services – analyses, management, and operations – aims to support improved operations in order to increase efficiency, and develop and improve the quality of the work performed in the organizations.

- The services include qualified investigations, analyses, audits or evaluations to be used as decision materials. Strategic advice to management teams on issues related to operations is also included.
- The area refers to support to management and control of the organization in order to develop it and increase its efficiency.
- The needs can include support and core activities. Audits can refer to the client's own materials or materials provided by other (second opinion).
- The services can be delivered as projects in which the supplier takes the main responsibility, projects in which the client organization participates and projects referring to various kinds of support and advice.
- The services can refer to the entire client organization, parts of it or particular needs within the government agency. The projects can also refer to operations in several agencies, or in other organizations.

---

[1] See www.avropa.se/ramavtal/utgangna-ramavtal/Ovriga-tjanster/Management konsulttjanster/Managementkonsulttjanster-analys/.

Below are generic examples of support that the government agencies might ask the suppliers to deliver:

- The need can include competences to perform qualified, independent investigations; knowledge of management control (particularly in the state); experience and knowledge of state administration, including legal-administrative matters, business and organizational development.
- There might be a need for quick actions, for example based on political decisions or other, external influences. The need might also be relevant for one or several agencies or stakeholders.

Examples of needs are:

- Investigations and analyses within support or core activities.
- Evaluations and audits regarding performance and effects.
- Overview of the agency's organization and control to manage changes internally or externally.
- Meeting the needs from external stakeholders and the need to collaborate externally.
- Managing changes in the agency's mission and assignment.
- Evaluations of performed actions and organizational changes.

Examples of specific areas:

- Increased efficiency in the control of existing operations
- The organization's quality and economy
- Sustainability
- Information security
- Sourcing
- Governance of IT from an organizational perspective and IT-audits
- Security/risk management

The request for proposal includes a catalogue with demands that government agencies can use to make their demands more precise. Staffing services are not included in this agreement.

Selected suppliers:

- Acando Consulting AB
- Capgemini Sverige AB
- Deloitte AB

- Ernst & Young AB
- Governo AB
- McKinsey & Co.
- Ramböll Management Consulting AB

Management Services: Development of Managers, Group. Supply of Competence

Time Period: 11 November 2016–30 April 2018. Option of Prolongation to Max. 31 October 2020

The framework agreement refers to services related to the development of managers, leaders, groups and co-workers in their respective roles. Strategic supply of competences is also included.

The framework agreements provide government agencies with access to services in relation to different kinds of development actions for their employees. The projects can refer to both advisory services and services in which the supplier takes responsibility for the project, and includes both client-tailored support and general support. The services must be adjusted to the operations in government agencies.

Below are generic examples of services that the government agencies might need. The services refer to support in development programmes that the agencies run for their staff. The projects can be relatively long and extensive, or can be limited to certain parts in a programme. The services can be performed as coaching, in groups or individually, as counselling, as education or in similar forms.

Leader and Management Development 1

To Work as Manager in the State 1.1

The services refer to the employer role in government agencies. The content of the services can be to mediate knowledge on regulation in the state, work environment, legal matters, economy and business planning. Examples of such areas are basic knowledge for new managers and further development of senior managers.

To Lead the Organization 1.2

The services aim to support the manager's management and collaboration with employees to achieve the set goals. The services include the development of leadership skills, based on the organization's control documents and values, and support a good work climate. The content can include:

- Coaching in how a manager, in dialogue with the employees, can clarify goals and expectations, motivate, support, receive feedback and make follow-ups.
- Developing the ability to lead during organizational changes.
- Theory and practice in group development.

Other Support 1.3

The services include other types of support in the manager role, such as:

- Communication and managing conflicts.
- Developing communication skills.
- Self-reflection, insights into how oneself and others function in various situations.
- Individual support and coaching, based on the organization's needs.

Development of Leaders, Groups and Employees 2

The services refer to the development of leaders, groups and employees in their respective roles.

Co-Working 2.1

The purpose of this is to support an active co-working team built on participation and responsibility. The aim can be to support a change in work practices to reach set organizational goals. The services can include:

- To improve the ability to manage changes
- Value and culture-related issues
- The role of civil servants
- Improved communication

Support to Work Groups 2.2

The services can include methods and coaching to support the work climate in the group so it can complete its tasks.

Management Team Development 2.3

The services refer coaching to management teams to develop and increase efficiency in their work, to oversee roles and collaborations to improve control. The development can refer to management teams at various levels in the organization.

Strategic Supply of Competences 3

The services refer to methods and planning to develop strategies for supply of competences. The purpose is to improve the methods for developing, recruiting and retaining employees. The services can include:

- Support with the planning of strategies for the supply of competences to create work practices.
- Strategies for re-using experiences and improve learning at work.
- Mapping the competences.
- Support in the introduction of new methods for strategic supply of competences.

Other 4

In this agreement, strategic supply of competences refers to generic actions taken to improve planning and methods in the government agency's supply of competences. Individual actions or education within the agency's field of expertise are not included. Recruitment and staffing services are not included. The request for proposal includes a catalogue with demands that government agencies can use to make their demands more precise.

Selected suppliers:

- Ekan AB
- Ernst & Young AB
- Gaia Leadership AB

- Indea AB
- IPF AB
- Riddarfjärden Implement AB
- Sandahls Partners Stockholm AB
- Öhrlings PricewaterhouseCoopers AB

Management Services: Business and Organizational Development

Time Period: 1 August 2016–31 January 2018. Option of Prolongation to Max. 31 July 2020

The framework agreement refers to services supporting organizational changes aiming to increase efficiency and develop, follow-up and improve quality. The services included are reviewing the business, organization and economy, analyses of results, follow-ups and evaluations. The projects can include the development of decision material for organizational changes, as well as goal-setting, strategies, process mapping, governance models, business planning, change management, evaluation, need specification in procurements and change of processes and organizations. A central tenet of the services is collaboration in order to achieve improvements regarding governance, structures and methods and show their utility after the project is completed. The projects can be performed in various ways: the supplier can take the main responsibility, the client organization can participate and the supplier can offer different types of support and advice. The services can include the entire development chain, parts of it or specific needs in the client organization.

Examples of services:

- Support/advice in governance, project management, prioritizations, taking an overall perspective and co-ordinating development work.
- Development of decision materials, documentation, reports, etc.
- Support in implementation work and working actively to drive decided changes forward.
- Support/advice or responsibility for delivering a specified result with or without participation from the government agency's staff.
- Prioritization and implementation of development actions.
- Support and coordination in development work.
- Support to managers/leaders and others in organizational changes.

Examples of areas:

- Overview of the organization's goals, visions and values within the state, governance forms and documents, the government agency's strategy and policy.
- Overview of processes.
- Organizational planning.
- Managing and leading change.
- Follow-ups and evaluations of performed changes.
- Analysis of utility, consequences and risks.
- Strategy and development needs regarding external stakeholders, citizens and customers; e.g. interaction, customer meetings and collaboration between organizations.
- Internal communication regarding the project.
- Support in the implementation of management systems/system administration.
- Overview of organization structures.
- Questions regarding changes in responsibilities and roles.
- Management control, means to achieve financial balance, cost and revenue analysis, key ratios, KPIs and evaluation methods.
- Internal control.

The request for proposal(s) includes a catalogue of 'demands' that government agencies can use to make their requests more precise.
Selected suppliers:

- Capgemini AB
- Ekan AB
- IBM Svenska AB
- Karlöf Consulting AB
- PA Consulting Group AB
- Preera AB
- Syntell AB
- Öhrlings PricewaterhouseCoopers AB

References

ABC (Australian Broadcasting Commission). 1999. 'The Consultocracy', Background Briefing, June 20 broadcast, Transcript: www.abc.net.au/ra dionational/programs/backgroundbriefing/the-consultocracy/3563694

Abelson, Donald E. 2002. *Do Think Tanks Matter? Assessing the Impact of Public Policy Institutes*. Kingston: McGill-Queen's University Press.

Abelson, D. E. 2007. Any Ideas? Think Tanks and Policy Analysis in Canada. In L. Dobuzinskis, M. Howlett and D. Laycock (eds.), *Policy Analysis in Canada: The State of the Art*. Toronto: University of Toronto Press: 298–310.

Aberbach, J. D. and B. A. Rockman. 1989. On the Rise, Transformation, and Decline of Analysis in the US Government. *Governance* 2 (3): 293–314.

ABS (Australian Bureau of Statistics). 2017. 5206.0 Australian National Accounts: www.abs.gov.au/ausstats/abs@.nsf/mf/5206.0.

ACCA. 2010. Management Consultants and Public Sector Transformation. The Association of Chartered Certified Accountants: www.accaglobal.com/content/dam/acca/global/PDF-technical/public-sector/tech-afb-mcps.pdf.

Adams, D. 2004. Usable Knowledge in Public Policy. *Australian Journal of Public Administration* 63 (1): 29–42.

Alvesson, M. and A. W. Johansson. 2002. Professionalism and Politics in Management Consultancy Work. In T. Clark and R. Fincham (eds.), *Critical Consulting. New Perspectives on the Management Advice Industry*. Oxford: Blackwell Business: 221–246.

ANAO. 2001. *Developing Policy Advice*, Auditor-General Audit Report No. 21 2001–2002 Performance Audit. Canberra: Australian National Audit Office.

Anderson, G. 1996. The New Focus on the Policy Capacity of the Federal Government. *Canadian Public Administration* 39 (4): 469–488.

APSC (Australian Public Service Commission). 2017. Statistical Bulletin 2016–2017: www.apsc.gov.au/aps-statistical-bulletin-2016-17

Archer, J. N. 1968. Management Consultants in Government. *O&M Bulletin* 23 (1): 23–33.

Armbrüster, T. 2006. *The Economics and Sociology of Management Consulting*. Cambridge: Cambridge University Press.

Arnold, P. J. and C. Cooper. 1999. A Tale of Two Classes: The Privatisation of Medway Ports. *Critical Perspectives on Accounting* 10 (2): 127–152.

Asplind, J. 2013. Generaldirektör. I rikets tjänst på politikens villkor. [Director General. In the Kingdom's Service on the Terms of Policy and Politics.] Bågspännaren Asplind Consulting.

Aucoin, P. 2012. New Political Governance in Westminster Systems: Impartial Public Administration and Management Performance at Risk. *Governance* 25 (2): 177–199. doi:10.1111/j.1468-0491.2012.01569.x

Auditor-General. 2017. *Australian Government Procurement Contract Reporting*, ANAO Report No. 19 Information Report, Canberra.

Auditor-General of Nova Scotia. 2005. *Report of the Auditor General to the Nova Scotia House of Assembly*. Halifax: Nova Scotia.

Australian Government. 2017. *AusTender*, www.tenders.gov.au/

Ayres, R. 2001. *Policy Markets in Australia*, PhD thesis, University of Canberra.

Bakvis, H. 1997. Advising the Executive: Think Tanks, Consultants, Political Staff and Kitchen Cabinet. In P. Weller, H. Bakvis and R. A. W. Rhodes (eds.), *The Hollow Crown: Countervailing Trends in Core Executives*. London: Macmillan: 84–115.

Ball, S. J. 2011. Academies, Policy Networks and Governance. In H. M. Gunter (ed.), *The State and Education Policy*. London: Continuum: 146–158.

Ball, S. J. 2012. *Global Education Inc. New Policy Networks and the Neo-Liberal Imaginary*. Abingdon: Routledge.

Ball, S. J. and C. Junemann. 2012. *Networks, New Governance and Education*. Bristol: Policy Press.

Banks, G. 2009. Evidence-based Policy Making: What Is It? How Do We Get It? ANZ/ANU Public Lecture Series, 4 February: www.pc.gov.au/__data/assets/pdf_file/0003/85836/cs20090204.pdf

Barber, M. 2007. *Instruction to Deliver*. London: Politico Press.

Bekke, H. A. G. M. and F. M. van der Meer. 2000. *Civil Service Systems in Western Europe*. Cheltenham: Edward Elgar.

Bennett, Scott and Margaret McPhail. 1992. Policy Process Perceptions of Senior Canadian Federal Civil Servants: A View of the State and Its Environment. *Canadian Public Administration* 35 (3): 299–316.

Berglund, J. and Werr, A. 2002. The Invincible Character of Management Consulting Rhetorics. *Organization* 7 (4): 633–655.

Berit, Ernst and Alfred Kieser. 2002. In Search of Explanations for the Consulting Explosion. In K. Sahlin-Andersson and L. Engwall (eds.), *Expansion of Management Knowledge: Carriers, Flows, and Sources*, 1st ed. Redwood: Stanford Business Books: 47–73.

Berg, van den, C. F. 2011. *Transforming for Europe: The Reshaping of National Bureaucracies in a System of Multi-level Governance*. Leiden: Leiden University Press.

Berg, van den, C. F. 2017. Dynamics in the Dutch Policy Advisory System: Externalization, Politicization and the Legacy of Pillarization. *Political Science 50*: 63–84.

Berg, van den, C. F. 2018. The Netherlands: The Emergence and Encapsulation of Ministerial Advisers. In R. Shaw and C. Eichbaum (eds.), *Ministers, Minders and Mandarins: An International Study of Relationships at the Executive Summit of Parliamentary Democracies*. Cheltenham: Edward Elgar: 129–144.

Berg, van den, C. F. and G. S. A. Dijkstra. 2015. Wetgevingsjuristen ten prooi aan New Political Governance? Een inventarisatie (2002–2015). *RegelMaat* 30 (4): 247–266.

Berg, van den, C. F., A. Schmidt and C. van Eijk. 2015. Externe advisering binnen de Nederlandse overheid: Naar een empirisch en theoretisch onderbouwde onderzoeksagenda. *Bestuurskunde* 24 (3): 17–31.

Beveridge, R. 2012. Consultants, Depoliticization and Arena-Shifting in the Policy Process: Privatizing Water in Berlin. *Policy Science* 45 (1): 47–68.

Bevir, M. and R. A. W. Rhodes. 2001. Decentering Tradition: Interpreting British Government. *Administration & Society* 33 (2): 107–132.

Bevir, M. and R. A. W. Rhodes. 2003. *Interpreting British Governance*. Abingdon: Routledge.

Bevir, M. R., A. W. Rhodes and P. Weller. 2003. Traditions of Governance: Interpreting the Changing Role of the Public Sector. *Public Administration* 81 (1): 1–17.

Bezes, P., D. Demazière, T. Le Bianic et al. 2011. New Public Management and Professions in the Public Administration: Beyond Opposition, What New Patterns Are Taking Shape? *Sociologie du Travail* 53 (3): 293–348: www.sciencedirect.com/science/article/pii/S0038029611000537

Bilodeau, N., C. Laurin and A. Vining. 2007. Choice of Organizational Form Makes a Real Difference: The Impact of Corporatization on Government Agencies in Canada. *Journal of Public Administration Research and Theory* 17 (1): 119–147.

Blair, T. 2015. Tony Blair – 1999 Speech on Modernising Public Services. www.ukpol.co.uk/tony-blair-1999-speech-on-modernising-public-services/

Bloomfield, B. P. and A. Best. 1992. Management Consultants: Systems Development, Power and the Translation of Problems. *The Sociological Review* 40 (3): 533–560.

Bloomfield, B. P. and A. Danieli. 1995. The Role of Management Consultants in the Development of Information Technology: The

Indissoluble Nature of Socio-Political and Technical Skills. *Journal of Management Studies* 32 (1): 23–46.

Blum, S. E. Fobé, V. Pattyn, M. Pekar-Milicevic and M. Brans. 2017. Scientific Policy Advice in Consensus-Seeking Countries: Close Friends or Mere Acquaintances? The Cases of Belgium and Germany. EGPA, Milan, 28 August–1 September.

Boaz, A. L. G., R. Levitt and W. Solesbury. 2008. Does Evidence-Based Policy Work? Learning from the UK Experience. *Evidence and Policy* 4 (2): 233–253.

Böhme, K. 2002. Much Ado about Evidence: Reflections from Policy Making in the European Union. *Planning Theory & Practice* 3 (1): 98–101.

Bolton, S. C., M. Houlihan, T. Andersson and S. Tengblad. 2009. When Complexity Meets Culture: New Public Management and the Swedish Police. *Qualitative Research in Accounting & Management* 6 (1/2): 41–56.

Booth, T. 1990. Researching Policy Research, Issues of Utilization in Decision Making. *Science Communication* 12 (1): 80–100.

Boston, J. 1994. Purchasing Policy Advice: The Limits to Contracting Out. *Governance* 7 (1): 1–30.

Boston, J. 1996. The Use of Contracting in the Public Sector – Recent New Zealand Experience. *Australian Journal of Public Administration* 55 (3): 105–110.

Boston, J., J. Martin, J. Pallot and P. Walsh. 1996. *Public Management: The New Zealand Model*. Auckland: Oxford University Press.

Bovens, M. A. P. P. 't Hart, M. J. W. van Twist, C. F. et al. 2017. *Openbaar Bestuur, beleid, organisatie en politiek*, 9th ed. Deventer: WoltersKluwer.

Brinkerhoff, D. W. and B. L. Crosby. 2002. *Managing Policy Reform: Concepts and Tools for Decision-Makers in Developing and Transitional Countries*. Bloomfield: Kumarian Press.

Brinkerhoff, D. W. 2010. Developing Capacity in Fragile States. *Public Administration and Development* 30 (1): 66–78.

Brinkerhoff, D. W. and P. J. Morgan. 2010. Capacity and Capacity Development: Coping with Complexity. *Public Administration and Development* 30 (1): 2–10.

Brint, S. 1990. Rethinking the Policy Influence of Experts: From General Characterizations to Analysis of Variation. *Sociological Forum* 5 (3; September): 361–385.

British Columbia. 2001. *Office of the Auditor General. Management Consulting Engagements in Government*. Victoria: Office of the Auditor General of British Columbia.

Broom, G. M. and G. D. Smith. 1979. Testing the Practitioner's Impact on Clients. *Public Relations Review* 5 (3; Autumn): 47–59.

Burnham, P. 2001. New Labour and the Politics of Depoliticisation. *British Journal of Politics and International Relations* 3 (2): 127–149.

Burns, J. P. and B. Bowornwathana. 2001. *Civil Service Systems in Asia.* Cheltenham: Edward Elgar.

Butcher, J., B. Freyens and J. Wanna. 2009. Policy in Action. *The Challenge of Service Delivery.* Sydney: University of New South Wales Press.

Butcher, J., B. Freyens and J. Wanna. 2010. *Policy in Action: The Challenge of Service Delivery.* Sydney: University of New South Wales Press.

Cabinet Office. 1999. *Modernising Government White Paper.* CM4310. London: TSO.

Cairney, P. 2016. *The Politics of Evidence-Based Policy Making.* London: Palgrave.

Cairney, P., K. Oliver and A. Wellstead. 2016. To Bridge the Divide between Evidence and Policy, Reduce Ambiguity as Much as Uncertainty. *Public Administration Review* 76 (3): 399–402.

Cameron, D. 2011. Prime Minister's Speech on Modern Public Service. www .gov.uk/government/speeches/prime-ministers-speech-on-modern-public-service.

Canbäck, S. 1998. The Logic of Management Consulting (Part One). *Journal of Management Consulting* 10 (12): 3–11.

Canbäck, S. 1999. The Logic of Management Consulting (Part Two). *Journal of Management Consulting* 10 (13): 3–12.

Caplan, N. 1979. The Two-Communities: Theory and Knowledge Utilization. *American Behavioural Scientist* 22 (3): 459–470.

Cappe, M. 2011. Analysis and Evidence for Good Public Policy. The Demand and Supply Equation. The 2011 Tansley Lecture, 19 April, Johnson-Shoyama Graduate School of Public Policy. Regina, Saskatchewan.

Carson E and L. Kerr. 2017. *Australian Social Policy and the Human Services*, 2nd ed. Melbourne: Cambridge University Press.

Cartwright, N. and J. Hardie. 2012. *Evidence-Based Policy. A Practical Guide to Doing It Better.* Oxford: Oxford University Press.

Cherney, A., B. Head, J. Povey, M. Ferguson and P. Boreham. 2015. Use of Academic Social Research by Public Officials: Exploring Preferences and Constraints that Impact on Research Use. *Evidence & Policy: A Journal of Research, Debate and Practice* 11 (2): 169–188.

Christensen, M. 2003. The Big Six Consulting Firms: Creating a New Market of Meeting a Public Policy Need? *Australasian Journal of Business and Social Inquiry* 1 (1): 24–32.

Clark, J. and A. Jones. 1999. From Policy Insider to Policy Outcast? Comite des Organisations Professionnelles Agricoles, EU Policymaking, and the EU's 'Agri-Environmental' Regulation. *Environment and Planning C, Government and Policy*, 17 (5): 637–653.

Clark, M. M. 2014. Whose Knowledge Counts in Government Literacy Policies and at What Cost? *Education Journal* 186. 20 January: 13–16.

Clark, M. M. (ed.). 2017. *Reading the Evidence*. Birmingham: Glendale Education.

Clark, T. 1995. *Managing Consultants: Consultancy as the Management of Impressions*. Buckingham: Open University Press.

Clark, T. and R. Fincham. 2002. *Critical Consulting: New Perspectives on the Management Advice Industry*. Oxford: Blackwell Business.

Clark, T. and G. Salaman. 1996. Telling Tales: Management Consultancy as the Art of Story Telling. In D. Grant and C. Oswick (eds.), *Metaphor and Organizations*. London: Sage Publications Ltd: 166–183.

Clarke, J. and J. Newman. 2007. *The Managerial State*. London: Sage.

Coen, D. 2007. Empirical and Theoretical Studies in EU Lobbying. *Journal of European Public Policy* 14 (April): 333–345.

Coffield, F. 2012. Why the McKinsey Reports will not Improve School Systems. *Journal of Education Policy* 27 (1): 131–149.

Cohen, N. 2006. Where Has All the Money Gone? *New Statesman*. 15 May: 15–16.

Colebatch, H. K. (ed.). 2006. *The Work of Policy: An International Survey*. New York: Rowman and Littlefield.

Colebatch, H. K., R. Hoppe and M. Noordegraaf. (eds.). 2011. *Working for Policy*. Amsterdam: Amsterdam University Press.

Consultancy.uk (2016) 10 Largest Management Consulting Firms of the Globe. www.consultancy.uk/news/2149/10-largest-management-consulting-firms-of-the-globe

Congressional Research Service (CRS). 2015. The Federal Acquisition Regulation (FAR): Answers to Frequently Asked Questions. Kate M. Manuel, Legislative Attorney; L. Elaine Halchin, Specialist in American National Government; Erika K. Lunder, Legislative Attorney. Michelle D. Christensen, Analyst in Government Organization and Management, 3 February: https://fas.org/sgp/crs/misc/R42826.pdf

Coopers and Lybrand. 1988. Local Management of Schools. *A Report to the Department of Education and Science*. London: DES.

Corbett, T. J. and K. Bogenschneider. 2011. *Evidence-Based Policymaking: Insights from Policy-Minded Researchers and Research-Minded Policy Makers*. New York: Taylor and Francis.

Corcoran, J. and F. McLean. 1998. The Selection of Management Consultants: How Are Governments Dealing with This Difficult Decision? An Exploratory Study. *International Journal of Public Sector Management* 11 (1): 37–54.

Courtney, S. J. 2015. Mapping School Types in England. *Oxford Review of Education* 41 (6): 799–818.

Craft, J. and J. Halligan. 2017. Assessing 30 Years of Westminster Policy Advisory System Experience. *Policy Sciences* 50 (1): 47–62.

Craft, J. and M. Howlett. 2013. The Dual Dynamics of Policy Advisory Systems: The Impact of Externalization and Politicization on Policy Advice. *Policy and Society* 32: 187–197.

Craig, D. and R. Brooks. 2006. *Plundering the Public Sector*. London: Constable.

Cross, W. 2007. Policy Study and Development in Canada's Political Parties. In L. Dobuzinskis, M. Howlett and D. Laycock (eds.), *Policy Analysis in Canada: The State of the Art*. Toronto: University of Toronto Press: 233–242.

Czarniawska, B. and C. Mazza. 2003. Consulting as a Liminal Space. *Human Relations* 56 (3): 267–290.

Czarniawska, B. and C. Mazza. 2013. Consulting University: A Reflection from Inside. *Financial Accountability & Management* 29 (2): 124–139.

Czarniawska-Joerges, B. 1989. Merchants of Meaning: Management Consulting in the Swedish Public Sector. In Barry A. Turner (ed.), *Organizational Symbolism*. Berlin: Walter De Gruyter Inc: 139–150.

Daalder, H. 2011. *State Formation, Parties and Democracy: Studies in Comparative European Politics*. Colchester: ECPR Press.

Dahlström, C. 2016. Introduction: Policy-Making in Sweden. In J. Pierre (ed.), *The Oxford Handbook of Swedish Politics*. Oxford: Oxford University Press: 631–633.

David, R. J. 2012. Institutional Change and The Growth of Strategy Consulting in the United States. In T. Clark and M. Kipping (eds.), *The Oxford Handbook of Management Consulting*. Oxford Handbooks Online: 71–92.

Davies, A. 2001. *Accountability: A Public Law Analysis of Government by Contract*. Oxford: Oxford University Press.

Davies, A. C. L. 2008. *The Public Law of Government Contracts*. Oxford: Oxford University Press.

Davis G., J. Wanna, J. Warhurst and P. Weller. 1993. *Public Policy in Australia*, 2nd ed., St Leonards: Allen and Unwin.

Daviter, F. 2015. The Political Use of Knowledge in the Policy Process. *Policy Sciences*, 48 (4): 491–505.

Denis, J. L., E. Ferlie and N. Van Gestel. 2015. Understanding Hybridity in Public Organizations. *Public Administration* 93 (2): 273–289.

Dent, H. 2002. Consultants and the Public Service. *Australian Journal of Public Administration* 61 (1): 108–113.

Deutsch, J. 1973. Governments and Their Advisors. *Canadian Public Administration* 16 (1): 25–34.

DfEE. 2000. *Influence or Irrelevance: Can Social Science Improve Government?* Secretary of State's ESRC Lecture, 2nd February. London: DfEE.

DfES/PwC. 2007. *Independent Study into School Leadership*. London: DfES.

Dickinson H. 2016. From New Public Management to New Public Governance. In J. Butcher and D. Gilchrist (eds.), *The Three Sector Solution: Delivering Public Policy in Collaboration with Not-for-Profits and Business*. Canberra: ANU Press: 41–60.

Dijkstra, G. S. A., F. M. van der Meer, C. F. van den Berg. 2015. Is er nu wel of niet sprake van een terugtredend openbaar bestuur? Het personeelsperspectief. In J. J. M. Uijlenbroek (ed.), *De Staat van de Ambtelijke Dienst*, 3rd ed. The Hague: CAOP.

Dilulio, J. J. 2016. Against Federal 'Leviathan by Proxy' and for a Bigger, Better Full-Time Federal Workforce. *Public Administration Review* 1 June: https://doi.org/10.1111/puar.12598.

Dluhy, M. 1981. Policy Advice-Givers: Advocates? Technicians? or Pragmatists? In J. E. Tropman (ed.), *New Strategic Perspectives on Social Policy*. New York: Pergamon Press: 202–216.

Dobuzinskis, L. and M. Howlett. 2018. *Policy Analysis in Canada*. Bristol: Policy Press.

Dobuzinskis, L., M. Howlett and D. Laycock. (eds.). 1996. *Policy Studies in Canada: The State of the Art*. Toronto: University of Toronto Press.

Dobuzinskis, L., M. Howlett and D. Laycock. (eds.). 2007. *Policy Analysis in Canada: The State of the Art*. Toronto: University of Toronto Press.

Doern, G. B. 1994. The Road to Better Public Services: Progress & Constraints in Five Canadian Federal Agencies. The Institute for Research in Public Policy.

DoF (Dept of Finance). 2017a. GAPS Contracts Export: https://data.gov.au/dataset/historical-australian-government-contract-data

DoF (Dept. of Finance). 2017b. AusTender CN CSV published up to 30 June 2017: https://data.gov.au/dataset/historical-australian-govern ment-contract-data

DoF (Dept. of Finance). 2017c. Additional Reporting on Consultancies: www.finance.gov.au/procurement/procurement-policy-and-guidance/buy ing/reporting-requirements/consultancies-reporting/practice.html

DoF (Dept. of Finance). 2017d. Procurement, Statistics on Australian Government Procurement Contracts: www.finance.gov.au/procurement/statistics-on-commonwealth-purchasing-contracts/

DoF (Dept of Finance). 2017e. AusTender Customised UNSPSC Codeset: Data.gov.au

DoF (Dept of Finance). 2018. Submission to Joint Committee of Public Accounts and Audit Inquiry Based on ANAO Report No. 19 (2017–18)

Australian Government Procurement Contract Reporting, Submission No. 4, JCPAA, Parliament of Australia: www.aph.gov.au/

DoFA (Dept of Finance and Administration). 1999. *Purchasing Statistics Bulletin*. Canberra: AGPS.

DoFA. 2004. *Gazette Publishing System (GaPS) User Guide*. Canberra: National Office for the Information Economy.

Dollery, B. and J. Drew. 2017. Paying the Piper: A Critical Examination of ACIL Allen's (2016) 'An Economic Assessment of Recasting Council Boundaries in South Australia', *Economic Analysis and Policy* 54: 74–82.

Dollery, B. F. Fiorillo and T. Burton. 2012 . Running the Big Smoke: A Critical Analysis of the KPMG (2008) Approach to Local Government Reform in the Sydney Metropolitan Area. *Australasian Journal of Regional Studies* 18 (2): 232–256.

Donaldson, D. 2018. 'Urgent': Former Secretaries Assess Public Service Capability. *The Mandarin*, 12 February.

DoT (Dept of the Treasury). 2017. Budget 2017/18, Budget Paper No. 4, Agency Resourcing: https://archive.budget.gov.au/2017-18/bp4/Budget2017-18_BP4.pdf.

Drew, J. and B. Grant. 2017. Multiple Agents, Blame Games and Public Policy-Making: the Case of Local Government Reform in New South Wales. *Australian Journal of Political Science* 52 (1): 37–52.

Drew, J., M. Kortt and B. Dollery. 2013. A Cautionary Tale: Council Amalgamation in Tasmania and the Deloitte Access Economics Report. *Australian Journal of Public Administration* 72 (1): 55–65.

Druckman, Alan. 2000. The Social Scientist as Consultant. *American Behavioral Scientist* 43 (10; 1 August): 1565–1577.

Easton, S. 2017. Meeting Global Standard for Open Procurement Data Might Cost Too Much. *The Mandarin*, 25 July.

Édes, Bart W. 2004. The Role of Government Information Officers. *Journal of Government Information* 27 (4; July): 455–469.

Edwards, M., J. Halligan, B. Horrigan and G. Nicoll. 2012. *Public Sector Governance in Australia*. Canberra: ANU E-Press.

Edwards, M., B. Head, A. Tiernan and J. Walter, 2017. The Decline in Policy Capacity: Trends, Causes and Remedies. *Australian Political Science Association Conference*, 25–27 September, Melbourne.

Efficiency Unit. 1988. *Improving Management in Government: The Next Steps*. London: HMSO.

Efficiency Unit. 1994. *The Government's Use of External Consultants*. London: HMSO.

Ehn, P. 2016. The Public Servant. In J. Pierre, *The Oxford Handbook of Swedish Politics*. Oxford: Oxford University Press: 332–346

Eichbaum, C. and R. Shaw. 2007. Ministerial Advisers and the Politics of Policy-Making: Bureaucratic Permanence and Popular Control. *The Australian Journal of Public Administration* 66 (4): 453–467.

Eichbaum, C. and R. Shaw. 2008. Revisiting Politicization: Political Advisers and Public Servants in Westminster Systems. *Governance* 21 (3): 337–363.

Elinder, M. and H. Jordahl. 2013. Political Preferences and Public Sector Outsourcing. *European Journal of Political Economy* 30: 43–57.

Ernst, B. and A. Kieser. 2002. In Search of Explanations for the Consulting Explosion. In K. Sahlin-Andersson and L. Engwall (eds.), *The Expansion of Management Knowledge: Carriers, Flows, and Sources*, 1st ed. Redwood: Stanford Business Books: 47–72.

Evetts, J. 2003a. The Sociological Analysis of Professionalism: Occupational Change in the Modern World. *International Sociology* 18 (2; 1 June): 395–415.

Evetts, J. 2003b. The Construction of Professionalism in New and Existing Occupational Contexts: Promoting and Facilitating Occupational Change. *International Journal of Sociology and Social Policy* 23 (4/5): 22–35.

FEACO. 2002. Survey of the European Management Consultancy Market. Brussels.

FEACO. 2010. Survey of the European Management Consultancy 2010/2011.

FEACO. 2016. Survey of the European Management Consultancy 2015/2016.

Ferlie, E., L. Fitzgerald, G. Mcgivern, S. Dopson and C. Bennett. 2011. Public Policy Networks and 'Wicked Problems': A Nascent Solution? *Public Administration* 89: 307–324.

Fincham, R. 1999. The Consultant–Client Relationship: Critical Perspectives on the Management of Organizational Change. *Journal of Management Studies* 36 (3): 335–351.

Fincham, R. 2012. The Client in the Client–Consultant Relationship. In M. Kipping and T. Clark (eds.), *The Oxford Handbook of Management Consulting*. Oxford: Oxford University Press: 411–426.

Fisher, F. 1990. *Technocracy and the Politics of Expertise*. Newbury Park: Sage.

Flynn, N. and A. Asquer. 2017. *Public Sector Management*. London: Sage Publications Ltd.

Ford, R. and D. Zussman. 1997. Alternative Service Delivery: Sharing Governance in Canada. Institute of Public Administration of Canada (Institut d'administration publique du Canada).

Forde, R., R. Hobby and A. Lees. 2000. *The Lessons of Leadership. A Comparison of Headteachers in UK Schools and Senior Executives in Private Enterprises*. London: Hay Management Consultants.

Freeman, J. 2000. The Contracting State. *Florida State University Law Review* 28 (155): 155–214.

Fulton, L. 1968. *The Civil Service, Report of the Committee 1966–1968 Volume 1, Cmnd 3638.* London: HMSO.

Garrett, G. A. and F. J. Beatty. 2011. Interesting Times for Government Contractors. *Contract Management* 51 (5): 12–14.

Garson, G. D. 1986. From Policy Science to Policy Analysis: A Quarter Century of Progress. In W. N. Dunn (ed.), *Policy Analysis: Perspectives, Concepts, and Methods.* Greenwich: JAI Press: 3–22.

Garsten, C. 1999. Betwixt and Between: Temporary Employees as Liminal Subjects in Flexible Organizations. *Organization Studies* 20 (4; 1 July): 601–617.

General Services Administration (FAR). 2005. Department of Defense, National Aeronautics and Space Administration. Federal Acquisition Regulation, issued March.

Genomförandeutredningen (SOU). 2014. *Nya regler om upphandling [New rules for public procurement].* Stockholm: Finansdepartementet.

Geva-May, I. and A. Maslove. 2006. Canadian Public Policy Analysis and Public Policy Programs: A Comparative Perspective. *Journal of Public Affairs Education* 12 (4): 413–438.

Gittins, R. 2016. Smarter Thinking on the Budget Deficit Is Long Overdue. *Sydney Morning Herald,* 28 November

Glassman, A. and M. Winograd. 2005. Public Sector Consultation. In L. Greiner and F. Poulfelt (eds.), *The Contemporary Consultant.* Mason: Thomson South-Western: 189–207.

Gomery, J. H. 2005. *Who Is Responsible? Fact Finding Report.* Ottawa: Commission of Inquiry into the Sponsorship Program and Advertising Activities.

Gomery, J. H. 2006. *Restoring Accountability: Recommendations.* Ottawa: Commission of Inquiry into the Sponsorship Program and Advertising Activities.

Gorard, S. 2018. *Education Policy.* Bristol: Policy Press.

Gov.uk. 2011. Thames Rolling Stock Project. www.gov.uk/government/publications/thameslink-rolling-stock-project–14.

Gov.uk. 2015. Government Saves £18.6 Billion for Hard Working Taxpayers in 2014 to 2015. www.gov.uk/government/news/government-saves-186-billion-for-hard-working-taxpayers-in-2014-to-2015.

Green, A. 2015. History as Expertise and the Influence of Political Culture on Advice for Policy since Fulton. *Contemporary British History* 29 (1): 27–50.

Green-Pedersen, C. 2002. New Public Management Reforms of the Danish and Swedish Welfare States: The Role of Different Social Democratic Responses. *Governance* 15 (2): 271–294.

Gregory, R. and Z. Lonti. 2008. Chasing Shadows? Performance Measurement of Policy Advice in New Zealand Government Departments. *Public Administration* 86 (3): 837–856.

Gross, A. C. and J. Poor. 2008. The Global Management Consulting Sector. *Business Economics* 43 (4): 59–68.

Grossman, E. and S. Saurugger. 2004. Challenging French Interest Groups: The State, Europe and the International Political System. *French Politics* 2 (2): 203–220.

Gunter, H. M. 2012. *Leadership and the Reform of Education.* Bristol: The Policy Press.

Gunter, H. M. 2017. Corporate Consultancy Practices in Education Services in England. In H. M. Gunter, D. Hall and M. Apple (eds.), *Corporate Elites and the Reform of Public Education.* Bristol: Policy Press: 147–160.

Gunter, H. M. 2018. *The Politics of Public Education: Reform Ideas and Issues.* Bristol: Policy Press.

Gunter, H. M. and C. Mills. 2016. Knowledge Production and the Rise of Consultocracy in Education Policymaking in England. In A. Verger, G. Steiner-Khamsi and C. Lubienski (eds.), *World Yearbook of Education 2016: The Global Education Industry.* London: Routledge: 125–141.

Gunter, H. M. and C. Mills. 2017. *Consultants and Consultancy: The Case of Education.* Cham: Springer

Gunter, H. M., E. Grimaldi, D. Hall and R. Serpieri. (eds.). 2016. *New Public Management and the Reform of Education.* Abingdon: Routledge.

Gunter, H. M., D. Hall and C. Mills. 2015. Consultants, Consultancy and Consultocracy in Education Policymaking in England. *Journal of Education Policy* 30 (4): 518–539.

Guttman, D. and B. Willner. 1976. *The Shadow Government: The Government's Multi-Billion-Dollar Giveaway of Its Decision-Making Powers to Private Management Consultants, 'Experts,' and Think Tanks.* New York: Pantheon Books.

Haddon, C. 2012. *Reforming the Civil Service. The Efficiency Unit in the early 1980s and the 1987 Next Steps Report.* London: Institute for Government.

Halffman, W. and R. Hoppe. 2005. Science/Policy Boundaries: A Changing Division of Labour in Dutch Expert Policy Advice. In S. Maassen and P. Weingart (eds.), *Democratization of Expertise? Exploring Novel Forms of Scientific Advice in Political Decision-Making.* Berlin: Springer Verlag: 135–151.

Hall, J. and E. Jennings. 2010. Assessing the Use and Weight of Information and Evidence in US State Policy Decisions. *Policy and Science* 29 (2): 137–147.

Halligan, J. 1995. Policy Advice and the Public Service. In B. G. Peters and D. J. Savoie (eds.), *Governance in a Changing Environment*. Ottawa and Montreal: Canadian Centre for Management Development and McGill-Queen's University Press: 138–172.

Halligan, J. 2000. Public Service Reform Under Howard. In G. Singleton (ed.), *The Howard Government: Australian Commonwealth Administration 1996–1998*, Sydney: UNSW Press: 49–64.

Halligan, J. (ed.). 2003. *Civil Service Systems in Anglo-American Countries*. Cheltenham: Edward Elgar.

Halligan, J. 2008. The Search for Balance and Effectiveness in the Australian Public Service. In C. Aulich and R. Wettenhall (eds.), *Howard's Fourth Government: Australian Commonwealth Administration 2004–2007*. Sydney: UNSW Press: 13–30.

Halligan, J. 2011. The Australian Public Service: New Agendas and Reforms. In C. Aulich and M. Evans (eds.), *The Rudd Government: Australian Commonwealth Administration 2007–2010*. Canberra: ANU E Press: 35–54.

Halligan, J. and J, Power. 1992. *Political Management in the 1990s*. Melbourne: Oxford University Press.

Halpin, D. R. and B. Frausen. 2017. Conceptualising the Policy Engagement of Interest Groups: Involvement, Access and Prominence. *European Journal of Political Research* 56: 3.

Hamilton-Howard, J. 2000. The Consultant Market: A User's Guide. *Canberra Bulletin of Public Administration*, IPAA, 97: 7–17.

Hammerschmid, G., S. Van de Walle, R. Andrews and P. Bezes. (eds.). 2016. *Public Administration Reforms in Europe: The View from the Top*. Cheltenham: Edward Elgar.

Hawke, G. R. 1993. *Improving Policy Advice*. Wellington: Victoria University Institute of Policy Studies.

Hawker, G. 2001. Consultants to the Commonwealth. *Canberra Bulletin of Public Administration* 99: 60–63.

Head B. 2015a. Policy Analysis and Public Sector Capacity. In B. Head and K. Crowley (eds.), *Policy Analysis in Australia*. Bristol: Policy Press: 53–68.

Head, B. W. 2015b. Toward More Evidence-Informed Policy Making? *Public Administration Review* 76 (3): 472–484.

Head, B. 2008. Wicked Problems in Public Policy. *Public Policy* 3 (2): 101–118.

Head, B. W. 2010. Reconsidering Evidence-Based Policy, Key Issues and Challenges. *Policy and Society* 29 (2): 77–94.

Head, B. W. 2013. Evidence-Based Policymaking – Speaking Truth to Power? *Australian Journal of Public Administration* 72 (4): 397–403.

Helden, van, G. J., H. Aardema, H. J. ter Bogt and T. L. C. M Groot. 2010. Knowledge Creation for Practice in Public Sector Management Accounting by Consultants and Academics: Preliminary findings and Directions for Future Research. *Management Accounting Research* 21 (2): 83–94.

Heringa, A. W., J. van der Velde, L. F. M. Verhey and W. van der Woude. 2018. *Staatsrecht*. Deventer: WoltersKluwer.

Hird, J. A. 2005. Policy Analysis for What? The Effectiveness of Nonpartisan Policy Research Organizations. *Policy Studies Journal* 33 (1): 83–105.

Hodge, G. and D. Bowman. 2006. The 'Consultocracy': The Business of Reforming Government. In G. Hodge (ed.), *Privatization and Market Development: Global Movements in Public Policy Ideas*. Cheltenham: Edward Elgar: 97–126.

Hogan, A., S. Sellar and B. Lingard. 2015. Network Restructuring of Global Edu-business. In W. Au and J. J. Ferrare (eds.), *Mapping Corporate Education Reform*. New York: Routledge: 43–64.

Hood, C. 1990. De-Sir Humphreyfing the Westminster Model of Bureaucracy: A New Style of Governance? *Governance: An International Journal of Policy and Administration* 3 (2): 205–214.

Hood, C. 1991. A Public Management for All Seasons? *Public Administration* 69 (1): 3–19.

Hood, C. 2013. *The Blame Game: Spin, Bureaucracy, and Self-Preservation in Government*. New Jersey: Princeton University Press.

Hood, C. and M. Jackson. 1991. *Administrative Argument*. Aldershot: Dartmouth Publishing Company Limited.

Hood, C. and H. Z. Margetts. 2007. *The Tools of Government in a Digital Age*. Basingstoke: Palgrave Macmillan.

Hood, C. and B. G. Peters. 2004. The Middle Aging of New Public Management: Into the Age of Paradox? *JPART* 14: 267–282

Hood, C., H. Rothstein and R. Baldwin. 2004. *The Government of Risk*. Oxford: Oxford University Press.

Hoppe, R. 2009. Scientific Advice and Public Policy: Expert Advisers' and Policymakers' Discourses on Boundary Work. *Poiesis and Praxis* 6 (3: 235–263.

House of Commons. 2014. *Government Procurement Service Annual Report and Accounts 2013/14*. London: The Stationery Office Ltd.

House of Commons Committee of Public Accounts. 2006. Central Government's Use of Consultants. *Thirty-first Report of Session 7*. London: The Stationery Office Limited.

House of Commons Committee of Public Accounts. 2007. Central Government's Use of Consultants. *Thirty-first Report of Session 2006–2007*. London: The Stationary Office Limited.

House of Commons Committee of Public Accounts. 2010. Central Government's Use of Consultants and Interims. *Twelfth Report of Session 2010–11*. London: The Stationery Office Limited.

House of Commons Committee of Public Accounts. 2016. *Use of Consultants and Temporary Staff*. London: The Stationery Office.

House of Commons Committee on Health. 2009. The Use of Management Consultants by the NHS and the Department of Health. *Fifth Report of Session 2008–09*. London: House of Commons.

House of Commons Hansard. 2012a. Transport. 23rd January 2012, Vol. 539. https://hansard.parliament.uk/Commons/2012-01-23/debates/1201 232000002/Transport?highlight=consultants#contribution-1201232 000005

House of Commons Hansard. 2012b. Pay and Consultants (Public Sector). 13th March 2012, Vol. 542. https://hansard.parliament.uk/Commons/20 12-03-13/debates/12031352000001/PayAndConsultants(PublicSector).

House of Commons Hansard. 2013. Consultants. 17th July 2013, Vol. 566. https://hansard.parliament.uk/Commons/2013-07-17/debates/13071768 000003/Consultants?highlight=consultants#contribution-13071768 000010

House of Commons Health Committee. 2009. The Use of Management Consultants by the NHS and the Department of Health. *Fifth Report of Session 2008–9*. London: The Stationery Office.

House of Commons Public Administration Select Committee. 2011. Good Governance and Civil Service Reform: 'End of Term' Report on Whitehall Plans for Structural Reform. *Eleventh Report of Session 2010–12*. London: The Stationery Office.

House of Commons Public Administration Select Committee. 2013. Government Procurement. *Sixth Report of Session 2013–14*. London: Stationery Office.

House of Lords Hansard. 2012. NHS: Management Consultants 13th February 2012, Vol. 735. https://hansard.parliament.uk/Lords/2012-02-13/debates/1202131000179/NHSManagementConsultants

Houten, D. R. V. and P. Goldman. 1981. Contract Consulting's Hidden Agenda: The Quest for Legitimacy in Government. *The Pacific Sociological Review* 24 (4; October): 461–493.

Howard, C. 2005. Policy Cycle: A Model of Post-Machiavellian Policymaking? *Australian Journal of Public Administration* 64 (3): 3–13.

Howard, M. 1990. The Use of Consultants by the Public Sector in Australia: Recent Evidence and Issues, Working Paper No. 4.

Howard, M. 1996a. A Growth Industry? Use of Consultants Reported by Commonwealth Departments, 1974–1994. *Canberra Bulletin of Public Administration*, IPAA, no 80: 62–74.

Howard, M. 1996b. A Sea Change in Staffing Mode? Commonwealth Departmental Spending on External Consultants and In-House Employees, 1988/89 to 1993/94. *Canberra Bulletin of Public Administration*, IPAA, no 80: 75–83.

Howard, J. 1997a. Consultants to Commonwealth Departments: Market Structure and Type of Consultancies, 1987-93. *Canberra Bulletin of Public Administration*, no 83: 86–97.

Howard, J. 1997b. Consultants and Public Policy. In M. Howard (ed.), *The Rise of Consultants: Enhancing or Eroding Public Sector Expertise?* Selected Proceedings of Seminar 13 October 1995, PSRC Seminar Papers No. 19. UNSW: Public Sector Research Centre: 102–113.

Howard, M. 2004. Comprehensive and Significant? The Consulting Activities of the 'Big Six' Accounting Firms for Fourteen Commonwealth Departments, 1987-93. Public Policy in Transition: Refereed Papers Presented at the 2004 Public Policy Network Conference, QUT: 88–113.

Howard, M. 2005. *Income and 'Expenditure': The Big Accounting-Consulting Firms and Their Pathways of Promotion within the Political and Bureaucratic System.* Dunedin: Refereed Papers of the Australasian Political Studies Association Conference.

Howard, M. 2006. Are Consultants Used for Advice on Corporate Services or Programme Content? *Public Administration Today*, IPAA, 7: 52–66.

Howard, M. 2017. Accretion of Influence: Mapping the Work of the Big Accounting-Consulting Firms for Federal Government Agencies in Australia, 1987–2017. *International Public Policy Association 3rd Biennial Conference*, Singapore.

Howlett, M. 1998. Predictable and Unpredictable Policy Windows: Institutional and Exogenous Correlates of Canadian Federal Agenda-Setting. *Canadian Journal of Political Science* 31 (3): 495–524.

Howlett, M. 2009a. Policy Analytical Capacity and Evidence-Based Policy-Making: Lessons from Canada. *Canadian Public Administration* 52 (2): 153–175.

Howlett, M. 2009b. A Profile of B.C. Provincial Policy Analysts: Troubleshooters or Planners. *Canadian Political Science Review* 3 (3): 55–68.

Howlett, M. 2009c. Policy Advice in Multi-Level Governance Systems: Sub-National Policy Analysts and Analysis. *International Review of Public Administration* 13 (3): 1–16.

Howlett, M. 2011. *Designing Public Policies, Principles and Instruments.* New York: Routledge.

Howlett, M. 2015. Policy Analytical Capacity. The Supply and Demand for Policy Analysis in Government. *Policy and Society* 34 (3–4): 173–182.

Howlett, M. P., C. Brouillette, J. Coleman and R. Skorzus. 2016. Policy Consulting in the USA: New Evidence from the Federal Procurement Data System – Next Generation. SSRN Scholarly Paper. Rochester: Social Science Research Network, 31 August. http://papers.ssrn.com/abstract=2834776

Howlett, M. and J. Craft. 2013. Policy Advisory Systems and Evidence-Based Policy. The Location and Content of Evidentiary Policy Advice. In S. Young (ed.), *Evidence-Based Policy-Making in Canada, A Multidisciplinary Look at How Evidence and Knowledge Shape Canadian Public Policy*. Oxford: Oxford University Press: 27–44.

Howlett, M. and E. Lindquist. 2004. Policy Analysis and Governance: Analytical and Policy Styles in Canada. *Journal of Comparative Policy Analysis* 6 (3): 225–249.

Howlett, M. and A. R. Migone. 2013a. The Permanence of Temporary Services. The Reliance of Canadian Federal Departments on Management Consultants. *Canadian Public Administration* 56 (3): 367–388.

Howlett, M. and A. R. Migone. 2013b. Policy Advice through the Market. The Role of External Consultants in Contemporary Policy Advisory Systems. *Policy and Society* 32(3): 241–254.

Howlett, M. and A. Migone. 2013c. Searching for Substance: Externalization, Politicization and the Work of Canadian Policy Consultants 2006–2013. *Central European Journal of Public Policy* 7 (1; June): 112–133.

Howlett, M. and A. R. Migone. 2014a. Assessing Contract Policy Work. Overseeing Canadian Policy Consultants. *Public Management and Money* 34 (3): 173–180.

Howlett, M. and A. R. Migone. 2014b. Making the Invisible Public Service Visible? Exploring Data on Policy and Management Consultancies in Canada. *Canadian Public Administration* 57 (2): 183–216.

Howlett, M., A. R. Migone and T. Seck. 2014. Duplication or Complementarity? External Policy Consulting and Its Relationship to Internal Policy Analysis in Canada. *Canadian Journal of Political Science* 47 (1): 113–134.

Howlett, M. and A. R. Migone. 2017. The Role of Policy Consultants: Consultocracy or Business as Usual. In M. Howlett, A. Wellstead and J. Craft (eds.), *Policy Work in Canada, Professional Practices and Analytical Capacities*. Toronto: Toronto University Press: 155–182.

Howlett, M. and J. Newman. 2010. Policy Analysis and Policy Work in Federal Systems. Policy Advice and Its Contribution to Evidence-Based Policy-Making in Multi-Level Governance Systems. *Policy and Society* 29 (1): 123–136.

Howlett, M., M. Ramesh and A. Perl. 2009. *Studying Public Policy: Policy Cycles and Policy Subsystems*, 3rd ed. Oxford: Oxford University Press.

Howlett, M.,T. Seck, A. R. Migone, A. Wellstead and B. Evans. 2014. The Distribution of Analytical Techniques in Policy Advisory Systems, Policy Formulation and the Tools of Policy Appraisal. *Public Policy and Administration* 29 (4): 271–291.

Howlett M., R. Stedman and A. Wellstead. 2010. Policy Analytical Capacity and Multi-Level Policy Work: A Structural Equation Model (SEM) Study of Canadian Policy Analysts. *Public Policy and Administration* 26 (3): 353–373.

Howlett, M. and A. Wellstead. 2011. Policy Analysts in the Bureaucracy Revisited. The Nature of Professional Policy Work in Contemporary Government. *Politics and Policy* 39 (4): 613–633.

Howlett, M. and A. Wellstead. 2012. Professional Policy Work in Federal States. Institutional Autonomy and Canadian Policy Analysis. *Canadian Public Administration* 55 (1): 53–68.

Howlett, M., A. Wellstead and J. Craft. (eds.). 2017. *Policy Work in Canada: Professional Practices and Analytical Capacities*. Toronto: University of Toronto Press, Scholarly Publishing Division.

Hudson, J. and S. Lowe. 2004. *Understanding the Policy Process: Analysing Welfare Policy and Practice*. Bristol: The Policy Press.

Hunn, D. K. 1994. Measuring Performance in Policy Advice: A New Zealand Perspective. In OECD (ed.), *Performance Measurement in Government: Issues and Illustrations*. Paris: OECD: 25–37.

Hyman, P. 2005. *One Out of Ten, From Downing Street Vision to Classroom Reality*. London: Vintage.

Jacobsson, B. 1994. *Organisationsexperiment i kommuner och landsting*. [Organizational experiments in municipalities and county councils]. Stockholm: Nerenius & Santérus.

Jacobsson, B. and G. Sundström. 2016. Governing the State. In J. Pierre (ed.), *The Oxford Handbook of Swedish Politics*. Oxford: Oxford University Press: 347–364

Jardine, B. 1997. NSW Government Employee Perspectives. In M. Howard (ed.), *The Rise of Consultants: Enhancing or Eroding Public Sector Expertise?* Selected Proceedings of Seminar 13 October 1995, Seminar Paper No. 19, Public Sector Research Centre. Sydney: UNSW: 86–90.

Jarl, M., A. Fredriksson and S. Persson. 2012. New Public Management in Public Education: A Catalyst for the Professionalization of Swedish School Principals. *Public Administration* 90 (2): 429–444.

Jarrett, M. C. 1998. Consultancy in the Public Sector. In P. Sadler (ed.), *Management Consultancy: A Handbook of Best Practices*. London: Kogan: 369–383.

JCPAA (Joint Committee on Public Accounts and Audit). 2018. Inquiry based on ANAO Report No. 19 – Complementary Submission Guidance. Parliament of Australia.

Jessop, B. 2002. *The Future of the Capitalist State*. Cambridge: Polity Press.

John, P. 2013. Political Science, Impact and Evidence. *Political Studies Review* 11 (2): 168–173.

Johnson, M. A. 2005. Five Decades of Mexican Public Relations in the United States: From Propaganda to Strategic Counsel. *Public Relations Review* 31 (1; March): 11–20.

Jupe, R. and W. Funnell. 2015. Neoliberalism, Consultants and the Privatisation of Public Policy Formulation: The Case of Britain's Rail Industry. *Critical Perspectives on Accounting* 29: 65–85.

Justitiedepartementet. 2010. *Kommittédirektiv. En ny organization för polisen? [Directions for the committee: A new police organization?]*. Stockholm: Justitiedepartementet.

Kagi, H. M. 1969. The Roles of Private Consultants in Urban Governing. *Urban Affairs Review* 5 (1): 45–58.

Kellner, P. and Lord Crowther-Hunt. 1980. *The Civil Servants*. London: Macdonald Futura Publishers Ltd.

Kickert W. J. M. and R. J. in't Veld. 1995. National Government, Governance and Administration. In W. J. M. Kickert and F. A. van Vught (eds.), *Public Policy and Administrative Sciences in The Netherlands*. London: Prentice Hall: 45–62.

Kingdon, J. W. 1993. How do Issues get on Public Policy Agendas? In W. J. Wilson (ed.), *Sociology and the Public Agenda*. Sage: 40–50.

Kipping, M. and T. Armbrüster. 2002. The Burden of Otherness: Limits of Consultancy Interventions in Historical Case Studies. In M. Kipping and L. Engwall (eds.), *Management Consulting: Emergence and Dynamics of a Knowledge Industry*. Oxford: Oxford University Press: 203–221.

Kipping, M. and L. Engwall. 2002. *Management Consulting: Emergence and Dynamics of a Knowledge Industry*. Oxford: Oxford University Press.

Kipping, M. and L. Engwall. (eds.). 2003. *Management Consulting: Emergence and Dynamics of a Knowledge Industry*. Oxford: Oxford University Press.

Kirby, J. 2017. Government spent £17.6m on consultants hired to draw up NHS cutbacks. www.independent.co.uk/news/uk/politics/nhs-cuts-crisis-government-consultancies-millions-paid-a7640176.html

Kitay, J. and C. Wright. 2004. Take the Money and Run? Organisational Boundaries and Consultants' Roles. *The Service Industries Journal* 24 (3): 1–18.

Kline, E. H. and C. G. Buntz. 1979. On the Effective Use of Public Sector Expertise: Or Why the Use of Outside Consultants Often Leads to the Waste of In-House Skills. *Public Administration Review* 39 (3; June): 226–229.

Knaggård, Å. 2014. What Do Policy-Makers Do with Scientific Uncertainty? The Incremental Character of Swedish Climate Change Policy-Making. *Policy Studies* 35 (1): 22–39.

Knill, C. 1999. Explaining Cross-National Variance in Administrative Reform: Autonomous versus Instrumental Bureaucracies. *Journal of Public Policy* 19 (2): 113–139.

Kubr, M. 2002. *Management Consulting – A Guide to the Profession*, 4th ed. Geneva: International Labour Office.

Lahusen, C. 2002. Commercial Consultancies in the European Union: The Shape and Structure of Professional Interest Intermediation. *Journal of European Public Policy* 9 (1): 695–714.

Lantto, J. 2001. NPM-reformerna och demokratin [NPM Reforms and Democracy]. *Ekonomi och Politik* 5 (3): 29–43.

Lapsley, I. and R. Oldfield. 2001. Transforming the Public Sector: Management Consultants as Agents of Change. *The European Accounting Review* 10 (3): 523–543.

Lapsley, I., P. Miller and N. Pollock. 2013. Foreword Management Consultants – Demons or Benign Change Agents? *Financial Accountability & Management* 29 (2): 117–123.

Lasswell, H. 1970. The Emerging Conception of the Policy Sciences. *Policy Sciences* 1 (1): 3–14.

Leys, C. 1999. Intellectual Mercenaries and the Public Interest: Management Consultancies and the NHS. *Policy & Politics* 27 (4): 447–465.

Light, P. C. 2006. *The New True Size of Government*. New York: NYU Wagner School Research, Brief no. 2.

Lijphart, A. 1999. *Patterns of Democracy*. New Haven and London: Yale University Press.

Lindblom, C. E. 1958. Policy Analysis. *American Economic Review* 48 (3): 298–312.

Lindquist, E. 1998. A Quarter Century of Canadian Think Tanks: Evolving Institutions, Conditions and Strategies. In D. Stone, A. Denham and M. Garnett (eds.), *Think Tanks across Nations: A Comparative Approach* . Manchester: Manchester University Press: 127–144.

Lippitt, R. 1975. *Consulting Process in Action: Examining the Dynamics of the Client–Consultant Working Relationship*. Development Publications.

Livingstone, D. N. 2007. Science, Site and Speech: Scientific Knowledge and the Spaces of Rhetoric. *History of the Human Sciences* 20 (2): 71–98.

Macdonald, D. 2011. *The Shadow Public Service: The Swelling Ranks of Federal Government Outsourced Workers*. Ottawa: Canadian Centre for Policy Alternatives.

Madigan, C. and J. O'Shea. 1997. *Dangerous Company: Management Consultants and the Businesses They Save and Ruin*. London: Penguin.

Majone, G. 1997. From the Positive to the Regulatory State. Causes and Consequences of Changes in the Mode of Governance. *Journal of Public Policy* 17 (2): 139–167.

Maley, M. 2000. Conceptualising Advisers' Policy Work: The Distinctive Policy Roles of Ministerial Advisers in the Keating Government, 1991–96. *Australian Journal of Political Science* 35 (3): 449–470.

Maley M. 2012. Politicisation and the Executive. In R. Smith (ed.), *Contemporary Politics in Australia: Theories, Practices and Issues.* Melbourne: Cambridge University Press: 237–248.

Martin, J. F. 1998. *Reorienting a Nation: Consultants and Australian Public Policy*. Aldershot: Ashgate.

Martin, W. 2017. Britain's Government Is Going to Pay Private Consultancies to Help It Deal with Brexit. http://uk.businessinsider.com/ government-tenders-15-million-brexit-consultancy-contract-2017-4

Mattson, I. 2016. Parliamentary Committees. A Ground for Compromise and Conflict. In J. Pierre (ed.), *The Oxford Handbook of Swedish Politics*. Oxford: Oxford University Press: 679–690.

Mayer, I., P. Bots and E. v. Daalen. 2004. Perspectives on Policy Analysis: A Framework for Understanding and Design. *International Journal of Technology, Policy and Management* 4 (1): 169–191

MCA. 2016. UK Consulting Industry in 'Vital Collaboration' with Government to Transform Public Services. www.mca.org.uk/news/press-releases/uk-consulting-industry-in-vital-collaboration-with-government-t o-transform-public-services

McGann, J. G. (ed.). 2007. *Think Tanks and Policy Advice in the US: Academics, Advisors and Advocates*. Abingdon: Routledge.

McGann, J. G. and E. C. Johnson. 2005. *Comparative Think Tanks, Politics and Public Policy*. Cheltenham: Edward Elgar.

McGivern, C. 1983. Some Facets of the Relationship between Consultants and Clients in Organizations. *Journal of Management Studies* 20 (3): 367–386.

McIntosh, N. 1997. Aspects of Change in the Canadian Federal Public Service. *Public Administration & Development (1986–1998)* 17 (1): 123–129.

McKenna, C. D. 1995. The Origins of Modern Management Consulting. *Business and Economic History* 24 (1): 51–58.

McKenna, C. D. 1996. Agents of Adhocracy: Management Consultants and the Reorganization of the Executive Branch, 1947–1949. *Business and Economic History* 25 (1): 101–111.

McKenna, C. D. 2006. *The World's Newest Profession: Management Consulting in the Twentieth Century*. Cambridge Studies in the

Management of Global Enterprise. New York: Cambridge University Press.

McKenna, C. D. 2010. *The World's Newest Profession: Management Consulting in the Twentieth Century.* Cambridge: Cambridge University Press.

McKeown, T. and M. Lindorff. 2011. Temporary Staff, Contractors, and Volunteers: The Hidden Workforce in Victorian Local Government. *Australian Journal of Public Administration* 70 (2; June): 185–201.

McLarty, R. and T. Robinson. 1998 . The Practice of Consultancy and a Professional Development Strategy. *Leadership & Organisational Development Journal* 19 (5): 256–263.

Mead, L. M. 2015. Only Connect, Why Government Often Ignores Research. *Policy Sciences* 48 (2): 257–272.

Meagher, G. and S. Goodwin (eds). 2015. *Markets, Rights and Power in Australian Social Policy.* Sydney: Sydney University Press.

Meer, van der, F. M. and G. S. A. Dijkstra. 2017. Omvang en kwaliteit van de ambtelijke dienst: Ontwikkelingen in de kabinetsperiode Rutte-II in perspectief. In J. Uylenbroek (ed.), *De Staat van de Ambtelijke Dienst: De motiverende overheid,* 3rd ed. The Hague: CAOP: 19–40.

Meer, van der, F. M. and L. J. Roborgh. 1993. Ambtenaren in Nederland. Omvang, bureaucratisering en representativiteit van het ambtelijk apparaat, Alphen aan den Rijn: Samsom HD Tjeenk Willink.

Meer, F. M. van der, J. C. N. Raadschelders and T. A. J. Toonen. (eds). 2015. *Comparative Civil Service Systems in the 21st Century.* London: Palgrave.

Meer, van der, F. M., C. F. van den Berg and G. S. A Dijkstra. 2012. *De ambtenaar in het openbaar bestuur: De inhoudelijke en juridische herpositionering van ambtenaren vanuit internationaal-vergelijkend perspectief (Academic Series).* Leiden: Leiden University Press.

Mennicken, A. 2013. 'Too Big to Fail and Too Big to Succeed': Accounting and Privatisation of the Prison Service in England and Wales. *Financial Accountability & Management* 29 (2): 206–226.

Meredith, H. and J. Martin. 1970. Management Consultants in the Public Sector. *Canadian Public Administration/Administration publique du Canada* 13 (4; December): 383–395.

Merton, R. K. 1949. *Social Theory and Social Structure.* New York: Free Press.

Mewett B. 1997. Are Consultants Taking Over from In-House Policy and Planning Sections. In M. Howard (ed.), *The Rise of Consultants: Enhancing or Eroding Public Sector Expertise?* Selected Proceedings of Seminar 13 October 1995, Seminar Paper No. 19, Public Sector Research Centre. Sydney: UNSW: 96–101.

Miller, C. and L. Orchard (eds). 2014. *Australian Public Policy: Progressive Ideas in the Neoliberal Ascendancy.* Bristol: Policy Press.

Ministerie van Binnenlandse Zaken en Koninkrijksrelaties. 2010. Nadere reactie op motie-Roemer inzake uitgavennorm externe inhuur [Further response to motion by Roemer regarding spending standard external hiring]. 2010–0000427652.

Ministerie van F. 2013/2017. Bijlage Rijksbegrotingsvoorschriften Externe Inhuur [Appendix: National Budget Regulations for External Hire].

Mintrom, M. 2007. The Policy Analysis Movement. In L. Dobuzinskis, M. Howlett and D. Laycock (eds.), *Policy Analysis in Canada: The State of the Art.* Toronto: University of Toronto Press: 71–84.

Miragliotta N., W. Errington and N. Barry. 2014. *The Australian Political System in Action.* Melbourne: Oxford University Press.

Mitchell, V.-W. 1994. Problems and Risks in the Purchasing of Consultancy Services. *The Service Industries Journal* 14 (3): 315.

Moor, L. 2008. Branding Consultants as Cultural Intermediaries. *The Sociological Review* 56 (3): 408–428.

Moran, M. 2003. *The British Regulatory State.* Oxford: Oxford University Press.

Moran, T. 2013. Reforming to Create Value: Our Next Five Strategic Directions. *Australian Journal of Public Administration* 72 (1): 1–6.

Murdoch, Z. 2015. Organization Theory and the Study of European Union Institutions: Lessons and Opportunities. *Organization Studies* 36 (12): 1675–1692.

Murray, C. 2007. The Media. In L. Dobuzinskis, M. Howlett and D. Laycock (eds), *Policy Analysis in Canada: The State of the Art.* Toronto: University of Toronto Press: 286–297.

National Audit Office. 2001. *Purchasing Professional Services. Report by the Comptroller and Auditor General.* HC 400 Session 2000–2001: 25 April 2001. London: The Stationery Office.

National Audit Office. 2003. *Getting the Evidence: Using Research in Policy Making.* London: National Audit Office.

National Audit Office. 2006. *Central Government's Use of Consultants.* London: The Stationery Office.

National Audit Office. 2010. *Central Government's Use of Consultants and Interims.* London: The Stationery Office.

National Audit Office. 2013. Cabinet Office, The Efficiency and Reform Group Report by the Comptroller and Auditor General. HC 956, Session 2012–13.

National Audit Office. 2016. *Use of Consultants and Temporary Staff.* London: The Stationery Office.

National Audit Office. 2006. *Central Government's Use of Consultants: Methodology*. London: National Audit Office.

Negus, K. 2002. The Work of Cultural Inter-Mediaries and the Enduring Distance between Production and Consumption. *Cultural Studies* 16 (4): 501–515.

New Zealand. 1994 Employment of Consultants by Government Departments. In *Report of the Controller and Auditor-General: Third Report for 1994*, 13–42. Wellington: Audit Office.

Newman, J. 2014. Revisiting the 'Two Communities' Metaphor of Research Utilisation. *International Journal of Public Sector Management* 27 (7): 614–627.

Newman, J. 2016. Deconstructing the Debate over Evidence-Based Policy. *Critical Policy Studies* 11 (2): 1–16.

Newman, J., A. Cherney and B. W. Head. 2017. Policy Capacity and Evidence-Based Policy in the Public Service. *Public Management Review* 19 (2), 157–174.

Newman, J. and B. W. Head. 2015. Beyond the Two Communities: A Reply to Mead's 'Why Government Often Ignores Research'. *Policy Sciences* 48 (3): 383–393.

Nicholson, J. 1997. Monitoring the Efficiency, Quality, and Effectiveness of Policy Advice to Government. In J. Maybe and E. Zapico-Goni (eds.), *Monitoring Performance in the Public Sector: Future Directions from International Experience*. New Brunswick: Transaction Publishers: 237–252.

O'Mahoney, J. and A. Sturdy. 2016. Power and Diffusion of Management Ideas: The Case of McKinsey & Co. Management Learning. *Management Learning* 47 (3): 247–265.

Öberg, P. 2016. Interest Organizations in the Policy Process: Interest Advocacy and Policy Advice. In J. Pierre (ed.), *The Oxford Handbook of Swedish Politics*. Oxford: Oxford University Press: 663–678.

O'Connor, A., G. Roos, T. Vickers-Willis. 2007. Evaluating an Australian Public Policy Organization's Innovation Capacity. *European Journal of Innovation Management* 10 (4): 532–558.

Office of Federal Procurement Policy. 2011 Service Contract Inventories; Report to Congress.

Office of the Auditor General of British Columbia. 2001. *Management Consulting Engagements in Government*. Victoria: Office of the Auditor General of British Columbia.

Office of the Procurement Ombudsman. 2010. Procurement Practices Review 2009–2010. *Chapter 4: Environment Canada – Review of Procurement Practices Related to Management Consulting and Other Professional Services*. Ottawa: Office of the Procurement Ombudsman.

Office of the Under Secretary of Defense. 2013. Reporting Inherently Governmental Functions Indicators to the Federal Procurement Data System. Memorandum for Commander, United States Special Operations Command (Attn: Acquisition Executive) Commander, United States Transportation Command (Attn: Acquisition Executive) Deputy Assistant Secretary of the Arivly (Procurement) Deputy Assistant Secretary of the Navy (Acquisition and Procurement) Deputy Assistant Secretary of the Air Force (Contracting) Directors of the Defense Agencies Directors of the Dod Field Activities, 25 February.

Oldersma, J. W. P. and M. Janzen-Marquard. 1999. The Iron Ring in Dutch Politics Revisited. *Public Administration* 77: 335–360.

O'Shea, J. 2002. *Dangerous Company: The Consulting Powerhouses and the Businesses They Save and Ruin*. Collingdale: Diane Pub. Co.

Osborne, D. and E. Gaebler. 1992. *Reinventing Government*. Reading: Addison-Wesley.

PA Consulting. 2017. Government and Public Sector. www.paconsulting .com/industries/government-and-public-sector/

Page, E. C. 2010. Bureaucrats and Expertise: Elucidating a Problematic Relationship in Three Tableaux and Six Jurisdictions. *Sociologie du Travail* 52 (2): 255–273

Page, E. C. and B. Jenkins. 2005. *Policy Bureaucracy: Governing with a Cast of Thousands*. Oxford: Oxford University Press.

Painter, M. and J. Pierre. 2005. *Challenges to State Policy Capacity: Global Trends and Comparative Perspectives*. London: Palgrave Macmillan.

Panchamia, N. and P. Thomas. 2014. *The Next Steps Initiative*. London: Institute for Government.

Parliament (UK). 2000. Select Committee on International Development Eighth Report. https://publications.parliament.uk/pa/cm199900/cmse lect/cmintdev/475/47508.htm

Parsons, W. 2004. Not Just Steering but Weaving. Relevant Knowledge and the Craft of Building Policy Capacity and Coherence. *Australian Journal of Public Administration* 63 (1): 43–57.

Paton, C. 1999. Commentary on 'Intellectual Mercenaries and the Public Interest: Management Consultants and the NHS. *Policy & Politics* 27 (4): 467–470.

Pattenaude, R. L. 1979. Introduction to Symposium on Consultants in the Public Sector. *Public Administration Review* 39 (3; June): 203–205.

Pearton, M. 1982. *The Knowledgeable State*. London: Burnett Books.

Peled, A. 2002. Why Style Matters: A Comparison of Two Administrative Reform Initiatives in the Israeli Public Sector, 1989–1998. *Journal of Public Administration Research and Theory* 12 (2): 217–240.

Pemer, F., L. Börjeson and A. Werr. 2014. Government Agencies' Use of Management Consulting Services in Sweden – An Explorative Study. SSE Working Paper Series in Business Administration No. 2014:3. Stockholm School of Economics.

Pemer, F. and T. Skjølsvik, 2017. Adopt or Adapt? Unpacking the Role of Institutional Work Processes in the Implementation of New Regulations. *Journal of Public Administration Research and Theory* 28 (1): 138–154.

Perl, A. and D. J. White. 2002. The Changing Role of Consultants in Canadian Policy Analysis. *Policy, Organisation & Society* 21 (4): 49–73.

Peters, B. G. 1996. *The Policy Capacity of Government*. Ottawa: Canadian Centre for Management Development.

Peters, B. G. and J. Pierre. (eds.). 2004. *Politicization of the Civil Service in Comparative Perspective: The Quest for Control*. Abingdon: Routledge.

Peters, M. A. 2016. From State Responsibility for Education and Welfare to Self-Responsibilisation in the Market. *Discourse: Studies in the Cultural Politics of Education* 38 (1): 138–145.

Petersson, O. 1994. *The Government and Politics of the Nordic Countries*. Stockholm: Fritzes

Pierre, J. 2016. Introduction: The Decline of Swedish Exceptionalism? In J. Pierre (ed.), *The Oxford Handbook of Swedish Politics*. Oxford: Oxford University Press: 1–18.

Pierre, J., B. Jacobsson and G. Sundström. 2015. *Governing the Embedded State: The Organizational Dimension of Governance*. Oxford: Oxford University Press.

Pierre, J. and G. B. Peters. 2000. *Governance, Politics and the State*. Basingstoke: Palgrave.

Pollitt, C. 2003. *The Essential Public Manager*, Maidenhead: McGraw-Hill Education (UK).

Pollitt, C. 2007. New Labour's Re-Disorganization. *Public Management Review* 9 (4): 529–543.

Pollitt, C. and G. Bouckaert. 2004. *Public Management Reform: A Comparative Analysis*. New York: Oxford University Press.

Pollitt, C. and G. Bouckaert. 2011. *Public Management Reform: A Comparative Analysis: New Public Management, Governance, and the Neo-Weberian State*. Oxford: Oxford University Press.

Pollitt, C. and G. Bouckaert. 2017. *Public Management Reform: A Comparative Analysis – Into the Age of Austerity*, 4th ed. Oxford: Oxford University Press.

Pollitt, C. and H. Summa. 1997. Trajectories of Reform: Public Management Change in Four Countries. *Public Money and Management* 17 (1): 7–18.

Pollitt, C. and C. Talbot. 2004. *Unbundled Government: A Critical Analysis of the Global Trend to Agencies, Quangos and Contractualisation.* London: Routledge.

Poulfelt, F. and A. Paynee. 1994. Management Consultants: Client and Consultant Perspectives. *Scandinavian Journal of Management* 10 (4; December): 421–436.

Prince, M. J. 1979. Policy Advisory Groups in Government Departments. In G. B. Doern and P. Aucoin (eds.), *Public Policy in Canada: Organization, Process, Management.* Toronto: Gage: 275–300.

Prince, M. 1983. *Policy Advice and Organizational Survival.* Aldershot: Gower.

Prince, M. J. 2007. Soft Craft, Hard Choices, Altered Context, Reflections on 25 Years of Policy Advice in Canada. In L. Dobuzinskis, M. Howlett and D. Laycock (eds.), *Policy Analysis in Canada, The State of the Art.* Toronto: University of Toronto Press: 95–106.

Project on Government Oversight. 2011. *Bad Business: Billions of Taxpayer Dollars Wasted on Hiring Contractors.* Washington, DC: Project on Government Oversight.

Public Service Commission. 2010. *Use of Temporary Help Services in Public Service Organizations.* Ottawa: Public Service Commission.

Radaelli, C. M. 1995. The Role of Knowledge in the Policy Process. *Journal of European Public Policy* 2 (2): 159–183.

Radcliffe, S. 2010. Non-rational Aspects of the Competition State: The Case of Policy Consultancy in Australia. *Policy Studies* 31 (1): 117–128.

Radin, B. A. 1997. Presidential Address: The Evolution of the Policy Analysis Field: From Conversation to Conversations. *Journal of Policy Analysis and Management* 16 (2): 204–218.

Ranald, P. 1997. Commonwealth Government Employee Perspectives on Use of Consultants. In M. Howard (ed.), *The Rise of Consultants: Enhancing or Eroding Public Sector Expertise?* Selected Proceedings of Seminar 13th October 1995, Seminar Paper No. 19, Public Sector Research Centre. Sydney: UNSW: 77–80.

Rasiel, E. M. and P. N. Friga. 2002. *The McKinsey Mind.* New York: McGraw-Hill.

Raudla, R. 2013. Pitfalls of Contracting for Policy Advice: Preparing Performance Budgeting Reform in Estonia. *Governance* 26 (4): 605–629.

Rehfuss, J. 1979. Managing the Consultantship Process. *Public Administration Review* 39 (3; May): 211–214.

Rhodes, R. A. W. 1994. The Hollowing Out of the State. *Political Quarterly* 65 (2): 138–151.

Riddell, N. 2007. *Policy Research Capacity in the Federal Government.* Ottawa: Policy Research Initiative.

Rihoux, B., A. Spretizer and R. Koole. 2015. The Impact of European Intergration on Within-Party Organization Dynamics: More or Less Consensus Politics? In H. Vollaard, J. Beyers and P. Dumont (eds.), *European Integration and Consensus Politics in the Low Countries*. London: Routledge: 69–91.

Rochet, C. 2004. Rethinking the Management of Information in the Strategic Monitoring of Public Policies by Agencies. *Industrial Management & Data Systems* 104 (3): 201–208.

Rombach, B. 1997. *Den marknadslika kommunen – en effektstudie [The municipality as a market – Analysing the effects]*. Stockholm:Nerenius & Santérus.

Rose, D. 2012. The Firm that Hijacked the NHS: MoS Investigation Reveals Extraordinary Extent of International Management Consultant's Role in Lansley's Health Reforms. www.dailymail.co.uk/news/article-2099940/NHS-health-reforms-Extent-McKinsey–Companys-role-Andrew-Lansley s-proposals.html

Rose, N. 1991. Governing by Numbers: Figuring Out Democracy. *Accounting Organizations and Society* 16 (7): 673–692.

Rosenblum, R. and D. McGillis. 1979. Observations on the Role of Consultants in the Public Sector. *Public Administration Review* 39 (3; June): 219–226.

Rosenthal, U., A. B. Ringeling, M. A. P. Bovens, P. T. Hart and M. J. W. van Twist. 1996. *Openbaar Bestuur: Beleid Organisatie en Politiek*, 5th ed. Alphen aan den Rijn: Samson Tjeenk Willink.

Saint-Martin, D. 1998a. Management Consultants, the State, and the Politics of Administrative Reform in Britain and Canada. *Administration & Society* 30 (5; November): 533–568. https://doi.org/10.1177/0095399798305003.

Saint-Martin, D. 1998b. The New Managerialism and the Policy Influence of Consultants in Government: An Historical-Institutionalist Analysis of Britain, Canada and France. *Governance: An International Journal of Policy and Administration* 11 (3): 319–356.

Saint-Martin, D. 2000. *Building the New Managerialist State*. Oxford: Oxford University Press.

Saint-Martin, D. 2001. How the Reinventing of Government Movement in Public Administration Was Exported from the US to Other Countries. *International Journal of Public Administration* 24 (6): 573–604.

Saint-Martin, D. 2004. *Building the New Managerialist State: Consultants and the Politics of Public Sector Reform in Britain, Canada and France*. Oxford: Oxford University Press.

Saint-Martin, D. 2005. The Politics of Management Consulting in Public Sector Reform. In C. Pollit (ed.), *Handbook of Public Management*. Oxford: Oxford University Press: 84–106.

Saint-Martin, D. 2006. Le Consulting et l'Etat : Une Analyse Comparée de l'offre et de La Demande. *Revue Française d'administration Publique* 120 (4): 743–756. https://doi.org/10.3917/rfap.120.0743.

Saint-Martin, D. 2007. Management Consultancy. In E. Ferlie, L. Lynn and C. Pollitt, *The Oxford Handbook of Public Management*. Oxford: Oxford University Press: 671–694.

Saint-Martin, D. 2012. Governments and Management Consultants: Supply, Demand and Effectiveness. In M. Kipping and T. Clark (eds.), *The Oxford Handbook of Management Consulting*. Oxford, Oxford University Press: 447–464.

Saint-Martin, D. 2013. Making Government More 'Business-Like': Management Consultants as Agents of Isomorphism in Modern Political Economies. In J. Mikler (ed.), *The Handbook of Global Companies*. Hoboken: John Wiley & Sons Ltd: 173–192. http://onlinelibrary.wiley.c om/doi/10.1002/9781118326152.ch10/summary.

Sanderson, I. 2006. Complexity, 'Practical Rationality' and Evidence-Based Policy Making. *Policy and Politics* 34 (1): 115–132.

Savoie, D. J. 2015. *What Is Government Good At? A Canadian Answer*. Montreal: McGill-Queen's University Press.

Schwartz, M., W. Ginsberg and J. F. Sargent Jr. 2015. Defense Acquisitions: How and Where DoD Spends Its Contracting Dollars. Library of Congress Congressional Research Service, 30 April.

Scott, J. C. 1998. *Seeing Like a State*. New Haven: Yale University Press.

SCP. 2017. Burgerperspectieven 2017|4, The Hague: www.scp.nl/Publicati es/Alle_publicaties/Publicaties_2017/Burgerperspectieven_2017_4.

SCP. 2018. *Burgerperspectieven*. no. 4 The Hague: SCP.

Shah, S. 2016. Government Consultancy Spends Spirals out of Control Once Again – So What Now? www.computing.co.uk/ctg/feature/2449925/gov ernment-consultancy-spend-spirals-out-of-control-once-again-so-what-now#

Shamir, R. 2008. The Age of Responsibilization: On Market-Embedded Morality. *Economy and Society* 37 (1): 1–19.

Shaw, R. and C. Eichbaum. 2018. *Ministers, Minders and Mandarins: An International Study of Relationships at the Executive Summit of Parliamentary Democracies*. Cheltenham: Edward Elgar.

Shergold, P. 2013. My Hopes for a Public Service for the Future. *Australian Journal of Public Administration* 72 (1): 7–13.

Siefken, S. and M. Schulz. 2013. The Governance of Policy Advice: Regulation of Advisory Commissions and Councils in Germany and The Netherlands. 1st International Conference on Public Policy. 26–28.6.2013, Grenoble.

Simon-Davies, J. 2010. How Many Are Employed in the Commonwealth Public Sector. Commonwealth Parliament, Parliamentary Library, Research Publications, Background Notes series.

Sin, C. H. 2008. The Role of Intermediaries in Getting Evidence into Policy and Practice: Some Useful Lessons from Examining Consultancy–Client Relationships. *Evidence & Policy: A Journal of Research, Debate and Practice* 4 (1; January): 85–103.

Smith, B. L. R. 1977. The Non-Governmental Policy Analysis Organization. *Public Administration Review* 37 (3; June): 253–258.

Smith, K. and K. Desouza. 2015. How Data Privatization Will Change Planning Practice. *Planetizen*, 20 July: www.planetizen.com/node/79680/how-data-privatization-will-change-planning-practice

South Australia. 2005. Use of External Consultants by Government Departments. 20 June: www.parliament.sa.gov.au/Committees/Standing/HA/EconomicandFinanceCommittee/CompletedInquiries/07ReportExternalConsultants/.

Souto-Otero, M. (ed.). 2015. *Evaluating European Education Policy-Making*. Basingstoke: Palgrave Macmillan.

Speers, K. 2007. The Invisible Private Service, Consultants and Public Policy in Canada. In L. Dobuzinskis, M. Howlett and D. Laycock (eds.), *Policy Analysis in Canada: The State of the Art*. Toronto: University of Toronto Press: 339–421.

Spoehr, J. 1999. *Beyond the Contract State: Ideas for Social and Economic Renewal in South Australia*. Adelaide: Wakefield Press.

SSCFPA (Senate Standing Committee on Finance and Public Administration). 2003. Estimates Hearings Transcripts, 6 November, pp. 78–81: www.aph.gov.au.

State Services Commission. 1999. *Essential Ingredients: Improving the Quality of Policy Advice*. Wellington: New Zealand State Services Commission.

Stewart, J. and M. Maley. 2013. The Public Sector. In A. Fenna, J. Robbins and J. Summers (eds.), *Government and Politics in Australia*. NSW: Pearson: 71–86.

Stirrat, R. L. 2000. Cultures of Consultancy. *Critique of Anthropology* 20 (1): 31–46.

Stone, D. 2008. Global Public Policy, Transnational Policy Communities and Their Networks. *The Policy Studies Journal* 36 (1): 19–38.

Stone, D. and A. Denham. 2004. *Think Tank Traditions: Policy Research and the Politics of Ideas*. Manchester: Manchester University Press.

Stone, D., A. Denham and M. Garnett. 1998. *Think Tanks across Nations: A Comparative Approach*. Manchester: Manchester University Press.

Stritch, A. 2007. Business Associations and Policy Analysis in Canada. In L. Dobuzinskis, M. Howlett and D. Laycock (eds.), *Policy Analysis in Canada: The State of the Art.* Toronto: University of Toronto Press: 242–259.

Sturdy, A. 2011. Consultancy's Consequences? A Critical Assessment of Management Consultancy's Impact on Management. *British Journal of Management* 22 (3): 517–530.

Sturdy, A., A. Werr and A. F. Buono. 2009. Editorial: The Client in Management Consultancy Research: Mapping the Territory. *Scandinavian Journal of Management* 25 (3): 247–252.

Sturdy, A. 1997. The Consultancy Process: An Insecure Business? *Journal of Management Studies* 34 (3): 389–413.

Suleiman, E. N. 2003. *Dismantling Democratic States.* New Jersey: Princeton University Press.

Svanborg-Sjövall, K. 2014. Privatising the Swedish Welfare State. *Economic Affairs* 34 (2): 181–192.

Teelken, C. 2015. Hybridity, Coping Mechanisms, and Academic Performance Management: Comparing Three Countries. *Public Administration* 93 (3): 307–323.

Thaler, R. H. and C. R. Sunstein. 2008. *Nudge.* New Haven: Yale University Press.

Thameslink Programme. 2017. The Government-Sponsored Thameslink Programme Is Transforming North–South Travel through London: www.networkrail.co.uk/our-railway-upgrade-plan/key-projects/thameslink-programme/

Thomson, P. 2015. Prime Minister Malcom Turnbull: Don't Turn Australian Public Service into a Glorified Mail Box. *Canberra Times,* 23 September.

Thomson, S. and S. John. 2007. *Public Affairs in Practice: A Practical Guide to Lobbying.* Kogan Page Publishers.

Tingle, L. 2015. *Political Amnesia: How We Forgot to Govern, Quarterly Essay,* No. 60. Melbourne: Black Inc.

Tisdall, P. 1982. *Agents of Change: The Development and Practice of Management Consultancy.* Portsmouth: Heinemann.

Toshkov, D., E. Schmidt and C. F. van den Berg. 2018. Slanker maar topzwaar, meer vrouwen maar vergrijsd: Het veranderende gezicht van de Rijksoverheid 2002–2015 (Slimmer but Top Heavy, More Women but Greyed Out: The Changing Face of the Government, 2002–2015) *Beleid en Maatschappij* 45 (1): 23–43. DOI:10.5553/BenM/138900692018 045001003

Toynbee, P. 2011. This Benefit Bonanza Is More Big Serco than Big Society. *The Guardian,* 5 April: www.theguardian.com/commentisfree/2011/apr/04/benefits-bonanza-big-serco-welfare.

Traynor, M. P., M. E. Begay and S. A. Glantz. 1993. New Tobacco Industry Strategy to Prevent Local Tobacco Control. *JAMA: The Journal of the American Medical Association* 270 (4; July 28): 479–486.

United Stations Government Accountability Office (GAO). 1991. Government Contractors: Are Service Contractors Performing Inherently Governmental Functions? Report to the Chairman, Federal Service, Post Office and Civil Service Subcommittee, Committee on Governmental Affairs, US Senate, November. http://archive.gao.gov/t2pbat7/145453 .pdf

United Stations Government Accountability Office (GAO). 2011. Managing Service Contracts: Recent Efforts to Address Associated Risks Can Be Further Enhanced. *Report to the Committee on Homeland Security and Governmental Affairs*, US Senate, December.

United Stations Government Accountability Office (GAO). 2012. Civilian Service Contract Inventories: United Stations Government Accountability Office. Defense Contracting: Improved Policies and Tools Could Help Increase Competition on DOD's National Security Exception Procurements. Report to Congressional Committees, January.

Upphandlingsutredningen (SOU). 2013. *Goda affärer – en strategi för hållbar offentlig upphandling [Good Business – A Strategy for Sustainable Public Procurement]*. Stockholm: Finansdepartementet.

USASpending.Gov. FAQs: www.usaspending.gov/references/Pages/FAQs .aspx

Verheijen, T. 1999. *Civil Service Systems in Central and Eastern Europe*. Cheltenham: Edward Elgar.

Verschuere, B. 2009. The Role of Public Agencies in the Policy Making Process. *Public Policy and Administration* 24 (1): 23–46.

Veselý, A. 2017. Policy Advice as Policy Work, A Conceptual Framework for Multi-Level Analysis. *Policy Sciences* 50 (1): 139–154.

Veselý, A., A. Wellstead and B. Evans. 2014. Comparing Sub-National Policy Workers in Canada and the Czech Republic. Who Are They, What They Do, and Why It Matters?*Policy and Society* 33 (2): 103–115.

Vincent-Jones, P. 2000. Contractual Governance: Institutional and Organizational Analysis. *Oxford Journal of Legal Studies* 20 (3): 317–351.

Vincent-Jones, P. 2006. *The New Public Contracting, Regulation, Responsiveness, Relationality*. Oxford: Oxford University Press.

Vocino, T., S. J. Pernacciaro and P. D. Blanchard. 1979. An Evaluation of Private and University Consultants by State and Local Officials. *Public Administration Review* 39 (3; June): 205–210.

Vromen, A. and P. Hurley. 2015. Consultants, Think Tanks and Public Policy In B. Head and K. Crowley (eds.), *Policy Analysis in Australia*. Bristol: Policy Press: 167–182.

Wagner, P. and H. Wollman. 1986. Social Scientists in Policy Research and Consulting: Some Cross-National Comparisons. *International Social Science Journal* 110: 601–617.

Walker, B. and B. C. Walker. 2000. *Privatisation – Sell Off or Sell Out?: The Australian Experience*, Sydney: ABC Books.

Waller, M. 1992. Evaluating Policy Advice. *Australian Journal of Public Administration* 51 (4):440–449.

Wanna, J., J.Butcher and B. Freyens. 2010. *Policy in Action: the Challenge of Service Delivery*. Sydney: UNSW Press.

Ward, S. C. 2012. *Neoliberalism and the Global Structuring of Knowledge and Education*. New York: Routledge.

Watts, R. 2014. Truth and Politics. Thinking about Evidence-Based Policy in the Age of Spin. *Australian Journal of Public Administration* 73 (1): 34–46.

Weber, M. 1968 [1921]. *Economy and Society*. Oakland: University of California Press.

Weible, C. M. 2008. Expert-based Information and Policy Subsystems: A Review and Synthesis. *Policy Studies Journal* 36 (4): 615–635.

Weiss, C. H. 1977. Research for Policy's Sake: The Enlightenment Function of Social Science Research. *Policy Analysis* 3 (4): 531–545.

Weiss, C. H. 1979. The Many Meanings of Research Utilization. *Public Administration Review* 39 (5): 426–431.

Weiss, C. H. 1980. Knowledge Creep and Decision Accretion. *Science Communication* 1(3): 381–404.

Weiss, C. H. 1986. The Circuitry of Enlightenment. Diffusion of Social Science Research to Policymakers. *Knowledge, Creation, Diffusion, Utilization* 8 (2): 274–281.

Weller, P. 2015. Policy Professionals in Context: Advisors and Ministers. In B. Head and K. Crowley (eds.), *Policy Analysis in Australia*. Bristol: Policy Press: 23–36.

Weller, P. and B. Stevens. 1998. Evaluating Policy Advice. The Australian Experience. *Public Administration* 76 (3): 579–589.

Wellstead, A. M. and R. C. Stedman. 2010. Policy Capacity and Incapacity in Canada's Federal Government: The Intersection of Policy Analysis and Street Level Bureaucracy. *Public Management Review* 12 (6): 893–910.

Wellstead, A. M., R. C. Stedman and E. A. Lindquist. 2009. The Nature of Regional Policy Work in Canada's Federal Public Service. *Canadian Political Science Review* 3 (1): 1–23.

Wesselink, A.,H. Colebatch and W. Pearce. 2014. Evidence and Policy: Discourses, Meanings and Practices. *Policy Sciences* 47 (4): 339–344.

Wesselink, A. and A. Gouldson. 2014. Pathways to Impact in Local Government. The Mini-Stern Review as Evidence in Policy Making in the Leeds City Region. *Policy Sciences* 47 (4): 403–424.

Whitehall Monitor. 2017a, Workforce: www.instituteforgovernment.org.u k/publication/whitehall-monitor-2017/workforce.

Whitehall Monitor. 2017b. Summary: www.instituteforgovernment.org.uk/ publication/whitehall-monitor-2017/summary.

Wildavsky, A. B. 1979. *Speaking Truth to Power. The Art and Craft of Policy Analysis*. Boston: Little-Brown.

Wilding, R. W. L. 1976. The Use of Management Consultants in Government Departments, *Management Services in Government* 31 (2): 60–70.

Woldendorp, J. J. 1995. Neo-corporatism as a Strategy for Conflict Regulation in the Netherlands. *Acta Politica* 2, 212–252.

Wollmann, H. 1989.Policy Analysis in West Germany's Federal Government: A Case of Unfinished Governmental and Administrative Modernization? *Governance* 2 (3): 233–266.

Yeatman, S. 1997. Contract, Status and Personhood. In G. Davis, B. Sullivan and A. Yeatman (eds.), *The New Contractualism*. Melbourne: Macmillan Education Australia Pty Ltd: 39–56.

Yin, R. K. 2009. *Case Study Research: Design and Methods (Applied Social Research Methods)*. Thousand Oaks: Sage Publications.

Young, S. (ed.). 2013. *Evidence-Based Policy-Making in Canada: A Multidisciplinary Look at How Evidence and Knowledge Shape Canadian Public Policy*. Oxford: Oxford University Press.

Index

300